They Did Not Grow Old

They Did Not Grow Old

Teenage Conscripts on the Western Front, 1918

TIM LYNCH

First published 2013
by Spellmount, an imprint of The History Press

The Mill, Brimscombe Port
Stroud, Gloucestershire, GL5 2QG
www.thehistorypress.co.uk

British Library Cataloguing in Publication Data.
A catalogue record for this book is available from the British Library.

ISBN 978 0 7524 8916 2

Typesetting and origination by The History Press
Printed in Great Britain

Contents

Preface

Thursday 28 September 1899. At the end of a long, hot and stormy summer, Robina Carr cradled her baby for the first time, blissfully unaware that the war that would one day claim him had just moved another step closer. As Robina, the British-born daughter of a German immigrant, proudly introduced their first-born child to his father, British troops were arriving in the diamond mining town of Kimberley in South Africa, where special correspondent J. Angus Hamilton reported:

> There is much solemn speculation upon the date of hostilities. The fact is that no one here can, with any certainty, predict an hour. A shot anywhere will set the border-side aflame. Moreover, the Boers are daily growing more impudent. At Borderside, where the frontiers are barely eighty yards apart, a field cornet and his men, who are patrolling their side of the line, greet the pickets of the Cape Police who are stationed there with exulting menaces and much display of rifles. But if the Dutch be thirsting in this fashion for our blood, people at home can rest confident in the fact that there will be no holding back upon the part of our men once the fun begins.[1]

There was, he said, an atmosphere of keen excitement in the town, where 'crowds of interested spectators besieged the railway station and thronged the dusty thoroughfares of the town. The Imperial men detrained very smartly to the sound of the bugle, off-loading the guns and ammunition to the plaudits and delights of an admiring crowd.'[2] As war loomed, Britain was riding high on a wave of jingoism fuelled by its success a year earlier when its army had slaughtered 11,000 Sudanese for the loss of just twenty-eight of its own men at the Battle of Omdurman, followed soon afterwards by another victory when a French military force was compelled to withdraw from the strategic Sudanese town of Fashoda after a bitter diplomatic row and the intervention of the Royal Navy that saw Britain and France brought to the brink of war. To the British public, it was unthinkable that the might of the British Empire could be challenged by Boer farmers, and a rush of volunteers came forward as it became 'every man's ambition to take his own share in "whopping" Kruger'.[3] For tuppence, British children could buy a Kruger doll complete with a tiny coffin to bury him in, whilst those from poorer families made do with a clay doll and a matchbox. It was, after all, only a matter of time before the might of the British Army crushed the upstarts.

Victory in the Franco-Prussian War of 1870–71 had led to the amalgamation of the various Germanic states into a unified Germany that under Bismarck's leadership began an aggressive policy of colonisation, making it the third largest player in the late nineteenth century's 'scramble for Africa'. Now, the Kaiser's open military support for the Boers would turn his country – long regarded by generations of Britons as sharing a common Saxon ancestry and therefore as a natural ally – into Britain's chief rival in the struggle for world power. When the Russo-Japanese War of 1904–05 threatened to draw Britain in to honour its treaty with Japan at the same time as France came under pressure to support its treaty with Russia, it became clear that Britain could no longer follow its policy of 'splendid isolation' from European affairs if it were to be able to defend its overseas territories from its European rivals. The signing of the *entente cordiale* in 1904 would once again make Britain a part of European politics. As a result, ten years later Britain would join its oldest enemy in battle with its closest kin. All that, though, could mean nothing to John and Robina in their Bradford home on the first day of their son's life. They named him after his father and wondered what life would hold for him.

At that moment, the same scene was being played out in other homes across the West Riding of Yorkshire. High on the Pennine Hills straddling the Lancashire border, railway signalman Fred Pickering and his wife Ada held their third child, Charles Edward. In Halifax John and Mary Jane Ambler welcomed the arrival of their fourth son, Arnold. On the outskirts of Huddersfield, Sarah Whitwam's first child Harold was making his presence known just as tailor Thomas Gaines and his wife Ruth gazed upon their son Frederick as he lay sleeping beside his mother in their Leeds home. To the north, in the town of Keighley, the Wiseman family – James, Elizabeth and their children James and Christiana – greeted the arrival of another son, also named Harold, with a mixture of joy and trepidation. As the family grew, their income had to be stretched further. Gone was the large home on the edge of town and their servant as the family slid slowly down the social scale.

Six boys among the thousands born on that Thursday. Six boys whose lives would be forever entwined by the events of a single day. On 20 July 1918, Arnold Ambler, John Carr, Frederick Gaines, Charles Pickering, Harold Whitwam and Harold Wiseman would rise up together and walk into a champagne vineyard against a barrage of fire they would hear for the rest of their lives. Six ordinary young men, now forgotten even by their families, among the millions who served. This is the story of those unknown warriors.

1

'Filth and squalor
reign supreme ...'

T he world those six boys were born into was a harsh one, as Elizabeth
Wiseman knew only too well. In July 1898 her second son, Frederick, had
died aged just 13 months in the same month as her third son, John, had
been born. John had died in January 1899 at the same time as she became preg-
nant with Harold. By 1911, three of Mary Jane Ambler's twelve children were dead,
as were two of Ada Pickering's and two of Ruth Gaines'; the odds were stacked
against a newborn surviving its first year in an industrial town. As historian Gordon
Corrigan has shown, the First World War is remembered as four years of carnage
on an unprecedented scale that cost Britain a generation of its youth, taking the lives
of around 8.3 per cent of the men mobilised for the military – approximately one in
twelve of those serving.[1] Yet in Leeds, birthplace of Frederick Gaines, the death rate
for infants in their first year ran at 262 per 1,000 for the quarter July to September
1899 – 26.2 per cent – more than one in four. The average yearly rate for the city
was around 170 to 180 deaths per 1,000 births[2] or, put another way, over twice the
death rate of the trenches as disease, malnutrition, accidents and even infanticide
in poverty-stricken households all took their toll. It was, as reformers were later to
argue, a situation in which the infantryman on the Western Front in 1914–18 stood a
greater chance of survival than a baby born in the West Riding of Yorkshire.

This was not the Yorkshire of wide open moors and clear streams familiar from
nostalgic TV dramas but the industrial heartland of empire, drawing thousands of
British and European migrants in search of work in the burgeoning textile industry. The vast county had never been a single entity. Instead it was divided into the
Old Norse *thrydings*, meaning 'thirds', which evolved into the 'Ridings' (North, East
and West), and each had a very different character: the East included the Yorkshire
coast and the flat, open farmland of the Vale of York whilst the North held large
swathes of open moorland and hill farms. By contrast, at the end of the nineteenth
century the West Riding became a mix of all that was good and bad in Victorian

Keighley 1900. Already polluted by industrial waste, rivers and streams acted as open sewers in the densely populated towns and waterborne epidemics were common.

England. Stretching 93 miles from Sedbergh in the extreme northwest to Bawtry in the southeast and almost 50 miles across at its widest point, it was, as Joseph Morris explained in 1911, 'a county of almost violent contrasts'.[3] The northern part encompassed what is today the Dales National Park, with its open spaces and settled communities of sheep farms, whilst the far south contained the cramped and dirty mining and steel towns that evolved into today's South Yorkshire. Between these two extremes lay the mill communities of modern West Yorkshire, ideally situated to combine the raw materials of the wool fleeces supplied by the north with the coal from the south to power thousands of looms producing woollen textiles. It was to these mill towns that the mass migrations of the nineteenth century had been drawn. Towns typically grew quickly. Keighley went from a population of just 6,864 to 41,564 in the ninety years between 1811 and 1901, Bradford from 5,000 in 1750 to 103,771 by 1851 and 280,000 by 1901 – a 5,600 per cent increase in just 150 years. In the ten-year period from 1891 to 1901 alone, the population of the industrial West Riding had grown by almost 305,000 people. Such rapid growth in urban areas lacking sanitation and clean water supplies inevitably created squalid slums in the already overburdened towns. 'Here,' wrote Morris, 'misery, filth and squalor reign supreme. In his quest for ancient churches it has been the duty of the writer to explore these unpleasant districts with some diligence – certain it is that he does not desire to ever visit them again.'[4]

Even within the industrial areas, though, there were differences. The six boys had been born into the wool textile producing towns of the Aire and Calder valleys where woollen mills nestled in steep-sided valleys and where, Morris pointed out, 'What matter if the [valley] bottom be defiled by ugly mills; if the highways be infested by vile electric tramways; if the waters of the brooks and rivers run fishless and polluted? Always it is possible to escape from this corruption to the solitude and silence of the ridges.'[5] But if the mill towns at least offered an escape onto open moorland, further south the landscape changed again. 'Those who ride out of rural Yorkshire across the border of the coal field may well be pardoned if they experience for the moment a sense of bewilderment', continued Morris:

> Gone in a moment are the wholesome green fields, the pleasant country lanes and the quiet red brick cottages. Instead we have piles of accumulating refuse; dusty roads, with unspeakable surface; footpaths grimy with cinders and coal dust; long gaunt rows of unlovely houses, set down anyhow by the highways and hedges; scraps of walled yard instead of garden; monotonous lines of monstrous ash-bins; dirty children at play in the street; everywhere misery, filth and squalor. It is difficult to believe that this outside unloveliness is not faithfully reflected in the lives of the people.[6]

Eighteenth-century indentures had made demands that servants should not be expected to eat poor men's food such as fresh salmon from the rivers more than three times per week. By 1850 those rivers were little more than open sewers. In 1851, near where the Wiseman family now began to raise their son Harold, 44-year-old Rebecca Town brought the town notoriety when it was reported that she had died having lost no fewer than thirty children in their infancy, in an area where average life expectancy had fallen to just 25.8 years.[7] A few paternalistic mill owners sought to create decent affordable housing for their workers, but most resorted to 'back-to-back' terraced housing where two houses shared a rear wall. Cheap to produce and usually built of low quality materials, these houses often had just two rooms, one on each floor. Because three of the four walls of the house were shared with other buildings and therefore contained no doors or windows, back-to-back houses were notoriously ill-lit, poorly ventilated and sanitation was minimal at best. Even these cramped, dark and airless places, though, were considered an improvement on what had gone before.

Between 1846 and 1847, the Irish potato crops failed and thousands of people fled their homes seeking work so that soon Keighley drew one in twenty of its population from Ireland. They settled in the poorer sections of town where a single privy shared between twenty houses was common, leaving cesspools overflowing and one street described as 'almost impassable from excrement'. The streets were described in a contemporary report as 'a filthy open drain from top to bottom' where 'foul and offensive liquid matter' seeped through walls and into cellars.[8] Frequently, those cellars were occupied by entire families and, in cases where the cellars abutted churchyards, what seeped through the walls could be more than just unpleasant.

In February 1851, William Ranger was sent to investigate living conditions in the Amblers' home town of Halifax and compiled his *Report to the General Board of Health*,

Keighley in the 1890s.

on a Preliminary Inquiry as to the Sewage, Drainage and Supply of Water, and the Sanitary Conditions of the Inhabitants of the Town of Halifax in the County of York. In it, he drew on evidence from a Mr Garlick, the medical officer for the township, who spoke of local housing as 'frequently closely built, badly ventilated and lighted, and abounding in accumulations of offensive matter'.[9] Like many of the period, Garlick was keenly interested in the need for fresh air and complained about the 'most close, confined quarters of town, where the fresh air has the greatest difficulty in penetrating' and homes 'surrounded by collections of filth and refuse which contaminate the air'.[10] The houses were overall, he said, in 'bad repair, deficient in the accommodations required by common decency, and still more in those of purification ventilation'. Nor was it only the older dwellings that suffered. Ranger reported that the proper ventilation was also lacking in the newer houses, especially those built as back-to-backs.

Worse, though, was to come. As many other places, Halifax had a considerable number of cellar dwellings. Mr Garlick considered these lodgings, often a single room measuring around 13ft by 12ft in area and 7ft in height,[11] to be 'unfit for human beings to live in ... provided with neither air, light, nor ventilation' and 'almost always damp, dirty, and unhealthy'.[12] For many, though, these rooms were the only shelter they could afford and the only alternative to living on the streets or in the workhouse.

Fifty years later, Arnold Ambler was born to a family living in Woolpack Yard, a cluster of slum houses attached to a pub built in the 1830s. Lacking all but the most basic facilities, Woolpack Yard had been home to one John Ambler back in 1841 and little had changed since then. Disease remained rampant, especially around the polluted river that served as the town's main sewer and, in the crowded conditions, spread quickly – an outbreak of scarlet fever in the town killed 762 people in the year of Arnold's birth.

Ten miles away, in Bradford, John and Robina Carr lived more comfortably. Robina's father was a successful glass manufacturer from an established Bohemian family and John himself ran a printing business. Not rich by any means, the family were at least comfortable and able to afford a home away from the town centre and near a park. In nearby Leeds, tailor Thomas Gaines and his family lived on the edge of the city centre in a recently built back-to-back terrace within an easy walk of nearby parks. In Keighley, the Wiseman family had suffered a loss of status. James, the head of the household, had been born in Liverpool but came from a long established family of lead miners and farmers in the Kettlewell area, about 20 miles to the north of his new home. In the general depression affecting the country in the late nineteenth century, he had made his way to the town and found work in an engineering company. His wife, Elizabeth, was born in Glasgow but moved to Keighley with her family at about the same time, her father setting up a moderately successful confectionery business. Soon after they were married, James and Elizabeth moved into a home together and could afford to employ a domestic servant, but as the family grew, their finances shrank and they relocated from their new home on the outskirts of town into a terrace near the centre, an embarrassing move in class-conscious Edwardian society.

For most of the six families, it was possible for the mother to remain at home to look after the children, but for those like the Amblers it was often necessary not only for the father to hold two or more jobs, but also for anyone else in the family capable of working to start earning as soon as possible. Arnold would later recall being sent out as a young child to comb the slag heaps of a nearby pit for any usable coal that had been dumped there. When railwayman Fred Pickering died in 1901, his wife was forced to find any work she could to support herself and young Charles.

This created serious problems for families like theirs. Following the Boer War, a number of investigations were carried out into the physical wellbeing of the nation and in 1908 the Acland Report commented on the worrying state of pre-school care. There were, it said, a great many mothers who, for whatever reason, could not care for their children during the working day. It concluded:

> the Committee find that there are only two courses open to her. She can leave her children unattended, either indoors or out of doors, or she can send them to be taken care of either by a neighbour or by a professional 'minder' … Where the mother is away all day and cannot attend to the children's meals or supervise their play, or where the homes are in 'slum' districts, the Committee cannot admit that the children can safely be left unattended all day in the streets or lanes. Apart from the physical dangers due to accidents, cold, wet, and dirt, children are often subjected under such conditions to very serious adverse moral influences. The Committee think that, difficult as it may be to estimate the extent to which these evils prevail, there is no doubt as to their gravity, and they consider that little children should be saved from unnecessary exposure to them.[13]

Where possible, the committee felt, the care of a suitable neighbour was sufficient but, then as now, not everyone could find affordable childcare and some had to turn to the services of less motivated childminders:

> The professional 'minder' is almost always unsatisfactory. The Committee are informed that it is a common practice in some districts for ignorant women to earn a living by minding their neighbour's children. The 'minders' make on an average a charge of about 8d a day per child, in return for which they undertake to watch and feed it. But there is at present no inspection or control over such places, which are often dirty and insanitary, and sometimes conducted by women of the grossest ignorance. It is a well-proved fact that it is a common practice in such places for children to be drugged in order to keep them quiet. A witness, who

supported his statement with careful reference to dates and facts, informed the Committee that in certain districts it was by no means unusual for children to be dosed night and morning with various sedative medicines generally containing opium. In some places gin and soothing syrup are used, and in others laudanum and opium pills are often administered to children. It may be added that it appears that these drugging practices apply almost entirely to children under three years of age. But they affect the children's health after three, and they show the nature of the places to which children over three are sometimes sent.[14]

As late as 1912, Bradford MP Frederick William Jowett told the House of Commons that:

with the exception of one or two instances, the income available for feeding and clothing after rent is paid only amounts to 3 [shillings] per head per week. In 55 per cent of the cases the family, when the rent has been paid, has actually less than 2 [shillings] per head per week. It is absolutely impossible for a family to live on any such amount.[15]

In other words, for some families, one day's care from a poor quality minder could cost a third of the entire week's budget to feed and clothe the child.

The Ranger Report was just one of many investigations into social conditions carried out around the turn of the century. Charles Booth in London and Seerbohm Rowntree in York had both long argued that Britain would ignore the needs of the lower orders at its cost. Rowntree's study, published in 1901, found that 27.8 per cent of the population of York lived in total poverty. This, he explained, included all those families 'whose total earnings are insufficient to obtain the minimum necessities for the maintenance of merely physical efficiency' and families 'whose total earnings would be sufficient for the maintenance of merely physical efficiency were it not that some portion of it is absorbed by other expenditures, either useful or wasteful'.[16] Referring to these categories as 'primary' and 'secondary' poverty, respectively, Rowntree claimed they accounted for just under 10 per cent and 18 per cent of the population of York. In defining 'primary poverty', Rowntree left no room for doubt about its severity:

A family living upon the scale allowed for in this estimate must never spend a penny on railway fare or omnibus. They must never go into the country unless they walk. They must never purchase a halfpenny newspaper or spend a penny to buy a ticket for a popular concert. They must write no letters to absent children, for they cannot afford to pay the postage. They must never contribute anything to their church or chapel, or give any help to a neighbour which costs money. They cannot save, nor can they join a sick club or Trade Union, because they cannot pay the necessary subscriptions. The children must have no pocket money for dolls, marbles or sweets. The father must smoke no tobacco, and must drink no beer. The mother must never buy any pretty clothes for herself or for her children, the character of the family wardrobe as for the family diet being governed by the regulation, 'nothing must be bought but that which is absolutely necessary for the maintenance of physical health, and what is bought must be of the plainest and most economical description.' Should a child fall ill, it must be attended by the parish doctor; should it die, it must be buried by the parish. Finally, the wage-earner must never be absent from his work for a single day.[17]

The embarrassing performance of the British Army in the Boer War, where failings in equipment, training and logistical management saw Britain being taught, as Kipling put it, 'no end of a lesson', served to highlight the problem. Around 7,500 soldiers died in battle against the Boers whilst over 13,000 died of disease as they tried to survive in extreme weather conditions without the appropriate clothing and often without rations. Worse still, although volunteers came forward to join the army to keep it up to strength, it was found that most failed to meet the physical standards for enlistment, due largely to illnesses linked directly to poverty and malnutrition.

Children gather to mark the coronation of King Edward in August 1902. Most of the boys in this picture would see action by 1918.

'Half-timers' gather outside a woolen mill waiting for their shift to start. Few could aspire to more than the most basic education and became family breadwinners before they finished school.

Although the rejection rate was often exaggerated, it drew attention to the failures of Victorian-era laissez-faire politics in which government refused to accept any responsibility for the welfare of the population. Working-class people – from whom the men needed to guard Britain's empire would be drawn – had been left to fend for themselves in an economy that was geared towards maximising profit for a relatively small and wealthy elite. With wages at subsistence level, few could afford to provide an adequate diet for their families and fewer still the luxury of medical and dental treatment. Poor dental health, for example, would continue to create a problem for the military into the early days of the Great War for the simple reason that men with damaged or missing teeth could not chew the hard tack biscuits that would form a major part of their rations on active service. The rejection of so many potential recruits could not be ignored. The inter-departmental Committee on Physical Deterioration was set up to investigate and report on the state of the nation's health and quickly established the link between poverty, malnutrition and failing health standards.

Inside a typical working-class home. A 'two up, two down' house would often accommodate large families.

At the same time, the political landscape was changing. In 1900, the Labour Representation Committee was formed to champion the interests of the working classes and of the growing trade union movement and, in the 'khaki election' of that year, secured two seats in Parliament. Aided by the Liberal Party in an attempt to break the Conservatives' grip on power, the Labour Party brought a new impetus to the campaign to improve the lot of the urban poor. The findings of the Committee on Physical Deterioration supported much of what the Liberal and Labour parties were demanding by showing that if the government wanted to maintain an army strong enough to retain the empire, it needed to ensure that the next generation of soldiers would be fit enough to serve. Noting the extent of Britain's urban squalor, former Prime Minister Lord Rosebery said that 'in the great cities, in the rookeries and slums ... an imperial race cannot be reared ... The survival of the fittest is an absolute truth'.[18]

Alongside that, Britain's place as a world leader in industry was under threat. Foreign manufacturing, particularly in Germany and the US, had not only caught up with Britain, but was edging ahead. A poorly educated workforce struggled to keep up with advances in technology and it was becoming increasingly clear that despite the signs posted outside factories and mills, the workforce could no longer be expected to be just 'hands'. As German production outstripped British, observers pointed to the social welfare system established in Germany as a crucial motivating factor. Whilst the British worker felt alienated from the country, the German worker felt he had an investment in the state and all it stood for. If the British Government intended to keep its position as a world leader, it needed popular support to do it. It needed to make its people believe in it. In 1904, across the West Riding, the boys started school.

2

'Cannot will otherwise than what you wish him to will'

Believing that an efficient modern state could not afford for its people to be illiterate, Frederick William I of Prussia instituted compulsory state-run primary education in 1717, establishing a model that would eventually be copied around the world. Declaring that 'an educated people can be easily governed', his son, Frederick the Great, strengthened the system so that by 1763, the Prussian Government was enforcing compliance with the threat of fines or even the removal of children from families who failed to maintain attendance requirements. The near disastrous war against Napoleon further encouraged reforms at all levels within the military and government and, although it stopped short of abolishing serfdom, Prussia instigated new approaches allowing greater opportunities for the lower classes, encouraged immigration and granted equality for Jewish immigrants already settled in the country, lessened the power of the guilds and weakened that of the Church, all of which stimulated industry and the economy. But if some saw universal education as part of the effort to modernise the country, others saw things somewhat differently.

Johann Fichte, a philosopher whose work was influential in the development of the German school system, had written that schools 'must fashion the person, and fashion him in such a way that he simply cannot will otherwise than what you wish him to will'.[1] In Britain, philosophers like John Stuart Mill agreed with Fichte and argued that state-run schools for the general population served to curtail civil liberties. In that light, the German policy of educating the masses was seen in Britain as a sinister attempt to create a purely militaristic society: 'The first lesson instilled into the mind of the German boy is that he has come into the world in order to take his part in the defence of the Fatherland. Army organisation and education are therefore parts of one coherent whole.' Dr M.E. Sadler wrote:

> Side by side with the influences of German education are to be traced the influences of German military service. The two sets of influence interact on one another

and intermingle. German education impregnates the German army with science. The German army predisposes German education to ideas of organization and discipline. Military and educational discipline go hand in hand.[2]

Despite these concerns, the introduction of state-funded education was part of a package of measures that by the end of the nineteenth century had seen Prussia elevated from a European backwater to a strong, independent state that in 1871 could bring together the various Germanic principalities into a single unified nation capable of challenging its European neighbours for political and economic supremacy. In marked contrast, when Arnold, Harold and the other boys started school in 1904, free compulsory elementary education for all was still a new phenomenon in Britain and the elementary school system was struggling, as Alan Penn put it, to 'serve the twin criteria of social utility and cheapness of operation'[3] in order to instil the basic skills necessary for pupils to take their place in the workforce at the lowest possible cost.

Although a wide variety of local institutions ranging from Sunday schools to Industrial, Reformatory, Poor Law and the so-called Ragged Schools were already in existence, educational provision in urban areas was patchy and it was not until the Liberal MP for Bradford, William Edward Forster, pushed through the Elementary Education Act of 1870 that state funding was made available to ensure a school place for every child in the country. The establishment of local school boards and their funding was intended to provide places for those children previously unable to obtain any sort of education but the act was, at best, a compromise. Board schools would fit into the gaps left by other forms of education, but were permitted to continue to charge tuition fees that made education a luxury beyond the means of large, low income families. Boards were elected to ensure the building of schools in areas identified as needing them and they were given the power to create by-laws regarding attendance, but although these allowed them to fine parents who did not send their children to school there were often exemptions for children living a mile or more from the school or where the child was deemed – by widely varying criteria – to have met the minimum standard of education. The so-called 'Dunce's Certificate', for example, allowed children to leave education solely on the basis of the completion of 250 school attendances regardless of whether they had been taught anything. As a result, the parents of the boys' generation often had little or no education themselves and had developed little respect for it. It was, to a great many, simply a luxury they could not afford until a further act of 1891 made elementary education free for all pupils for the first time.

Even then, though, there were problems. In the 1880s, the Bradford School Board was dealing with around 10,000 'half timers' – children attending school for part of the day before going out to exhausting but poorly paid work and who, as the Committee on Physical Deterioration had found, were in very poor physical condition. In 1887, the headmaster of Bradford's Wapping Road

Teaching was not just about the three Rs but also about becoming British. When, in 1915, the threat of German air raids increased, these children were taught how to react.

School began using his own money to buy bread, jam and tea after several pupils fainted from hunger during school assembly and an 1889 report indicated that over 50,000 pupils in London alone were attending school 'in want of food'. By 1902 the Bradford Education Committee had begun providing meals for poor children but the practice was difficult to support since it was illegal to use public funds for that purpose. Two members of the board, Margaret McMillan and future Bradford MP Fred Jowett, lobbied Parliament and in 1906 Bradford became the first area allowed to provide free school meals at state expense for children deemed to be in poverty. The following year, the Bradford school medical officer, Dr Ralph Crowley, was given a grant of £50 to study the effects of the programme. By measuring the weight of a test group, Crowley found that during the Whit holiday when schools were closed for a week, his test group lost the weight they had previously gained from their school meals and took two weeks to recover full fitness.

Perhaps not surprisingly, against this backdrop of poverty and hunger in which education took lower priority than physical survival, the board schools became, as W.A.L. Blyth put it, 'a whole educational process in themselves and one which is by definition limited and by implication inferior; a low plateau, rather than the foothills of a complete education'.[4] The overall aim, Blyth argued, was not to educate the masses beyond what was necessary to maintain an efficient workforce and offered little or no prospect of further education. Teachers were of varying quality, some genuinely dedicated and innovative but often with minimal training and knowledge. The 1900 guidelines, for example, suggested that school trips to local museums and art galleries were to be actively encouraged but inspectors soon found that teachers 'seem afraid to undertake visits to Museums ... some tell me that they would not like to explain objects to their classes because there would generally be experts near at hand who would easily detect any mistakes that they might make while others say that they are not sure of the kind of reception that they would meet with on the part of the Curators ...'[5]

From the outset, as the Acland Report was later to comment, the children attending board schools were often those who had experienced poor or virtually non-existent childcare from an early age and in many cases they had been left to fend for themselves as 'feral' children. Schools were segregated into boys and girls with separate entrances for each. Around fifty to sixty pupils per class was commonplace and up to seventy not unusual, with discipline a significant issue, especially in the boys' classes. Older pupils were frequently relied on as 'monitors' to act as teaching assistants and there was a genuine need to establish acceptance of the teacher's authority, the importance of punctuality, obedience and conformity simply as a practical measure to ensure that any sort of teaching could take place. As a response, the teaching of drill movements became standard in all elementary schools to instil obedience.

It started young. Writing in 1905, Katherine Bathurst, one of the few female school inspectors for the Board of Education, described one class of 'babies' being drilled by their teacher in an infant class:

Fold arms – Sit up – eyes on ceiling (all the heads are raised) – Eyes on floor (all the heads are bent) – Eyes to the right – Eyes to the left – Eyes on blackboard – Eyes on me (all the sixty baby heads are wagged in unison).

This, she said, might be followed by twenty minutes in which all the children were required to do was thread needles. 'The discipline,' she said, 'is military rather than maternal, and can only be maintained at the expense of much healthy, valuable, and, as far as the children are concerned, necessary freedom.'[6] Often, schools in built-up areas lacked space for playgrounds, but enterprising teachers found ways to get their children to perform drill movements – in some cases climbing onto flat roofs, in others getting children to stand on benches in the classrooms or in the aisles between desks to perform synchronised arm and leg movements under the general heading of 'Swedish Drill'. Elsewhere, if space permitted, military-style marching was the preferred form of exercise. It was cheap, required no equipment and fulfilled the need to discipline the children. Teachers turned to Parts 1 and 2 of the army's 1870 'Field Exercise Book' and schools were encouraged to purchase (at just tuppence each) copies of a short *Manual of Elementary Military Exercise and Drill* developed for army-run schools for serving military families.

In a report on Church of England schools in 1871, the Reverend H.W. Bellars claimed:

> The drill in our schools is generally bad; I should like to see a regular system of military drill introduced, with marching tunes and, where practicable, with drum and fife bands. Arrangements with the adjutants of the militia and volunteers for providing the necessary teaching might easily be made, and the expense of it by employing drill sergeants would not be great.[7]

By 1875, like many others around the country, the board schools of the West Riding had embraced the need for boys to be disciplined through drill lessons. Her Majesty's Inspectorate of Schools recommended around two hours per week 'for not more than twenty weeks in the year' in school time and even that Saturday morning sessions could be held – each of which would count towards the infamous 'Dunce's Certificate'. The Bradford Board had employed Sergeant J. Ryan as its Drill Instructor; an 1892 report by the Chief Inspector of Schools in nearby Leeds shows that they, too, had taken on a full-time Drill Instructor who visited each school once a fortnight and the authority held annual field days in which schools competed for banners awarded for the best drill displays.

But whilst many argued the need to create discipline in order to manage schools, others grew concerned about the increasingly militaristic tone of the training. Parliament debated the possibility of providing formal military training as part of the school curriculum with Sir Lauder Brunton, later a founder member of the Boy Scout movement's national committee, suggesting that weapons training using wooden rifles should begin at the age of four and progress throughout the school years.[8] In some areas, school boards had gone as far as obtaining weapons, equipment and uniforms and even provided shooting practice and tactical training for pupils. Trade unions and religious groups expressed their concerns, but in the wake of the Boer War, calls increased for the introduction of compulsory military training, with schools being identified as the ideal starting point. During a debate in the House of Lords in 1905 Lord Meath, founder of the Lads' Drill Association and a proponent of conscription, even went as far as proposing that the War Office and Board of Education set up a committee to consider the use of War Office funding to provide weapons training for all boys. After lengthy discussion it was agreed that it would be impractical to provide the proposed two to three years of training in the northern schools because of the impact this would have on the already restricted education of the half-timer children.

Outside schools, the phrase 'muscular Christianity' was being widely used to describe the prevailing attitude across religious denominations. Drawn from the New Testament teachings of St Paul and others who used athletic metaphors to help describe the challenges of the Christian life, the term was first adopted in the

1850s to describe the characteristics of the novels of writers like Charles Kingsley and Thomas Hughes, both of whom were keen sportsmen and advocates of active lifestyles as an antidote to what they saw as the 'effeminacy' of 'education and bookishness'.[9] Hughes used the term in his 1861 novel *Tom Brown at Oxford*, saying that it was 'a good thing to have strong and well-exercised bodies', and that even 'the least of the muscular Christians has hold of the old chivalrous and Christian belief, that a man's body is given him to be trained and brought into subjection, and then used for the protection of the weak, the advancement of all righteous causes, and the subduing of the earth which God has given to the children of men'. The premise of Victorian muscular Christianity – that participation in sport could contribute to the development of Christian morality, physical fitness and a 'manly' character – fitted perfectly with ideals of helping the poor, weaker members of society, and from the 1880s onwards, church and civic leaders began enthusiastically promoting healthy, active and above all morally uplifting pastimes for the nation's youth.

Starting in Glasgow in 1883, W.A. Smith's Boy's Brigade used military structure, ranks and discipline and was founded on ideals of Christian manliness expressed through gymnastics, summer camps, religious services and classes as well as rifle drill and other forms of paramilitary training. Enormously popular, by 1910 there were some 2,200 companies connected with different churches throughout the United Kingdom, the British Empire and the United States, with 10,000 officers and 100,000 boys.[10] It was followed in 1891 by the founding of the Church Lads' Brigade with its sister organisation, the Church Nursing and Ambulance Brigade for Young Women and Girls, which became the Church Girls' Brigade in 1901. Other groups, such as the Jewish Lads' Brigade and the Catholic Boys' Brigade, followed suit and, in 1907, Lord Robert Baden-Powell held an experimental camp on Brownsea Island near Poole in Dorset to try out ideas he had developed during reconnaissance operations in South Africa and at the 1899–1900 siege of Mafeking. On his return to the UK, Baden-Powell had written about the importance of training troops in fieldcraft and tracking both to increase their military skills and to improve their ability to use their own initiative. The book proved enormously popular, not only with the military, but also among teachers and youth organisations looking for ways to inspire the boys in their classes.

Although Baden-Powell had some concerns about the military organisation of the Boys' Brigade and promoted the ideal of an international movement emphasising peace and co-operation, he believed his ideas could offer interesting and useful activities for such groups to take part in and set about writing a new version of his military manual with youth groups in mind. *Scouting for Boys* was published in 1908 in six fortnightly parts at 4*d* a copy. Sales of the book were enormous and what had been intended as a training aid for existing organisations became the handbook of new, spontaneously created Scout Patrols formed by groups of boys on their own initiative. In September 1908, Baden-Powell set up an office to deal

Although based on a pacifist ideal of co-operation, the Boy Scout Movement owed much to its military origins. Here scouts tackle a military assault course.

with enquiries pouring in about what he began to refer to as 'the Movement' and it quickly became established in its own right. No fan of Liberal politics, in 1911 Baden-Powell complained that 'Free feeding and old age pensions, strike pay, cheap beer and indiscriminate charity do not make for the hardening of the nation or the building up of a self-reliant, energetic manhood'.[11]

Despite their popularity, concerns were voiced about the quasi-military nature of such groups (the Boys' Brigade, for example, would continue to practise rifle drill until the 1920s) but even among Quakers there was support for uniformed groups:

> While concerns about militarism were never far away, Friends emphasised the benefits of uniformed youth organisations for the training of young people's character. For example, Martha Baker of Willesden argued that the Boys' Life Brigade – *not* the Boys' Brigade – could 'supply the elements needed, both as to out-door exercise, physical drill, discipline, brotherliness, self-sacrifice, and patriotism'.[12]

By the time the Scouts were established, the Earl of Meath's own youth groups, the Lads' Drill Association and the Duty and Discipline Movement had been incorporated into the National Service League. Founded to provide 'systematic physical and military training of all British lads and their instruction in the art of the rifle', Meath's campaign left little doubt that he regarded preparation for war (almost certainly against Germany) as vital to future British interests. Stressing its tenets of 'discipline, duty, mutual service and patriotism', the movement attracted many senior establishment figures – including Winston Churchill – as supporters. By 1907 it was actively campaigning for compulsory military training at school as part of the National Service League's agenda to bring in peacetime conscription in order to create a reserve army in case of war and claimed over 91,000 members by 1911 but, as Ian Beckett records, its support came largely from the Church of England, with a number of Anglican bishops among its more prominent backers. As such, in the West Riding, where Non-Conformist religions held sway, there was little interest.

Things came to a head in 1910 when youth groups came under pressure to become part of the newly formed national cadet force scheme linked directly to the Territorial Force and funded by the War Office with the threat of penalties against those who failed to sign up. Despite its strong military leanings, the Boys' Brigade resisted and, with its huge membership, was able to survive the threats to its existence, as did the Scout Movement. The creation of the cadet force, though, brought another layer to the mix. Public schools had long had cadet forces which were seen as officer training schools for future military leaders. Now, another cadet force would be open to ordinary youths as a stepping stone to service in the Territorial Force, cutting down on the need for basic military training by drawing in those who already knew how to march and drill and who had the basic fieldcraft skills for camp.

In his study of Youth Movements in the early twentieth century, historian Paul Wilkinson used a survey by the Mass Observation Archive to show that between 1901 and 1920, 34 per cent of British males were, at one time or another, members of the Boy Scouts. A further 14 per cent said they had been part of the Boys' Brigade. Even allowing for some dual membership, he says, a conservative estimate would have around 40 per cent of young male Britons having been part of one or other organisation.[13] To this figure we can add a wide variety of other youth groups, sports teams and clubs to suggest that a substantial majority of the generation growing up in the first decade of the twentieth century were members of some sort of organised social group. Among the reinforcement draft to which the six boys would eventually be posted, membership of the Scouts, the Temperance Band of Hope and Church missions was commonplace. The problem was that there is evidence to suggest these groups tended to attract more upwardly minded youths from upper working-class families than the disadvantaged urban poor they were aimed at.

By 1901, muscular Christianity was influential enough in England that Cotton Minchin, in his account of the influence of public schools on English history, could praise 'the Englishman going through the world with rifle in one hand and Bible in the other' and add, 'If asked what our muscular Christianity has done, we point to the British Empire'.[14] Inevitably, such thinking heavily influenced both the school boards and the School Inspectorate when they set about attempting to impose some sort of standardisation on the various types of school in operation. In 1900 the government issued guidelines requiring all schools to provide 'suitable instruction in the elementary things' and 'simple lessons on common things'. For 'older scholars' aged 7 years and upwards, a course of instruction 'to be taken as a rule in all schools' involved 'Lessons, including object lessons, on geography, history, and common things'.[15] The inclusion of history and geography into the recommended syllabus owed much to Disraeli's 'one nation' belief that as societies develop, members within them have increasing levels of duty towards each other, and in particular an emphasis on the obligation of the upper classes to care for those classes below them. As the threat of revolution spread across Europe, it was clear that the two-tier class system could not be maintained forever and that there was a need to harness the political support of the wider population for a common political goal. The teaching of geography would give children a sense of the role their country played in a world in which they, as Britons, owed a duty of care to the people of the less developed regions of the empire. At the same time, history could be used to create a sense of nationhood by teaching children about the role models provided by a variety of real and fictional British (or more often English) heroes.

Specific lessons in history were initially few and far between, but the statutory inclusion of history in the curriculum in 1902 saw a massive rise in the teaching of the subject and between 1890 and 1903 the number of elementary schools offering separate lessons in history rose from just over 400 to around 23,000. Writing in 1901, educationalist H.L. Withers noted:

It has no doubt been the case in many schools, in which History has not been presented as a class subject, that nevertheless, lessons in history have been given. And in every school without exception the rule had held good that out of the three reading books in every class above the Second Standard one has been a 'History reader'.[16]

'Readers' became big business for publishers since they could serve a dual purpose, thus keeping costs down. In a 1906 teaching manual, James Welton claimed:

If the term 'reading book' be confined to those books which are used mainly for oral reading, then we see that the contents should be of value as literature rather than as information. The attempt to combine the two, like most endeavours to kill two birds with one stone, usually hinders the attainment of the result which should be sought from each. The chief exception is the history reader, which, if well chosen, is at once literature and the medium of conveying definite information.[17]

The phrase 'if well chosen' was the key. History 'readers' were being produced from a variety of sources, some more reliable than others. In his 1904 teaching manual, A.H. Garlick argued that historical learning in elementary school should not encourage jingoistic sentiments, but instead should 'help to break away national *prejudice* by giving us some knowledge of other countries' (Garlick's emphasis). He continued: 'Bias against, and hatred and contempt for other nations, are often the results of ignorance.'[18] James Welton's manual followed suit, arguing that in addition to being in poor taste, the history produced in textbooks was considered largely *un*historical:

A good textbook should be one written by an **author who is competent at once as a scholar and a teacher**. Too many of those in common use are mere pieces of hackwork, the study of which engenders prejudice and false notions even when it does not lead to disgust with the whole subject. [Welton's emphasis][19]

Despite the warnings, school texts continued to be produced on the basis of profit over accuracy. Charles Fletcher and Rudyard Kipling's 1911 *A School History of England*, for example, was heavily criticised by the *Educational Times* for being too bloodthirsty and militaristic but sold well. A glance at some of its content helps to illustrate the degree to which such readers could be used as political propaganda. The authors make clear their own social Darwinian beliefs in noting 'improvements in medicine and surgery have saved and prolonged countless useful, as well as many useless, lives'.[20] What constitutes a 'useless' life is left undefined, but the theme of some form of racial or social superiority pervades the book. Discussing the Roman invasion, the authors consider it 'a misfortune for Britain that Rome never conquered the whole island', leaving 'no traces of civilization' in Scotland and never attempting to invade Ireland; 'So Ireland never went to school, and has been a spoilt child ever since … incapable of ruling herself, and impatient of rule by others.'[21]

Elsewhere, in discussing the history of the nineteenth century, there is an acknowledgment that readers might learn of this period from older family members who experienced them, 'and so it is desirable for me, in this last chapter, rather to state what did take place than to try to *guide your opinions*' (author's emphasis).[22] It then goes on to discuss the Prince Regent ('mean, cowardly and an incredible liar'), William IV ('stupid honest old man') and Queen Victoria ('No sovereign ever so unweariedly set herself to win the love of her people, to be the servant of her people. And her people rewarded her with a love that she had more than deserved'). Prince Albert of Saxe-Coburg-Gotha is described as 'the wise and prudent statesman, the peace-lover, the peacemaker of Europe, the noble English gentleman'. These comments are offered to children as facts, not opinions, offering little scope for discussion. It concludes with a comparison between Britain and other nations and the warning that future war could be disastrous: 'But I don't think there can be any doubt that the only safe thing for all of us who love our country is to learn soldiering at once, and to be prepared to fight at any moment.'[23]

The original caption explains that these scouts were taking the wounded out 'for an airing'. Scouts like Arnold Ambler and Harold Wiseman enthusiastically wore their uniforms even to work in the early days of the war and were actively involved in assisting the wounded and refugees.

The teaching of history and geography, many argue, was not to broaden the children's minds, but to create a sense of nationhood by teaching a view of Britain as a united nation with an innate racial superiority over all others. Written predominantly by middle-class English men, they tended to view 'British' and 'English' as synonymous with a heavy emphasis on an Anglo-Saxon, rather than Celtic, heritage. In an age characterised by a widespread support for Social Darwinism and the survival of the fittest, the Anglo-Saxon 'race' was considered to be the pinnacle of achievement. Book I of *The Britannia History Readers* in 1902 explained:

England is only part of the island called Great Britain, the other parts of which are Scotland and Wales. To the west of Great Britain is another island, called Ireland. The two together are known as the British Isles. From the first, Englishmen have had much to do with the inhabitants of the other parts of the British Isles, that it is impossible to write about them quite separately. And they are all now under one sovereign, and form the kingdom of Great Britain and Ireland. The British Isles are only a small part of the dominions of the British Sovereign, to whom new lands belong all over the world. It is said that upon the British Empire the Sun never sets … English history has to tell, among other things, how it is that we have come to possess such a large part of the world.[24]

It was a theme continued by G.T. Warner's 1899 school textbook, *A Brief Survey of British History*, which told children:

When we look at a map of the world, and we see how wide is the red that marks the British Empire, we may feel proud … Our race possesses the colonial spirit which French, Spaniards and Germans do not possess: the daring that takes men into distant lands, the doggedness that keeps them steadfast in want and difficulties, the masterful spirit that gives them power of Eastern races, the sense of justice that abuses them from abusing this power.[25]

Readers like this were, at best, of limited value as textbooks. Their main purpose, after all, was in teaching children to read, not to analyse history. As one school inspector noted of a Wakefield school:

I have sometimes been puzzled, in schools where history is taught through a reading-book, to discover without reference to the time-table whether a lesson was one in history or in reading, lessons marked on the time-table as reading being overburdened with questions on the historical subject-matter, and lessons marked as history being taken up with the correction of faults of phrasing.

Elsewhere, another reported:

The children are attentive and interested while their teachers are talking to them [of history and geography]; but, except in the best schools, very little of the information is returned to the teacher; the children appear to remember scarcely anything. One head teacher's view is that it is not necessary that the children should be able to answer questions on these subjects nowadays.[26]

'Ultimately,' argues Peter Yeandle:

it was intended that these readers would confer a sense of the national past to which scholars felt they belonged. Readers, to some extent, were invitations into middle class perceptions of national identity. The working classes had previously little reason to feel themselves part of the Empire project. Now – in order to promote a sense of national belonging and national pride concomitant with selling the values and legitimacy of imperialism – the common man (and to a much lesser extent woman) was to be written into national narrative. It was the intention that working class schoolchildren would, in identifying with the national past, identify with the nation in its present, and be prepared to serve the national wellbeing in the future.[27]

Whatever its faults, the elementary education system stressed the teaching of the three Rs of reading, writing and 'rithmetic above all else so that by 1900, the overwhelming majority of the population had become literate to some degree. A crude measure of the success of the efforts of Forster and his colleagues comes from research into marriage registers which showed that in 1872, 29 per cent of adults were unable to sign their own name. By 1880, the figure had fallen to 11 per cent and by 1900, just 5.5 per cent of newlyweds were unable to write.[28] This massive increase in literacy brought with it a new market for publishers and for newspaper owners with the appearance of new national papers such as the *Daily Mail* (1896), the *Daily Express* (1900) and the *Daily Mirror* (1904), all aiming at the middle and aspiring working classes.

Of these, the *Daily Mail*, founded according to legend on owner Lord Northcliffe's belief that his paper should provide a daily hate figure, would prove to be immensely influential on public thinking in the years before the outbreak of war. Selling at half the penny cost of other papers, it quickly achieved huge circulation figures and became the best-selling paper in the world, with over a million copies sold a day by 1902. Claiming not to shape public opinion but only to reflect it, Northcliffe's editorial stance could be confusingly flexible:

When Lord Northcliffe set out to feed the war flame in South Africa, he did so, I think, without any real feeling against the Boers. He is not, I fancy, a man who bears malice. For to bear malice involves attachment to some point of view, indicates some reality of character. Had the Boers won he would probably have written them a letter of congratulation. But the mood of the country was high and turbulent. We were full of such boastings as the Gentiles use, and lesser breeds without the law.

And his conception of journalism is to give the public the meat it craves for. If it wants a war, then it is his duty to paint the enemy black and horrific; if it wants a sensation, then it is his task to provide it. Does the temper of the moment demand the immolation of France, then he is the fiercest of Francophobes:

If the French cannot cease their insults (he says in 1899), their Colonies will be taken from them and given to Germany and Italy. The French have succeeded in thoroughly convincing John Bull that they are his inveterate enemies … England has long hesitated between France and Germany. But she has always respected the German character, whereas she has gradually come to feel a contempt for France. Nothing like an entente cordiale can subsist between England and her nearest neighbour.

Does the mood change and Germany become the object of national suspicion, then who so ready to throw faggots on the flame:

Yes, we detest the Germans and we detest them cordially (he says in 1903). They render themselves odious to the whole of Europe. I would not tolerate that anyone should print in my journal the least thing which might to-day wound France; but, on the other hand, I would not like anyone to insert anything that could please Germany.[29]

In the late nineteenth century, anti-Semitic pogroms in Eastern Europe sent thousands of refugees fleeing to Britain, often as a stopover on the way to the United States. By the turn of the century, a popular and media backlash had begun with groups like the British Brothers League campaigning to avoid the country becoming a 'dumping ground for the scum of Europe', which led to the passing of the Aliens Act of 1905 to curb immigration. In the public mind, 'Russia' and 'Prussia' were one and the same and rumours of a German/Jewish conspiracy began to circulate, especially after Germany's open support for the Boers. A whole genre of popular fiction about a German invasion of England had emerged, with Erskine Childers' 1903 spy novel about a planned attack across the North Sea selling so well that 'for the next ten years Childers' book remained the most powerful contribution of any English writer to the debate on Britain's alleged military unpreparedness'.[30] By coincidence, Childers' plot bore some semblance to the 'Schroder Plan' developed by Germany in 1897, when war planning included a scenario in which an attack on England might be made, and the book was published shortly before the government announced the building of its long planned naval base covering the North Sea. This last move gave Childers credibility as a man of vision – indeed he objected to his publisher's insistence on marketing the book as a novel, fearing his warning would be lost. So great was Childers' influence that when war broke out in 1914 Churchill personally ordered the Director of Naval Intelligence to employ him.

Whilst Childers wrote well, it was another writer who would most influence British thinking in the years before the Great War. William Le Queux's *The Invasion of 1910*, published in 1906, provided a detailed account of an invasion by Germany made possible by cuts to the army budget and failures to introduce compulsory military training. Written as a military history, the book described in detail the landing of German troops at Grimsby and their inexorable march southwards to London. Typical of his style is the description of fighting involving the regiments to which the boys of the West Riding would flock in 1914:

> The [German] independent cavalry advance continued through Doncaster until dusk, when Rotherham was reached, during which advance scattered bodies of British Imperial Yeomanry were met and compelled to retreat, a dozen or so lives being lost. It appears that late in the afternoon of Sunday news was brought into Sheffield of what was in progress, and a squadron of Yeomanry donned their uniforms and rode forward to reconnoitre, with the disastrous results already mentioned.
>
> The sensation caused in Sheffield when it became known that German cavalry were so close as Rotherham was enormous, and the scenes in the streets soon approached a panic; for it was wildly declared that that night the enemy intended to occupy the town. The Mayor telegraphed to the War Office, appealing for additional defensive force, but no response was received to the telegram. The small force of military in the town, which consisted of the 2nd Battalion Yorkshire Light Infantry, some Royal Artillery, and the local Volunteers, were soon assembled, and going out occupied the strong position above Sheffield between Catcliffe and Tinsley, overlooking the valley of the Rother to the east.
>
> The expectation that the Germans intended an immediate descent on Sheffield was not realised, because the German tactics were merely to reconnoitre and report on the defences of Sheffield, if any existed. This they did by remaining to the eastward of the river Rother, whence the high ground rising before Sheffield could be easily observed.
>
> Before dusk one or two squadrons of Cuirassiers were seen to be examining the river to find fords and ascertain the capacity of the bridges, while others appeared to be comparing the natural features of the ground with the maps with which they all appeared to be provided.
>
> As night fell, however, the cavalry retired towards Doncaster, which town was occupied, the Angel being the cavalry headquarters. The reason the Germans could not advance at once upon Sheffield was that the cavalry was not strongly supported by infantry from their base, the distance from Goole being too great to be covered in a single day. That the arrangements for landing were in every detail

perfect could not be doubted, but owing to the narrow channel of the Ouse time was necessary, and it is considered probable that fully three days must elapse from Sunday before the Germans are absolutely established.

An attempt has been made by the Yorkshire Light Infantry and the York and Lancaster Regiment, with three battalions of Volunteers stationed at Pontefract, to discover the enemy's strength and position between Askern and Snaith, but so far without avail, the cavalry screen across the whole country being impenetrable.[31]

The book continued in similar vein until the Germans reached London:

The hospitals were already full of wounded from the various engagements of the past week. The London, St. Thomas', Charing Cross, St. George's, Guy's, and Bartholomew's were overflowing; and the surgeons, with patriotic self-denial, were working day and night in an endeavour to cope with the ever-arriving crowd of suffering humanity. The field hospitals away to the northward were also reported full … Everywhere people were regretting that Lord Roberts' solemn warnings in 1906 had been unheeded, for had we adopted his scheme for universal service such dire catastrophe could never have occurred. Many had, alas! declared it to be synonymous with conscription, which it certainly was not, and by that foolish argument had prevented the public at large from accepting it as the only means for our salvation as a nation. The repeated warnings had been disregarded, and we had, unhappily, lived in a fool's paradise, in the self-satisfied belief that England could not be successfully invaded. Now, alas! the country had realised the truth when too late.[32]

Le Queux's account was presented as a 'forecast' based on 'all the available military and naval knowledge' and apparently the result of close co-operation with the retired commander-in-chief of the forces, Lord Roberts. Le Queux was the author of a number of pulp spy fiction novels and in 1894 had published *The Great War in England in 1897*, in which a Russian and French coalition attack scores significant successes until Germany enters the war in support of Britain. Now, in the wake of the Entente Cordiale, the enemies had changed but the plot remained very similar. Portrayed as a great military thinker, in 1914 Le Queux became convinced that the Germans were out to get him for 'rumbling their schemes' and demanded special protection from German assassins. The Metropolitan Police, however, regarded him as 'not a person to be taken seriously' and refused.[33] Far from being a strategic genius, Le Queux had been employed to write the book for serialisation in the *Daily Mail* and to write it to Lord Northcliffe's specifications. After taking advice from Roberts about likely German targets, Le Queux followed orders from Northcliffe to ignore it and to substitute towns with a large *Daily Mail* readership for the strategically relevant towns and villages Roberts named. Backed by an aggressive marketing campaign funded by the *Daily Mail* in which men dressed in Prussian uniforms paraded around Whitehall, the book became a million-seller and was said to have been translated into twenty-seven languages (including an unauthorised German edition). It was eventually released as a film in late 1914.

The works of Childers and Le Queux were only part of an outpouring of anti-German writings which, as John Ramsden put it, 'was beyond parody, for serious books had already hijacked the improbable, leaving no room for satire'.[34] The *Mail* was soon advising its readers that they should refuse to be served by German or Austrian waiters and to demand to see the passport of those claiming to be Swiss, whilst the million-selling *Boy's Own* paper advised its readers in 1906 that most German tourists in Britain were spies on the basis that they wore jackboots in bad weather. An 8-year-old Evelyn Waugh formed a gang dedicated to drilling and preparing for invasion whilst Guy du Maurier's play *An Englishman's Home* played to packed audiences in 1909 with its tale of the takeover of a middle-class house by foreign troops. Elsewhere, live performances of battles against German troops were staged at Crystal Palace, leading one observer to note: 'formerly one had to be able to read in order to be spooked by invasion scares; now a blind illiterate had access to scaremongering literature.'[35] The matter was not helped by speeches such as that given by Colonel Hind in Doncaster on 15 March 1913 as part of a recruitment

'An Englishman's Home', 1911. Years of novels about a German attack were followed by plays and, by 1913, films on the same subject.

drive for the understrength Territorial Force. The threat of German invasion, he claimed, was a real one. Germany had increased its spending on arms and now even had a fleet of thirty airships capable of flying troops or explosives across the North Sea at any time.[36]

As a result, the generation that went to war in 1914 was one for whom the threat to Britain's survival was taken as read and where training for military service was not just a matter of duty but seemingly about personal survival. It was a society conditioned at many levels, as Michael Howard put it, 'to accept military activity as necessary or desirable or both',[37] but the degree to which Edwardian Britain was a truly militarised society is the subject of much ongoing debate. Despite the acceptance of military need, the army was still largely seen as the last refuge of the unemployed and desperate, and soldiers in uniform were routinely banned from pubs, music halls and theatres. As Kipling had noted in 1892, only in wartime would soldiers and soldiering be valued.

When the boys who would travel to France in 1918 reached the end of their schooling, they had been thoroughly immersed in a world where the belief that Britain and the British stood supreme was unquestioned and in which notions of God, honour, discipline and duty had been focused, as Fichte had predicted, in such a way that they could not will otherwise than what their leaders would wish them to will.

3

'Murderous gang
of warmongers ...'

The increase in literacy rates over the previous generation had created a
market for reading material and Bradford alone had four daily newspapers
and one weekly edition by 1914. But if the ordinary men and women were
better informed about the world and more politically aware than their parents, the
murder on 28 June 1914 of an Austrian Archduke in a faraway Serbian city meant
little to the people of the West Riding. Even where the story was reported, papers
showed little sympathy for 'Austria's Idiot Arch-Dukes', themselves considered by
many as 'dangerous to liberal institutions'.[1] As a later history put it:

> The Austrian government regarded this crime as part of an organised move-
> ment by Servia [sic]. It stirred feelings of horror, true; but Leeds people, like other
> inhabitants of Great Britain, felt no particular apprehension as to the ability of
> statesmanship to compose the differences that arose. For several weeks our public
> and private affairs proceeded as usual. We had our own troubles – unrest in the
> industrial world, grave disorders in Ireland – but even these did not divert atten-
> tion from the ordinary routine of business and pleasure.[2]

Across the northern industrial towns the problems of the Austro-Hungarian
Empire were far less relevant than the events in March 1914 when the 'grave disor-
ders in Ireland' had begun to take a more sinister turn. In early 1912, the Liberal
coalition government under Asquith had introduced the third Home Rule Bill for
Ireland, which proposed the creation of a self-governing Irish Parliament in Dublin.
Unionists had objected to potential rule by a Dublin Parliament and had founded
the paramilitary Ulster Volunteers with the intention, if necessary, to fight against
the British Government and any future steps towards Irish Home Rule. During
1913 a number of senior British officers had warned Parliament that the British
Army would hesitate to act against the Ulster Volunteers, given that they both

believed Home Rule would threaten the very foundations of the British Empire they had sworn to preserve and defend, but matters came to a head in March 1914 when the General Officer Commanding in Ireland, Sir Arthur Paget, was ordered by the War Office to prepare to move troops to Ulster to counter any violence that might break out once the Home Rule Bill was passed. The troops were ordered to occupy government buildings and to guard five military armouries against thefts by the Volunteers. These orders to prepare for possible unrest were misinterpreted by Paget as a demand for him to march against the Ulstermen.[3]

Ireland had, for many years, been a major recruiting ground for the British Army and the threat of what the War Office termed 'active operations in Ulster' placed officers in a dilemma. Not only was there widespread sympathy with Unionism, but those with homes and families in the province would be put at enormous personal risk. Orders passed from the Secretary of State for War, John Seely, had recognised this and had:

> authorised that officers whose homes were actually in the province of Ulster who wished to do so might apply for permission to be absent from duty during the period of operations, and would be allowed to disappear from Ireland; that such officers would subsequently be reinstated and would suffer no loss in their careers; that any officer who from conscientious or other motives was not prepared to carry out his duty as ordered should say so at once, and that such officers would be at once dismissed from the Service ...[4]

On 20 March, Paget met in Dublin with the generals under his command to discuss what had been referred to as an 'ultimatum' and the impending 'active operations'. All agreed that these appeared to go far beyond precautionary measures and Seeley's instructions should be passed to the officers under their command. Hubert Gough, commanding the 3rd Cavalry Brigade, returned to his barracks to offer his officers their options, telling them that he himself would choose to resign rather than fight the Volunteers. Of the seventy officers at Curragh Camp, fifty-seven followed his lead. Technically, it was not mutiny since they had lost their commissions before being given any direct order, but it was a sometimes heart-breaking decision for men who had served loyally for thirty or forty years and who had little income to fall back on. One subaltern later wrote:

> Can you imagine a subaltern of 22–26 making up his mind in an hour as to whether he should shoot down Loyalists in Ulster or try to start a civil job without a bob? ... Imagine anything more criminal than making us decide a matter which might affect our whole careers, without giving us time to think or get advice from any one?[5]

Charles Fergusson's infantry division also showed signs of beginning to crack, but he himself was detained in Dublin and did not learn of the problems until the following day. Fergusson was often heard to say that it was 'the duty of leaders to lead' and he was not prepared to leave his officers, least of all the young ones, to face such a momentous decision by themselves. He ordered the battalions from Manchester and Suffolk to parade in the gymnasium at the Curragh, where he addressed them before travelling to units in Kildare, Newbridge and Dublin. Each time he gave the same message about the need for discipline and loyalty. It was, according to an officer of the East Surreys, a reminder that 'although we must naturally hold private political views, officially we should not be on the side of any one political party. It was our duty to obey orders, to go wherever we were sent and to comply with instructions of any political party that happened to be in power. There was no sloppy sentiment, it was good stuff straight from the shoulder and just what we wanted.'[6]

Claiming 'honest misunderstandings', the Asquith government backed down and reinstated the officers, publicly stating that British soldiers would not be used to enforce Home Rule, although those responsible for the statement later lost their jobs as a result. The situation was debated in Parliament and made worse in late April when, in an operation organised by Major Frederick Crawford and Captain Wilfrid Spender of the Ulster Unionist Council, over 200 tons of arms and ammunition, including thousands of German rifles, were smuggled ashore at Larne on the night of 24/25 April as the Ulster Volunteer Force mounted a full test mobilisation, manning roadblocks and patrolling the coast. Vehicles were brought to Larne to help distribute the weapons to arms dumps established around the province and newspapers later described how 'hundreds of motors reached the assembly point at an identical moment. It was an amazing sight to see this huge procession of cars nearly three miles in length descending upon the town with all their headlights ablaze ...'[7] After other smaller shipments, by June 1914 the Ulster Volunteers had some 37,000 rifles; so many, in fact, that at the outbreak of war the British Government asked to use some.[8]

The purchase and transportation of the shipment had been reported in the *London Times* as early as 1 April and the Curragh incident had shown that little, if any, action could be expected from the British authorities against the Ulster Volunteers, thus increasing the fears of the Irish nationalists who watched Ulster Volunteer Force numbers soar. Many thousands of Irish refugees had fled their homeland in the wake of the potato famines and had settled in towns across the north of England. In the West Riding, the numbers had been so large that Irish and English politics had become inextricably intertwined to the extent that the Independent Labour Party spoke of the Liberals taking the Irish for granted as 'the hewers of wood and drawers of water for the Liberal party'.[9] In 1893, the Irish National League had established itself in Keighley and declared that the town 'had contributed more money to the Executive for purposes of organization than either of the populous towns of Glasgow or Liverpool'.[10] The Liberal Party's commitment to Home Rule won them the unswerving loyalty of the Irish population at the turn of the century, to the point that it was a vital source of support for Asquith's government.

As the repercussions of the Sarajevo assassination echoed around Europe, Irish politics again came to the fore when on Sunday 26 July Erskine Childers, whose book *Riddle of the Sands* had done so much to fuel the fear of an invasion of England by Germany, landed a shipment of German arms destined for use by the Irish Nationalist movement. Just like the operation by the Ulster Volunteers, the delivery of the guns to Howth, near Dublin, was hardly discreet but the response was very different. The local Boy Scouts paraded in uniform before joining the procession of men marching in daylight to collect the weapons and marched back with each man armed but without ammunition. Around 160 soldiers of the King's Own Scottish Borderers had been mobilised to support the local police and a clash between the two groups took place along Howth Road and Malahide Road. The Irishmen's weapons were not loaded, so as the army approached they used their empty rifles as clubs. One Boy Scout was later described as having clubbed a soldier and taken his loaded rifle from him. Bayonets fixed, the soldiers attempted to control the crowd and at least one man was seriously wounded when he was stabbed by a soldier, later dying of his wounds. As the soldiers returned to barracks that evening, a crowd of between 500 and 600 people gathered around them and stones and missiles were thrown. About thirty soldiers were ordered to form a line across the street in order to cover the rest of the company's withdrawal into their barracks and, in the heat of the moment, shots were fired into the crowd. Three men and one woman died and many more were wounded and the nationalists quickly seized on the incident as a propaganda coup, fuelling anger that would see the Howth rifles deployed on the streets of Dublin in 1916.

Alongside the Irish troubles, the West Riding had its own unrest. A century earlier, a mill owner and militia officer named Cartwright had fortified Rawfolds Mill near Halifax against Luddite unrest. Armed workers and militiamen slept on the premises and a supply of acid was kept to hand ready to pour on attackers. On the night of 11/12 April 1812, a Luddite group had attempted to force their way into the mill, drawing fire from the six civilians and five soldiers garrisoning it. Two men later died of their wounds but the rest escaped. Following the incident the government flooded regular soldiers into the area until a combination of hangings and other harsh penalties brought the Luddites under control. Throughout the region, though, new mills and military barracks were built to be defensible with firing positions incorporated into factory designs as fears took hold of a British revolution and the relationship between workers and the military worsened. At the turn of the twentieth century, trade unionists and Labour supporters in the Halifax area were described as showing 'traditional hostility' towards the part-time Volunteers because they believed that they represented a force to be used against any action by workers demanding rights. Several verbal and even physical attacks on such units were carried out by mobs throughout the mid-nineteenth century, even as the threat of invasion grew again.[11]

A hundred years after the quashing of the Luddites, new industrial unrest was sweeping the West Riding. A period of depression and high unemployment in the first decade of the twentieth century was followed from 1910 by an unprecedented series of strikes as workers demanded higher wages to keep pace with inflation and better working conditions, particularly protection against bullying in the workplace. A strike by Leeds tramway workers in 1911 was followed almost immediately by a national railway strike marked by militant picketing to such a degree that on 19 August, 600 men of the West Yorkshire Regiment, reinforced by men of the Queen's Royal Lancers, took up positions around the city's two main stations. Armed with rifles and bayonets, the troops charged a crowd in City Square on 20 August despite the strike having ended that day and large, angry crowds booed the armed cavalrymen deployed to escort carters bringing supplies into the city, further deepening local hostility towards the military. At the same time, engineering apprentices went on strike for better wages and, with the threat of even more action, the Lord Mayor allowed the local council to vote in severe measures to police and control strikers without a proper debate or even forming a legitimate quorum for such an important decision. This, along with the use of Leeds University students as blackleg labour, did much to damage class relations and politicise what had been largely union matters. The following year saw the carters go on strike and in 1913–14, a widespread action even drew in shop assistants of the Leeds Co-operative Society and manual workers of the City Corporation[12] in an action that eventually cost the government some £22,000 to police. The twin problems of Irish politics and labour relations were highlighted on 6 and 7 February 1914 when bombs exploded at a municipal power station and at the Harewood Territorial Barracks, where police drafted in to police the municipal strike from as far afield as Liverpool were being accommodated. The attack, at 9 p.m., bore the hallmarks of similar devices used by the Irish Republican Army and appeared calculated to endanger lives; although the perpetrators were never found, the chief suspect was an Irishman seen shouting anti-British slogans a few days earlier who had been punched by a Territorial Force sergeant outside the barracks.[13]

Meanwhile, in Huddersfield, the day of Franz Ferdinand's assassination was also the day on which 400 engineers walked out of twenty local firms in a dispute about pay. By the end of June up to 2,000 men were on strike and the importation of blackleg labour from Manchester caused violence and resentment. The police were viewed as siding with the employers and the trials of picket-line offenders were packed, tense affairs as the six-week strike brought Huddersfield's engineering industry to the point of collapse. Across the moors, Keighley's engineers were also on strike and had been since the beginning of May. Their demand for a pay rise of 2 shillings per week had met with a sharp refusal from the Master's Federation of employers and the Keighley strike quickly became an acrimonious battle; two non-striking workers were followed home on the first day by a crowd of 200 people.

Crowds gather outside Buckingham Palace to await the declaration of war, August 1914.

By the following week 1,500 men were out and matters took a turn for the worse. Non-striking workers had to be escorted to and from home by the police, their homes and allotments were vandalised and tripwire ambushes were laid for cyclists as they attempted to reach their workplaces. Windows of businesses part-owned by the engineering companies were smashed, as was the front of the local cinema 'in which', reported the *Keighley News*, 'Mr H Smith, of Dean, Smith and Grace Ltd has a very small interest'. Another local employer's home was guarded at one point by fifty policemen drafted in from the surrounding area and accommodated in the local Drill Hall. An anonymous letter from non-strikers to the Amalgamated Society of Engineers (ASE) threatened that 'if this window smashing is not stopped we shall take the same game up and let them see that two can play the game of broken pots with your windows'. So great was the problem that the directors of the Keighley and District Mutual Plate Glass Insurance Society held an emergency meeting and concluded that they were not liable for 'breakage caused by civil commotion, tumult or riot'.[14]

The Wiseman family were among those affected by the Keighley strikes. Harold's father was a mechanical moulder and a member of the ASE, as was his 21-year-old son, James William (known as 'Jimmy'), and the family was struggling to manage the loss of income caused by their being off work. The number of children being fed by the local school board steadily increased and the unions attempted to provide at least some support by funding picnics and parties in nearby parks to maintain the morale of striking families. Harold himself, now at the end of his school days, was destined to follow his father and brother into the trade but now, in the summer of 1914, his attention was focused on the upcoming camp. A bugler for the YMCA Troop of the local Boy Scouts, Harold expected to join them on their annual trip over the August Bank Holiday; his brother Jimmy had already gone to camp at Marske in North Yorkshire on 26 July with the 6th Battalion of the Duke of Wellington's Regiment for the Territorial Force manoeuvres. For the Wiseman family, like many thousands of others, the Austrian ultimatum to Serbia on 23 July meant very little as the August Bank Holiday weekend approached.

When the ultimatum expired on Sunday, 26 July, the 'European Crisis' suddenly escalated beyond all expectations. The widely held assumption had been that a diplomatic solution could eventually be found and, as Arthur Marwick put it, 'war was widely expected as an eventual probability but it was scarcely visualised at all as an immediate contingency'.[15] With war only a week away, an editorial in the Conservative-leaning *Yorkshire Post* of 27 July asked, 'Is it conceivable that Europe can be on the eve of a conflict between the tremendous forces represented by all those great military nations? Happily we see no reason why Great Britain should be drawn in.' The speed at which war approached following Austria's declaration of war against Serbia and Russia's mobilisation to support its Serbian allies was shocking and brought anxious responses from Britain's anti-war lobby. The Socialist

International Congress held in Brussels on the 29th urged its constituent members to each apply 'the most vigorous pressure' on their respective governments to resolve the crisis through arbitration, but fell short of calling for an international general strike, whilst across Britain, trades unions and the Labour Party opposed war at every opportunity.

In Huddersfield, home to Harold Whitwam's family, the issue of Liberal politics, Irish support for the Liberal Party, Home Rule and the European Crisis created an atmosphere of confusion and concern. The local paper complained that there was, in the town, 'the uncomfortable feeling that the public were not in possession of all the facts about the commitments of this country in case of European war',[16] whilst the *Worker* newspaper called openly for any outbreak of war to be the catalyst for revolution against the government. Two meetings organised by the labour and socialist movements filled St George's Square in the centre of town and unanimously approved anti-war resolutions whilst another, at the Paddock Socialist Club, condemned the 'murderous gang of war mongers responsible for the present European crisis' and 'the efforts that are being made to involve this country in the bloody outrage on humanity'.[17]

Across the moors in Bradford, John Carr's family had most reason to be concerned. John's maternal grandfather, 62-year-old Joseph Richter, was born in Bohemia in 1852 and as a young man had moved with his family to England. After marrying and starting a family in Glasgow, the Richters had moved to Bradford thirty-four years earlier. By 1914 Joseph was running his own glass engraving business and had become part of the city's well established German community. By the mid-nineteenth century, Bradford had a growing German population centred around 'Little Germany' where immigrants had set up shop as wool merchants. By 1902, half the city's wool merchants and two-thirds of its yarn merchants were of German origin, with successful businessmen building fine villas for themselves on Heidelberg Road, Bonn Street and Mannheim Road. Over a quarter of the Bradford Chamber of Commerce were foreign born and by 1910–11 the city had its second German Lord Mayor. Composer Frederick Delius, portrait artist Sir William Rothenstein and poet Humbert Wolfe were all Bradford-born sons of German-born wool merchants and the community counted Justices of the Peace, a Lord Lieutenant of the County and various school and charitable benefactors among its numbers. The prospect of war between Britain and Germany held fears that overnight friends and neighbours would become enemies.

The last weekend of peace began disappointingly for the boys who would sail to France in 1918. Arnold Ambler and Harold Wiseman had both been looking forward to their now cancelled Scout camps. Strong winds and rain had affected the Great Yorkshire Show and smaller agricultural shows had seen marquees blown down. In Todmorden, Charles Pickering's annual treat – one of very few treats available since his father's death in 1901 – was to have been an outing with the local

Band of Hope but that, too, was delayed. Those who could afford it went away to the seaside or to visit friends and family for the holiday and thousands flocked to London to see the sights. Despite the growing unease, people seemed determined to carry on as normal. As a later history of Pickering's home town put it:

> On the 1st August, while the issue seemed still hanging in the balance, the streets of Todmorden were filled with the usual Saturday night crowds, and the European crisis was deemed hardly more important as a subject of discussion than Todmorden's prospects of winning the Lancashire League Cup or the proposed Sunday opening of the Free Library newsroom, subjects which were just then occupying public attention.[18]

The next day, congregations in churches and chapels across the country were urged to pray for peace and in London alone around 15,000 people attended an anti-war rally in Trafalgar Square, while many similar rallies were held in other cities throughout the day. Charles and his mother went home from chapel to news from Fred Pickering's old boss, local stationmaster Mr Thompson, that a War Office telegram had been received informing him: 'Naval Reserves mobilised. Honour warrants, and give every facility for transit.' That evening 'the town was thrown into a fever of excitement by the issue of a special edition of the Sunday papers reporting – without foundation, as it turned out later – a Naval engagement in the North Sea. Many people waited till the last possible moment on Sunday night to try to gain more definite information. None came, and morning brought no confirmation of the rumour, but made public the disquieting news that Germany had sent ultimatums to Russia and France.'

The next morning Todmorden's Drill Hall was besieged with inquiries about the possible movements of the local Territorials after rumours spread that they were destined for Limerick and that the Ambulance Corps had received orders to go to Cork, but staff there had no idea what was happening. Postmaster Mr Taylor received instructions that the Post Office was to remain open all night until further notice for telegraphic business as Monday evening's papers carried the first official news of England's attitude in relation to the crisis, 'and the opinion was freely expressed that our hope of remaining neutral was now practically at an end'.[19]

Despite this, people still held out hope. A full-page advert placed by the Neutrality League appeared in the *Yorkshire Post* on 4 August with an appeal to the population to 'keep your country out of this wicked and stupid war'. In the village of New Mill, about 6 miles from Huddersfield, the local 'bellman' had summoned a village meeting at 7.30 p.m. on Tuesday 4 August that was attended by about 500 people – probably the entire adult population of the village – who met and approved unanimously a resolution urging the government to maintain Britain's neutrality. A forlorn gesture, but one that meant the people of New Mill 'would always have the satisfaction of knowing that they had publicly expressed their convictions in favour of peace'.[20]

A similar meeting, with the same aim, had been called for in Todmorden but was over-taken by events: 'by tea time on Tuesday practically all doubts had been removed as to the ultimate outcome of the situation. The invasion of Belgian territory by German troops made it impossible for us to keep clear of the struggle.' That afternoon, about thirty German reservists had boarded the 2.15 p.m. train from Bradford to London, seen off by their families and friends and the German pastor whilst a band played. Still bound by the terms of their conscription, the men had been recalled and ordered to make their way to Germany if they could get out of England in time.

At 11 p.m., the ultimatum issued by Britain to Germany that it should respect Belgian neutrality expired. Britain was at war. Michael Macdonagh, parliamentary correspondent for *The Times*, later described having passed through Trafalgar Square on the evening of the 4th, where 'I found two rival demonstrations in progress under Nelson's Pillar – on one side of the plinth for war, and on the other against!' As the deadline approached, he joined a crowd outside Buckingham Palace as they waited:

No one came out of 10 Downing Street. No statement was made. There was no public proclamation that we were at war by a herald to the sound of trumpets and the beating of drums. [After hearing Big Ben strike 11 p.m.] The great crowd rap-idly dispersed in all directions, most of them running to get home quickly, and as they ran they cried aloud rather hysterically 'War!' 'War!' 'War!' They were eager, no doubt, to spread the dread news ...[21]

Today, the folk memory of August 1914 is, as Adrian Gregory has pointed out, of cheering crowds gathering outside Buckingham Palace, of long lines at recruit-ing offices, of soldiers marching away through crowded streets to the strains of 'Tipperary'. It is, in short, a view of the countries of Europe responding enthu-siastically, even eagerly, to the prospect of war. The reaction of holidaymakers in London for the Bank Holiday, especially after an evening in the pub, cannot be taken as representative of the reaction of the whole country. In fact, accord-ing to Gregory, 'the evidence for mass enthusiasm at the time is surprisingly weak ... Furthermore, discussion of responses to the war in Britain have been remark-ably blind to major divisions in Edwardian society, particularly along regional (or national), class and gender lines'.[22]

Across the West Riding, there had been no pro-war demonstrations to rival the thousands who had flocked to protest. In Huddersfield, Harold Whitwam's family and neighbours had made clear their opposition, as had the people around Charles Pickering in Todmorden. For the Gaines family in Leeds and the Wisemans in Keighley, the immediate concern was surviving the industrial actions gripping their towns. Arnold Ambler's family struggled on in Halifax where distrust of the military would now need to be rethought. And for John Carr and the citizens of Bradford, family, friends, trusted neighbours and civic leaders were now, suddenly, the enemy.

'When the English learned to hate ...'

For most people, the most immediate concern in the first few days of August was not the war itself, but the impact it would have on business. In Todmorden, Charles Pickering saw streets that were, according to the town's official record of the war 'crowded with excited groups, discussing the situation, especially its possible effect on the nation's trade'.[1] With so much of its production exported to Germany, the West Riding stood to lose a great deal by going to war since, as historian A.J.P. Taylor's pragmatic grandfather observed, 'can't they see as every time they kill a German they kills a customer?'[2] Yet it was not only the export trade that would suffer. Within two days the effects of the war were being 'seriously felt in the majority of trades in Leeds', according to the *Yorkshire Evening News* of 6 August. Shipping companies faced enormous insurance premiums now the country was at war and so kept their ships in port until they were commandeered by the government. Pre-existing plans had put the railways under government control immediately war was declared and now priority went to military transport, leaving civilian freight at depots and unable to move. With no way to move stock, many businesses went on to short working and some were forced to close. Elsewhere workers met with employers and agreed cuts to wages in an effort to keep companies afloat. The holiday trade, reliant on income generated over the summer months, abruptly found its livelihood threatened. The post office had employed many ex-servicemen who now found themselves recalled, seriously disrupting mail deliveries, and the requisitioning of horses and vehicles caused severe problems for transport businesses. Both the *Yorkshire Post* and the *Yorkshire Evening News* of 6 August considered Bradford – virtually a single industry town with Germany as its biggest export customer – to be facing imminent ruin. Within the first week, thousands of military-age men found themselves out of work.

In Leeds, the Gaines family were swept along in what 'was almost a panic caused by the sadden rise in food prices':

Alarmed by the thought of a possible scarcity, many people rushed heedlessly to buy more than they required of flour, bacon and other provisions. Thus a complete dislocation of supplies threatened until, after a day or two, the government regulated the position. There were fears of unemployment, too; there were doubts as to the instant effect on commerce and industry; there were difficulties foreshadowed by the calling-up of men in the police force and in the various municipal services.[3]

By the end of Wednesday 5 August, the Huddersfield Industrial Society had sold all its stocks of flour and was still filled with shoppers two hours after its normal closing time. Flour prices rose from 1s 11d to 2s 6d per stone in two days and bakers quickly passed on the price rise to their customers. Elsewhere, all other goods saw similar rises with sugar leaping up by as much as 7d per pound in a few days (equivalent to a rise of over £2.20 in 2012). 'This rise,' noted Sir John Hammerton, 'fell most heavily on small and struggling retailers in poor districts, who could not afford to keep large stocks. As a result they had to increase prices for their customers, and the poorer classes were made to pay.'[4] Across the country came reports of food riots and the looting of shops and the growing panic was only stopped by government intervention. After meeting with representatives of the large grocery firms and the Grocer's Federation, maximum retail prices were set for certain foods and a huge supply of sugar was compulsorily purchased by the government for sale at a fixed price. On Friday 7 August the banks reopened to ensure wages could be paid. Shortages of gold had already led to the introduction of the £1 and 10-shilling notes and legislation had been put in place allowing staff to refuse to allow individuals to make large withdrawals to prevent a run on the banks. Gradually, a sense of order began to emerge with the passing of what Hammerton called 'one of the most extraordinary legislative measures ever passed by the British Parliament'. The Defence of the Realm Act (DORA) was seen by many as a draconian measure giving the government sweeping powers, including the right to try civilians by court martial for a wide and loosely defined set of offences. 'In other words', Hammerton wrote:

> the military authorities could arrest any persons they pleased and, after court martial, inflict any sentence on them short of death. In addition, the military authorities were allowed to demand the whole or part of the output of any factory or workshop they required. They were also allowed to take any land they needed. This, in effect, made the civil administration of the country entirely subservient to the military administration.[5]

DORA reached almost every facet of daily life. Not far from the Wisemans' home in Keighley, Eva Leach, the daughter of the landlord of the King's Head Hotel, recalled how the pubs in the town were forced to shut for a few days because of the money crisis and by the time they re-opened, new regulations had been brought in to force them to stop serving alcohol at 9 p.m. After that, only soft drinks could be sold. 'Hoyle's, the local soft drinks people, made a killing with "Hop Ale",' she later explained:

> It looked like bitter beer – in colour only! – And there was another drink called 'After Nine Stout' which was a form of dandelion and burdock. There was also a horrible concoction called 'Vegale', a hot soupy drink that smelt to heaven of peas. Nobody bought it. We were also allowed to sell Bovril and Oxo but they weren't very popular with the men at the bar.[6]

Within a week, working-class people across the country had been hit by a drop in employment and by rocketing food prices, followed by the fact that the severe and wide-ranging powers of DORA were impacting even on their ability to enjoy a trip to the pub. Resentment quickly set in.

In the nineteenth century a series of pogroms had swept Eastern Europe. German states had stripped Jews of their rights to work, settle and marry and frequent outbreaks of violence had forced many to emigrate. A wave of revolutions in 1848 brought some protection to the Jews but added political refugees to the flood moving westward. Vicious pogroms in Russia thirty years later brought another wave of refugees westward, thereby adding to the growing tensions in Germany. Most were hoping to begin a new life in the United States, but many found themselves in the UK, either unable to afford the fare to America or victims of unscrupulous ship's captains who simply dumped their passengers on British docksides after assuring them they were in New York.

Many settled in the large cities. The West Riding textile industry also actively recruited immigrant labour to work in specialist fields such as dyeing, where specialists were continually developing new processes and finishes. Over 80 per cent of the chemicals used in Bradford were supplied by German companies and the businesses in Little Germany reflected the connection – Hertz, Lowenthal, Schuster and Schwabe were all familiar names to local workers. Sir Jacob Behrens had been among the first to arrive in 1832 and by 1874 the links were so firmly established that Danzig-born Charles Semon was elected mayor of the city. Affluent streets bore the names of the German towns the immigrants had left behind. When war came, the first commanding officer of the newly formed Bradford 'Pals' was Colonel Muller, the British-born son of German parents.

With thousands of Germans living in Britain at the outbreak of war, the Home Secretary announced that they would have until 10 August to leave the country. 'Thanks to this extraordinary permission, young German reservists, amounting in numbers to a division of the army, were enabled to return home, rejoin their colours, and fight.'[7] Those not intending to leave took their chances in what they had come to see as their new homeland. Roundups of 'known' German spies under DORA began immediately, but evidence for their being spies was often sketchy at best. Anyone could be suspect: waiters with foreign accents, young domestic servants and governesses and naturalised British citizens with German names (though the royal family were generally excused). Worse still, under the terms of the Naturalisation Act 1870, marriage to an 'alien' would cause a British woman to automatically lose her British subject status and be deemed to have acquired her new husband's nationality. Since such women might not in fact have acquired the husband's nationality by becoming naturalised subjects of his country, many effectively became stateless. The only concession made under the 1870 Act was that natural-born British subject women could apply to resume British nationality upon their husband's death, which meant that at the outbreak of war, thousands of British born women and children suddenly found themselves classified as 'enemy aliens' or 'hunwives'. The situation was rectified by the British Nationality and Status of Aliens Act 1914 which became law in January 1915 and which removed the automatic loss of status, but for a time even the children of naturalised British subjects might not be legally classified as British if they had not been included in the father's application for citizenship.

For a generation brought up on warning tales of German spies and planned invasion, the 'enemy within' were suddenly everywhere. As James Hayward reports, an English actor found himself the target of a sustained campaign by local villagers solely on the basis of his wearing a wide-brimmed hat. 'If he is not a spy,' asked the local schoolmistress, 'why does he wear a hat like that?'[8] Spy hunting became a popular pastime, not least for boys like Arnold Ambler and Harold Wiseman, whose Scout uniforms conferred a certain status amongst their civilian friends, but after Baden-Powell himself had been reported as having been shot as a German spy and to be actively engaged in covert missions in Germany, even the most enthusiastic spy hunters began to question just how real the menace was. It is not known whether John Carr's elderly grandfather was considered too old to be rounded up among them, but some 19,000 men of German and Austrian descent were arrested and detained in internment camps over the coming months as anti-German feeling grew.

As the German Army entered Belgium, and particularly as the British Expeditionary Force began its retreat, lurid tales of atrocities began to be heard. With very little hard news available, rumours spread like wildfire. By mid-August, up to a million Russians were 'known' to have landed in Scotland and travelled south by train and the *Daily Mail* reported a sighting of a million men passing through Stroud on a single night. Despite the sea voyage and the August heat, they arrived with snow still on their boots, ready for some undefined operation in France or possibly Germany itself. It was not until 14 September that the Press Bureau finally denied the story.[9] By then, wildly imaginative tales, eagerly passed on, told of 'Swiss' watchmakers secretly building bombs and German waiters poisoning food.

Years of anti-immigration campaigning came to a head with demands for anyone of German descent to be interned immediately. Protests quickly turned violent in many areas.

Newspapers encouraged their readers to check the papers of anyone claiming to be Swiss or whose accent sounded vaguely Germanic. As the hysteria reached its peak, German Shepherd dogs became 'Alsatians' and German Measles was renamed 'Belgian Flush'. Assistants at Boots the chemist explained to customers that the eau de Cologne they sold was made in Britain and had nothing to do with the city. Dachshunds were attacked in the streets and allegedly even killed. Lord Haldane, whose efforts to modernise the British Army had done much to make it ready for war, came under a barrage of abuse in the press as a German sympathiser because his dog was named Kaiser.[10]

During the Franco-Prussian war of 1870–71, the Germans had suffered casualties at the hands of civilian *franc-tireurs* forming a prototype resistance movement. Operating in groups, these *corps-francs* did not create many casualties but they diverted German resources away from the front lines to protect their lines of supply. If captured, the laws of war offered no protection and *franc-tireurs* faced summary execution; as early as 1915, Robert Graves claimed that British troops dismissed the colourful tales of atrocities but accepted that the killing of spies, *franc-tireurs* and obstructive local officials was both widespread and legitimate.[11] As the Germans moved through Belgium, hundreds of such suspects were shot – just as, a generation later, British troops would execute a great many 'fifth columnists' on the road to Dunkirk.[12] Alongside these alleged atrocities, though, were genuine cases of sanctioned war crimes. The sacking of the town of Louvain, for example, between 26 and 30 August came as retaliation for the panic caused among German troops during a counter-attack by Belgian forces through fears of *franc-tireur* activity. As an official German source explained, the 'only means of preventing surprise attacks from the civil population has been to interfere with unrelenting severity and to create examples which, by their frightfulness, would be a warning to the entire country'.[13] Meanwhile, in Germany itself, almost identical rumours spread of the savage treatment of civilians in East Prussia by invading Russians whilst in the German Army; wild tales of the torture and murder of wounded Germans by Belgian women and children fuelled the anger with which troops responded to real or imagined attacks by *franc-tireurs*. All sides, it seemed, were determined to portray the enemy as sub-human barbarians.

Terrible as the genuine atrocities like Louvain were, the British public were ever eager for more. At all levels of society, pornographic stories about the rape, torture and murder of women and children in Belgium circulated and were accepted without question. Lord Bryce, former Regius Professor of Civil Law at Oxford, Professor of Jurisprudence at Manchester and a respected historian for his work on the Holy Roman Empire, was commissioned to investigate 'Alleged German Outrages' and his report, published in 1915, was based on 1,200 unsworn depositions from unidentified Belgian refugees. None of the committee actually interviewed any of the supposed witnesses themselves and hearsay evidence was accepted as fact. Relying on Bryce's reputation alone to prove its reliability, the report was widely distributed and quoted in American newspapers, yet long before it was published, Bryce was aware that much, if not most, of the content was unreliable at best. In Britain Lord Northcliffe had offered £200 for any genuine photograph of a mutilated refugee, but the prize was never claimed[14] and American correspondent William Shepherd of United Press later recalled:

> I was in Belgium when the first atrocity stories went out. I hunted and hunted for atrocities during the first days of the atrocity scare. I couldn't find atrocities. I couldn't find people who had seen them. I travelled on trains with Belgians who had fled from the German lines and I spent much time amongst Belgian refugees. I offered sums of money for photographs of children whose hands had been cut off or who had been wounded or injured in other ways. I never found a first-hand Belgian atrocity story; and when I ran down second hand stories they all petered out.[15]

In September, Harold Whitwam's family in Huddersfield read the story of a Scottish nurse from Dumfries, 23-year-old Grace Hume, who had left home at the start of the war to work in a Belgian hospital. When German troops captured the hospital they murdered and beheaded the wounded men and cut off Nurse Hume's right breast, leaving her to die. As the national papers took the story, it grew. A second nurse named Millard wrote of how Hume had shot a German who attacked her patients and was tortured as a result. For almost two weeks the story ran in several papers until *The Times* revealed that not only did Nurse Millard not exist, but that Grace Hume had never left the country and was, in fact, working in Huddersfield. The whole story had been made up by her 17-year-old sister.[16] Nevertheless, most British civilians believed every word of the stories and were encouraged to do so by the government, the clergy and by official reports such as that by Bryce. By now, the Germans had become the direct descendants of the 'Huns' who had devastated Europe and destroyed the Roman Empire. Academics sought to demonstrate that these were not the noble Saxons with whom the British had long identified themselves, but Prussians with their blood diluted by genetic throwbacks to the Tartar hordes and with an innate pre-disposition toward sexual perversion, sodomy and child rape. Not pausing to consider the impact on Britain's Russian allies, Prussian bestiality was linked with a mongrel ancestry: 'at bottom either Germanised Slavs or at most the result of a mixture between Germans and Slavs.'[17]

After decades of anti-immigrant campaigning by right-wing groups like the British Brotherhood League, the problem of what to do about the streams of refugees fleeing the Hun barbarity and arriving in Britain was a tricky one. Miners in Yorkshire and Wales made it clear they would not be welcome in those areas and a handbook issued to the Belgians advised against taking British workers' jobs or working for lower wages than their British counterparts. Mill towns proved more welcoming, remembering that pre-war trade with the Low Countries had been profitable and finding work for weavers, but pity for their plight soon turned back to the usual complaints against incomers, with the standard joke among those who had taken in refugees being to ask, 'And how are your Belgian atrocities?'[18] Referring to the stories of brutal behaviour against the Belgians and later to the attacks by ship and aircraft against British civilians, this was the time, Kipling later wrote, 'when the English learned to hate', but it was a lesson they were already well prepared for and more than willing to learn.

Anti-German hysteria, rising food prices and the long running industrial dispute produced an explosive combination in towns across the country, nowhere more so than in Keighley. 'Because of the newspaper stories and gossip that went around,' wrote Eva Leach:

> I'm afraid we disliked the Germans very much. There were dreadful stories of the atrocities in Belgium, babies being bayoneted and women treated unspeakably. There were several small pork butchers in Keighley. Some of them had been there for generations, but they all had German names – there was Stein and Schultz and Schneider and Hoffman – and all these shops were attacked and looted.

Shortly after 9 p.m. on the night of 29 August, a drunk by the name of Kelly walked into a butcher's shop owned by a German family named Andrassy. An argument about the price of Polony sausage took place which led to Kelly being thrown out, claiming to have been assaulted by the shopkeeper. He returned two hours later with a group of friends and attacked the shop, smashing its windows. With her home at the King's Head Hotel just a few yards away, Eva Leach was able to witness the attack:

> It was a Saturday night and we children were playing in the upstairs sitting room while our parents were busy at the bar ... Near the pub was an Irish club. It was usually pretty noisy on Saturdays, so on the night of the riot we kids didn't take much notice of all the noise. Then my father came upstairs and he said, 'I want you children to see this. You'll never forget it!' We scurried into our clothes and went out with my father (my mother didn't approve so she stayed behind) ... There was a great crowd there, mostly Irish from the Turkey Street district which was a poor quarter, and they were mostly drunk.[19]

The Reverend Father Joseph Francis Russell from St Anne's Catholic church hurried into town and helped calm the situation and the police responded quickly, dispersing the mob and taking the Andrassy family and their servants to the police station for safety. But this was only the beginning.

Anticipating further trouble, the next day local police drafted in seventy reinforcements from surrounding towns. Shortly after 10 p.m. on the Sunday night, police reported a 'dense crowd' having formed in the town centre. Some witnesses later spoke of up to 1,000 people being involved as the mob again attacked Andrassy's shop in what the *Yorkshire Post* would describe the following day as 'an organised raid' and set it on fire. The mob then moved on to attack other pork butchers in the town, including those owned by the Hoffman and Schultz families – despite both families being naturalised British citizens. The shops were looted, as were nearby businesses totally unconnected with the original targets, including a bootmakers, and an unsuccessful attempt was made to loot a jeweller's. With the recent industrial unrest still causing resentment, the mob then turned its attention from Germans and towards Sir Prince Smith, one of the town's largest employers, who had been holding out against the strikers' demands. Leaving the town centre behind, the crowd marched towards his home on Spring Gardens Lane. As they approached the property, mounted and foot police hidden in the grounds charged the crowd and 'used their batons freely. Many people suffered'[20] as the crowd fell back towards the town centre, and rocks and bottles were hurled at the police. Another butcher's shop was looted and windows in the police station and forty panes of glass smashed at the home of Police Superintendent Birkhead. At around midnight, the police used their batons to clear the street and by 1 a.m. the riot was over.

On Monday, the task of clearing up began. Looters appeared in court after police found sides of ham and bacon stored in cellars. Arthur Little, a weaver who had previously served in the army, was given a week to re-enlist after being found guilty of being drunk and disorderly. Herbert Towers told how he saw others stealing from the shops and decided he should join in and was remanded to prison for stealing 9s worth of bacon. The mayor expressed his understanding of public anger over the atrocity reports, but condemned as 'cowardly and un-English' the attacks on 'unfortunate Germans who found themselves in England'. With mills closed on the Monday, sightseers came into town to witness the damage for themselves, some taking fragments of shattered glass as souvenirs. The police put on a show of force with 148 men, including eight mounted policemen in town; a further twenty-five officers stood by in Bradford in case of any further violence, and forces in nearby towns were alerted. For the authorities, the riots were hard to define – certainly anti-German sentiment had played a part, but the attack on Sir Prince Smith's home showed that the true causes were much harder to pin down. No similar large-scale attacks occurred in Bradford, despite – or because of – its large German population, nor indeed in any of the other West Riding towns where German shops had been established. Some measure of the confused attitudes of the time comes from Eva Leach's memories of the victims:

> The Schulz family were a nice couple with a baby. They lived next door to friends of ours in Low Street and they were all very good neighbours. When the looters started attacking their shop, the Schulzes rushed next door and sheltered with

The Defence of the Realm Act (DORA) granted wide-ranging powers to the military and fell only a little short of full martial law.

the Mitchells until the trouble died down. Mrs Schulz was in an awful state, quite terrified … Of course we were sorry for them, but we children thought that it was quite natural. After all, they were Germans![21]

Similar scenes played out to a lesser extent in Bradford and in other towns and would sporadically be repeated throughout the war. By the end of August, the British Army was in full retreat. Louvain and other towns had been sacked and nothing, it seemed, could prevent the Germans arriving in Britain just as the books, plays and newspapers had warned. When they did, the consequences would be too terrible for even those who opposed the war to contemplate. One woman recalled:

My brother, indeed the whole family were conscientious objectors … We were in mid-discussion when my brother suddenly stood up and said, 'You know, Mother, supposing people were to come into this room … and attack you and Emily … I shouldn't sit here and let them do it … I've got to go, the Germans are coming here, we all know the stories they are telling. I've got to protect you from them … I'm here as a defender and I've a right to defend you' … We did not want to go and fight anybody, we wanted to live in peace. However, we weren't allowed to because of Germany, it wasn't our fault.[22]

In the coming years, the threat of a German invasion never went away. Even in 1918, thousands of troops remained based along the east coast of Britain in case of attack across the North Sea. Those in the trenches fought not so much for king and country, but in fear of what might happen to their families if they failed to stop the Germans reaching home. During the week after the Keighley riot, when the situation appeared at its worst, recruiting across the country reached an all-time high.

5

Comb outs and roundups

On 5 August, Prime Minister Herbert Asquith appointed Field Marshal Lord Horatio Herbert Kitchener as Secretary of State for War, a post Asquith himself had been filling since the resignation of Seely over the Curragh incident earlier in the year. It was, in many ways, an odd choice given how deeply Kitchener divided opinion, and he was a particular target for Northcliffe's *Daily Mail* because whilst the public saw him as the high-profile hero of Omdurman and the Boer War, politicians and the military alike found him difficult to work with to the point where his death in 1916 sparked conspiracy rumours that he had been killed by rivals within the British Government. At 64 years old, Kitchener had spent most of his adult life in the Middle East, South Africa and India and was, at the time of his appointment, in England on leave from his role as Consul-General in Egypt. As a result, he had little experience of working in Whitehall and admitted: 'I don't know Europe; I don't know England; and I don't know the British Army.'[1] He was, however, astute enough to recognise that the coming war would not, as most seemed to believe, last for less than six months; instead he predicted a three-year, large-scale war. It was clear to him that Britain's existing army would need to expand massively if it was to play its part in the coming battles and that it would draw severely on all available British manpower. Kitchener considered the forces available to him and reached a drastic conclusion. This was not war in the far-flung reaches of empire against an under-equipped native army; this was a war against the professional army of a major European power. For Britain to survive, he would need to create a whole new army.

Prior to 1914, Britain had regarded itself as primarily a naval power. Its army was, in effect, not a national army but an imperial police force made up of individual regiments structured to support small deployments across the world to maintain British rule. Nor was it even a single entity. 'It should be remembered,' wrote Gary Sheffield, 'that the British army was a collection of individual regiments and corps,

each fiercely independent, with its own traditions and customs.'[2] Over and above
the tribal regimental system, there were two very separate armies still trying to find
a way to co-exist: the Regular Army with its full-time staff committed to overseas
service, and the Territorial Force, formed in 1908 by the amalgamation of various
Volunteer, Militia and Yeomanry units and earmarked for home defence duties.
Each had very different identities, culture and standards of training.

The Regular Army of 1914 was the product of over forty years of reforms
intended to streamline it and make it fit for purpose, although the Boer War had
shown only too well that it still fell far short of expectations. Between 1868 and
1874, hastened by the performance of the German Army in the Franco-Prussian
War of 1871, Secretary of State for War Edward Cardwell had abolished the system
of purchase for commissions in order to move away from the traditional 'gentleman
soldier' and to create instead a professional officer class. He also abolished flogging
as a punishment and the twenty-one-year service period, introducing instead a new
seven-year 'short service' contract for recruits in order to encourage enlistments.
He then pushed through the comprehensive Regulation of the Forces Act in 1871
which sought to localise recruitment, replacing the old 'General Service' enlistment
in which men could be sent to any regiment with a new system of sixty-six Brigade
Districts (later renamed Regimental Districts), based on county boundaries and
population density. All line infantry regiments would now consist of two regular
battalions based in a regimental depot associated with a specific recruiting area.
One battalion would then serve for a period overseas, while the other was stationed
at home for training. The Militia unit of that area could then become the third battalion, which could also provide recruit training.

Cardwell's reforms made the British Army into a more efficient imperial force
and were followed in 1881 by further changes introduced by Hugh Childers.
General Order 41/1881, issued on 1 May 1881, amended by G.O. 70/1881 dated
1 July, created a network of multi-battalion regiments each of which had two regular or 'line' battalions and two militia battalions. In addition, the various corps
of county rifle volunteers were to be designated as volunteer battalions. Each of
these regiments was linked by headquarters location and territorial name to its local
Regimental District and the reforms came into effect on 1 July. Most significantly,
from that date the old regimental seniority numbers were officially replaced by the
regimental district name, creating the 'county' regiments. Unofficially, the regiments were still referred to by their numbers by their officers and men, as tradition
and a point of pride, and several regiments lobbied to keep their distinct names as
part of their battalion titles, so that the 'Black Watch' and 'The Buffs' could continue to be known as such.

Despite the move to 'local' recruiting, the actual links to a locality were often
tenuous at best. There is a widespread and deeply held belief that the British Army
entered the First World War with strong local links, an assumption so strong that

many historians take it as read. In a typical aside, one noted military historian comments on the effect of the war on the Regular Army battalions of 19th Brigade, who were among the first to arrive in France in 1914 and who served there throughout the next four years. He writes of events later in the war that '[i]nto all these battalions trickled conscripts, who might have come from anywhere; certainly the Cameronians were obliged to welcome Cockneys from London's East End and the 2nd/Royal Welsh were compelled to take conscripts from Edinburgh or Glasgow'.[3] This belief that local affiliations were strong in 1914 but weakened by 1918 is not, however, supported by the evidence. According to the casualty lists published after the war as a series of volumes entitled *Soldiers Died in the Great War* (SDGW), the 1st Cameronian (Scottish Rifles) referred to above suffered some sixty-five fatalities in the period August–December 1914, of whom sixteen men, although perhaps not technically Cockneys, were born in London whilst only fourteen appear to have been born anywhere in Scotland. Repeating the exercise in September 1918, the battalion shows seventy-four casualties, for whom sixty-eight birthplaces are recorded, London accounting for one man England for a further eleven, along with two Irishmen and one New Zealander – a total of fifteen non-Scottish soldiers. In other words, taking the SDGW record as a snapshot of the battalion, the proportion of Scots serving in the Scottish Rifles rose from 21.5 per cent in 1914 to 88 per cent after the introduction of conscription. Likewise the other battalion mentioned,

A recruiting station in 1914.

the 2nd/Royal Welsh Fusiliers, underwent a similar transformation with its medical officer, Captain J.C. Dunn, later reporting:

> The battalion which arrived in France was largely English, the 'Birmingham Fusiliers', as it was chaffingly called, with a sprinkling of Irish. (Of the killed of 1914–15 there are about two English for one Welshman). By the beginning of this summer [1918] it had become about 85 per cent Welsh and there were fewer Irish. Three officers and two or three men, in my time, were Scots.[4]

In fact, SDGW shows four results for Glasgow, one of whom was a Welshman who had enlisted in the Highland Light Infantry in the city and later transferred. The pattern is repeated elsewhere, with David French reporting that in the pre-war Regular Army, only three regiments mustered more than 70 per cent local men with the Cameronians managing just 9.6 per cent, and most averaged no more than 50 per cent representation of their local recruiting areas.[5]

Although these reforms sought to make the army a more attractive prospect to potential recruits, in the years leading up to 1914 it remained much as it had been for centuries – a useful dumping ground for spare sons and otherwise unemployable men. For the urban poor, the problem of overcrowding could be resolved to some degree by sending girls into service and boys into the army, whilst for those further up the social scale it was generally accepted that second or third sons could go into the ministry or the army to give them something to do, thus creating an army marked by the two extremes of wealth and poverty. Writing about the officer class, Richard Holmes has shown that at a time when a sizeable London town house might cost £100 a year to rent, the War Office had reckoned that an infantry officer – the cheapest branch of the army – needed a minimum of £160 per year over and above his salary to be able to maintain himself.[6] As Gary Sheffield points out:

> There was an unofficial 'league table' of exclusivity with some regiments demanding a large private income of their officers. Indeed, by 1912 there was a shortage of officers in the cavalry of the line, and the War Office was forced to ask that Sandhurst cadets be acquainted with the fact that it was possible in some regiments to survive on an income of £300–400.[7]

It was said that one newly commissioned officer was bemused to find that he was actually being paid by the War Office, assuming it was his responsibility to pay subscriptions to join. Small wonder that in 1912 Major General M.F. Rimington warned that whilst it had once been possible to recruit officers to cavalry regiments because there was nothing to do, the expectation that they might be required to work as late as 3 p.m. would be disastrous since no one would pay to serve in the cavalry and then have to work for a pittance of War Office pay. Meanwhile, at the other end of the scale, soldiers earned 1 shilling per day before a bewildering array of deductions were taken back and were routinely barred from many pubs, music halls and theatres by a civilian population that viewed them with distrust and disdain. Few were able to list a trade on their attestment papers and soldiering remained, despite the reforms, a career most would seek to avoid. With peacetime soldiering held in such low esteem, the Regular Army battalions of the British Expeditionary Force sent to France in 1914 were woefully understrength when war broke out and were made up largely of recalled reservists fresh from the comforts of civilian life who were unfit and out of practice. They suffered badly in their opening clashes with the Germans and were soon on the retreat.

Hastily brought back from their summer camp, the West Riding Territorial Force received orders to mobilise at 6 p.m. on Tuesday 4 August and the next day, like many thousands of others, Harold Wiseman's older brother Jimmy received a long green envelope marked 'Mobilisation – Urgent' containing Army Form E635. Making his way to the Drill Hall in Keighley, Jimmy was forced to move his kit around the policemen billeted there against the town's strikers – many of whom were now sharing the same room. As yet it was unclear what was likely to happen, but as camp disbanded they had been addressed by the Earl of Harewood as Chairman of the West Riding Territorial Association. 'I am positively sure,' he told them. 'I am positively sure that if the Germans land on our shores you will give them such a warm reception that they will never come again.'[8] By the end of the week, Territorial Force units began to leave their home towns for serious training to repel the expected invasion.

Alongside the Regulars, the Haldane Reforms of 1907–08 had brought together a disparate group of part-time soldiers from the old Militia, Yeomanry and Volunteer groups that had developed over the previous century. Militia men had enlisted to serve for six years as a reserve force, liable for one month's training per year at their local regimental depot. The Yeomanry had developed in the late eighteenth century as a cavalry force officered by local landowners and farmers with men drawn from the officers' estates in which every man was required to own a horse – thereby excluding the vast majority of the poorer elements of the population and effectively creating a paramilitary police force to quell local disturbances. The Yeomanry gained notoriety after the infamous 'Peterloo Massacre' in Manchester in 1819, when in response to a request from local magistrates the Manchester and Salford Yeomanry had charged into a crowd demanding parliamentary reform, killing at least eleven (including an infant knocked from its mother's arms as the cavalry rode towards the area of the meeting) and injuring over 400. As they were reinforced by men from the Cheshire Yeomanry, a regular cavalry officer was heard trying to regain control of the soldiers as they drew swords and attacked the crowd, but the Yeomanry's discipline was very different to that of the regular cavalry also at the scene. Whilst the Hussars used the flat side of their sabres to knock protestors to one side, the Yeomanry simply lashed out with the blade. Similar units had also been involved in anti-Luddite policing across the West Riding and bad feeling remained, especially in the area around Huddersfield and Halifax where reprisals against Luddite activists had been particularly harsh. At their peak, operations against the protestors saw around 12,000 troops drafted into the West Riding, with over 1,000 in Huddersfield alone.[9]

Finally, 'Volunteer' units had emerged as a response to the threat of French invasion in the mid-nineteenth century. Liable to be called out in response to an invasion or rebellion, members of the Volunteer Rifle Corps were required to provide their own arms and equipment and pay all costs associated with training for up to twenty-four days per year. Not surprisingly, these conditions made the Volunteers an exclusive organisation which, by the time of the Haldane Reforms, had developed a club-like atmosphere, with officers and NCOs often chosen by election rather than merit. The Territorial Force that emerged from this amalgamation was marked by huge disparities between regiments and areas. Those inheriting facilities from wealthy Volunteer units might boast a drill hall with a bar,

MEDICAL OFFICER: "Sorry I must reject you on account of your teeth."
WOULD-BE-RECRUIT: "Man, ye're making a gran' mistake. I'm no wanting to bite the Germans, I'm wanting to shoot 'em."

With a surplus of willing volunteers, standards could be set high but many were genuinely rejected because of poor dental hygiene that would have made chewing the army's iron rations impossible.

billiards rooms and the latest equipment, while others struggled to provide even the basics. Some continued to charge fees to ensure the right sort of enlistments; the London Rifle Brigade, for example, charging recruits a guinea to join until as late as 1916.[10] High charges by elitist battalions deterred 'bobtails', while at the other extreme many employers resented their workers having time off to attend training camps and frequently refused to employ anyone who was a member of the Territorial Force. Not surprisingly, most found it difficult to maintain themselves at full strength. It is perhaps a mark of the status of the force in public opinion that in 1913 the commanding officer of the 4th Battalion King's Own Yorkshire Light Infantry received a personal letter of congratulations from the Secretary of State for War, General Seely, for managing to maintain the battalion at full strength for three years at a time when most battalions struggled to maintain anything like their expected establishment.

The use of Militia and Yeomanry units against workers' protests and trade union activities left a deep distrust of the part-time military in the industrial towns of Yorkshire so that in 1914 the Territorial Force in Halifax was the weakest in the West Riding, seven officers and 298 men understrength due, according to historian Patricia Morris, to 'working class hostility of long standing',[11] whilst outright and overt hostility could sometimes be shown towards troops marching through town.[12] As Major F.L. Watson, a pre-war Leeds Territorial, later put it:

> Before mobilization, we were greatly below establishment. Leeds was a very unmilitary city, and we had to face a good deal of veiled hostility from various quarters: partly genuine pacifism – that is, opposition to war in any circumstances, partly an ancient prejudice connecting soldiers with immorality and drink, and partly, a strong objection felt by Trade Union leaders to their young members coming under the personal influence of the 'boss class' to which they conceived the officers to belong.[13]

At the outbreak of war the Territorial Force (TF) rapidly expanded, in part because enlistment into it had the significant advantage of being seen to be doing one's bit without the obligation to actually go to war. The terms of service for Territorials meant that no man could be required to serve overseas unless he volunteered by signing the Imperial Service Obligation (ISO). Even then, a unit would not be regarded as having agreed to serve overseas unless 80 per cent of its men had signed the ISO (though by the end of August this had been reduced to 60 per cent). Prior to the outbreak of war only five TF units had agreed. By the end of August, the number of battalions committed to overseas service had risen to sixty-nine, but frequently these were composite units made up of whoever had come forward, often believing they would be sent to imperial garrisons to free up regular battalions for war service. The willingness of sixty-nine battalions to serve is often cited as an

g.   *R.*

Your King and Country Need You.

Another 100,000 Men Wanted.

Lord Kitchener is much gratified with the response already made to the Appeal for additional men for His Majesty's Regular Army.

In the grave National emergency that now confronts the Empire he asks with renewed confidence that another 100,000 men will now come forward.

TERMS OF SERVICE.

(Extension of Age Limit.)

Age of Enlistment, 19 to 35 ; Ex-Soldiers up to 45 and certain selected Ex-Non-Commissioned Officers up to 50. Height 5ft. 3in. and upwards. Chest, 34 inches at least. Must be medically fit.

General Service for the War.

Men enlisting for the duration of the War will be able to claim their discharge with all convenient speed at the conclusion of the War.

PAY AT ARMY RATES

and Married Men or Widowers with Children will be accepted, and will draw Separation Allowance under Army Conditions.

HOW TO JOIN.

Men wishing to join should apply in person at any Military Barracks or at any Recruiting Office ; the address of the latter can be obtained from Post Offices or Labour Exchanges.

GOD SAVE THE KING!

Kitchener's call for the 'Second Hundred Thousand' who would form the next cohort of the New Army.

example of the positive response to the outbreak of war, but this ignores the fact that there were 207 battalions in the TF in July 1914. Only a third had showed themselves willing to fight and some of those found that commanding officers had put in returns without even asking their men, so that original estimates of those who would sign the ISO went far beyond the numbers who actually did so and even the sixty-nine battalions sometimes struggled to fill their ranks with genuine volunteers.[14] Even where volunteers were forthcoming, the minimum age for TF service was 17, a year younger than that for the Regulars and two years below the minimum legal age for service overseas. The removal of 'Immatures' and men deemed no longer fit for front-line service quickly depleted the ranks still further and those eligible to serve were uncomfortably aware of how poor their state of training actually was.

According to Walter Nicholson, a staff officer with the 51st Highland Division, 'it was not cowardice that decided them to say they wouldn't fight, it was the belief that the Government had broken faith with them … The Territorial had not joined for foreign service, but to defend his country'. As one officer of the division put it, 'There must be something wrong if employers go out to fight alongside Regular private soldiers' and the feeling was that 'the Territorial Force was a last resort … it was not meant to come into the war until all the Regulars had been killed; a Regular was not playing the game if he let a Territorial come and fight alongside him so early in the war as this'.[15] There was a widespread sense of betrayal about even being asked the question and officers were reported to have counselled their men against signing. In part, given the role TF battalions would later play, the reluctance may have come from poor communication leading them to believe they were being asked to deploy immediately rather than an unwillingness to serve. A further argument came from the fact that the actual level of threat of a German invasion was unknown. As the BEF was pushed back from Mons, the possibility that the TF might be needed for its original purpose could not be ignored. Whatever the truth of the matter, as the second line 2/4th King's Own Yorkshire Light Infantry (KOYLI) gathered at Wellingborough station ready to leave England at the start of 1917, pre-war attitudes remained strong. The colonel's wife was heard to remark that she 'hoped that if the battalion suffered officer casualties, their replacements would be gentlemen'. But more tellingly, on another part of the platform, Captain Harry Greaves, 'seated mournfully on his luggage', confided to the wife of Captain Gerald Beaumont that 'if he had known he would have to go to France he would never have joined'.[16]

Faced with a Territorial Force that could not be legally required to serve over-seas unless its members chose to and which, in any case, was badly trained and frequently unfit for deployment, Kitchener's mistrust of amateur soldiering came to the fore as he told Sir Charles Harris that he 'could take no account of anything but regular soldiers'.[17] Rather than attempting to bring the various forces together, he would start from scratch with a brand new army. On 7 August, perhaps the most successful and iconic advertising campaign ever was launched as Kitchener's face appeared on posters across the country above the slogan 'Your Country Needs You'. Every Regular Army battalion was ordered to send one captain, two subalterns, two sergeants and thirteen other NCOs to their respective regimental depots to prepare for the arrival of 100,000 volunteers for the new Regular Army 'Service' battalions into which men aged 19 to 31 could enlist for three years or the duration of the war. By the end of August, the first 100,000 men had enlisted and, in the week following news of the retreat from Mons and the sacking of Louvain, recruiting began for K2, the second of what would become five New Kitchener Armies by January 1915.

The days after the outbreak of war had been marked by the arrival, in huge numbers, of young men at recruiting offices across the country. The war had already brought some industries to a standstill and Labour Exchanges actively encouraged men to enlist as an alternative to unemployment. Donald Hankey, a former officer who chose to enlist in the ranks of the New Army, noted that

"KEIGHLEY LADS, PLAY THE GAME!"

2nd Bradford — Pals' Battalion

Full Back:
LORD KITCHENER.

Three Quarter Backs:
General **FRENCH.**   Admiral **JELLICOE.**
LORD FISHER.   General **SMITH DORRIEN.**

Half Backs:
Gen. Sir **DOUGLAS HAIG.**   Admiral **BEATTY.**

WANTED AT ONCE
DASHING FORWARDS
FOR THE KEIGHLEY COMPANY.

Apply for all Particulars:
RECRUITING OFFICE :—DRILL HALL, KEIGHLEY.

Keighley enthusiastically joined the recruitment campaign to boost the local 'Pals' battalion of the West Yorkshire Regiment, despite the town's long-standing links with the West Riding Regiment.

'fear of starvation' had certainly played its part in encouraging some of his new comrades to join up[18] and this was particularly true in the case of the Bristol Poor Law Guardians who, in August, simply stopped paying any form of relief to paupers they regarded as able-bodied enough to enlist. Likewise, Lord Wemyss threatened to sack and evict any able-bodied labourers on his estate who failed to join up, while other employers offered bounties to rid themselves of single young men.[19] Alfred Mansfield, travelling to his new depot, was accompanied by eight servants of a peer who had decided that all the younger members of his staff should go.[20] Although widely regarded as reprehensible even in 1914, such coercion was commonplace and employers sometimes offered assurances of a guaranteed job on return, contributions towards pension funds or a top-up for army pay, but also sometimes announced that they were simply laying off all single men on their staff. As a result, the 'first hundred thousand' or K1

6th RESERVE BATTALION
DUKE OF WELLINGTON'S REGIMENT.
═══════════

1,000 MEN
WANTED IMMEDIATELY.

FOR THE ABOVE BATTALION. ALL MEN TO SOLDIER TOGETHER.
UPHOLD THE HONOUR OF YOUR TOWN
COME AND SERVE NOW.

YORKSHIRE with it road acres, dense population and strapping men, must not lag behind in this life and death struggle against the German military despot.

Your HOME, your WIFE, your MOTHER, your CHILDREN, your FUTURE, your EXISTENCE, depend on your decision. RECRUITS are needed urgently. Don't wait for your neighbour—set him an example. COME AT ONCE. Step into the ranks of those who are defending our shores before it is too late.

Remember the horrors of German Savagery in Belgium to men, women and children. Now is the time to put an end to this for all time. You can help if we are to emerge successfully, and AT ONCE, as delay will be fatal.

Terms of Enlistment:—4 years Home Defence, but a man of the Territorial Force must subject himself to liability to serve in any place outside the United Kingdom in the event of National Emergency. Men will be allowed to take their discharge at the termination of the War.

Apply :—DRILL HALL.

HELP OTHERS.   HELP YOURSELF.
GOD SAVE OUR KING AND EMPIRE.

Edward Foulds & Sons, Printers, &c., Excelsior Works, Dinley.

Harold Wiseman's brother Jimmy was already serving with the 6th West Ridings when the decision was made to double the battalion. Once 1,000 men had been recruited, the 6th battalion became the 1/6th and 2/6th, both eventually serving overseas.

volunteers were not significantly different to the type of recruit enlisting in the pre-war Regulars. The significant change began with K2.

The first Kitchener volunteers were destined to join 'Service' battalions under War Office control but at the end of August a plan was put forward intended to create an instant *esprit de corps* for the New Army based on suggestion of General Sir Henry Rawlinson that men would be more inclined to enlist if they knew that they were going to serve alongside their friends and work colleagues. He then appealed to London stockbrokers to raise a battalion of men from workers in the City of London to set an example and 1,600 men enlisted in the 10th (Service) Bn Royal Fusiliers, the so-called 'Stockbrokers' Battalion', within a week. A few days later, on the evening of 28 August, Edward Stanley, the 17th Earl of Derby held a meeting to encourage the formation of a battalion of men from Liverpool and told them that theirs should be 'a battalion of pals'. So great was the response that three battalions were raised within days and a fourth complete by October. Encouraged by Lord Derby's success, Kitchener promoted the idea of organising similar recruitment campaigns throughout the entire country founded around shared occupations, employers or some other common background. It was a phenomenal success, not least because Kitchener's call for volunteers offered these men a chance to enjoy a little excitement in a war few believed would last for long and, best of all, would not require a loss of status by mixing with the typical soldier class. The volunteers for the new 'Pals' units of Kitchener's New Army would not be expected to mix with the men Wellington had called 'the scum of the earth'.

'Today has seen the commencement of recruiting for the middle-class clerks and professional men, or the "black coated battalions",' noted the *Hull Daily Mail* of 2 September 1914. '[I]t must not be thought there is a desire for class distinction but just as the docker will feel at home amongst his every-day mates, so the wielders of the pen and drawing pencil will be better as friends together.' Hull would eventually produce four 'Pals' battalions, the 10th to 13th (Service) Battalions of the East Yorkshire Regiment, known respectively as the Hull Commercials, Hull Tradesmen, Hull Sportsmen and, to accommodate the rest, Hull T'Others. 'The advantage of the system described,' noted the *Yorkshire Observer* of 7 September 1914 on the formation of a battalion from Bradford,

> is that it restricts admission to the battalion to the right sort of men. An exact definition of suitability for this purpose can hardly be obtained, but the ideal to be aimed at is a congenial companionship and a community of interest and association, and the question of suitability in this respect will be in the discretion of employers who distribute the tickets or the responsible league representatives who will supervise the registration and form their own judgement upon each of the men who come forward.

Those judgements, the article noted, would then be used to direct a successful recruit to the most appropriate company:

A Company	Professional men and Bradford Trade Employers
B Company	Cashiers, foreign correspondents, higher grade office workers
C Company	Clerks
D Company	Warehousemen
E Company	Master Tradesmen
F Company	Tradesmen's Assistants
G Company	'Pals', meaning friends who wish to stand together despite differences of civilian occupation
H Company	Miscellaneous[21]

According to the *Yorkshire Observer* of 14 September 1914, eagerness to enlist 'seems to have taken firm root in the minds of young commercial and professional men of the city, who appear only too anxious to get started ...' Photographs taken at the time outside recruiting depots show not the flat caps of working-class men but smart straw boaters worn by men in suits. Massive social changes in the late Victorian and Edwardian periods had created a whole new class of office workers who now sought a break from a life very different to that of the role models they had been raised to believe marked the true Englishman.

For many men, though, the decision to enlist was a difficult one not to be taken lightly. For families already living at poverty level, army pay might just keep them afloat but for most workers, enlisting meant an often drastic cut in pay at a time when prices were rising sharply. In 1914, a soldier earned just 1 shilling per day. With Proficiency Pay awarded for extra skills he could earn up to eleven pence more – a total weekly wage (less stoppages of three and a half pence) of 11 shillings 4½ pence per week – around 2 shillings less than the average earnings of an unskilled agricultural labourer in the poorest paid area of Britain. By comparison, by March 1918, an unskilled man working in munitions averaged £2 12s 6d and unskilled females brought home £1 17s 6d. A skilled female copper band turner could earn up to £7 per week[22] – over twelve times as much as a front-line infantryman. Separation Allowances for married men were offered but, as one woman later recalled, 'the separation allowance was terrible. It really was. Starvation money, that's what you could call it.'[23] In response to unrest caused by the discrepancy between civilian and military pay, in September 1917 a government issued 'Memorandum on Soldiers and Sailors Pay' concluded that a soldier with a wife and two children received pay and benefits of between 47s 6d and 94s 6d per week and a single man somewhere between 30 shillings and 73s 6d.[24] Impressive as this sounded, it was based on such dubious calculations as that board and lodgings, were provided so the man's dugout in a muddy trench and tins of bully beef could be valued at 20 shillings per week as 'benefit in kind'.

After the initial shock of the outbreak of war, sections of British industry recovered quickly. As Scott's history of Leeds in the Great War put it:

> Only the clothing operatives were greatly perturbed. There were fears that the industry – of such vital importance to Leeds – might not recover from the emphatic check of war. Its 'good time', however, was not long in coming. Army orders soon gave ample employment. Contracts for boots, and for khaki cloth, too, rolled in. The early queues of workless grew smaller and smaller. Trade prospects all round brightened, though it meant a diversion of ways and means and some considerable adaptation to the novelty of the industrial situation ... At the beginning of November ... Leeds woke up to the fact that there was more employment in its midst than had been known for many a long month. Hunslet, Holbeck, Armley and every industrial quarter shared in the improvement. Engineering and textile firms alike were working at full pressure on Government orders, one group of which, by the way, related to no less than a million uniforms.[25]

Textile mills went onto overtime to produce cloth for uniforms. Ironically, before the war khaki dye was almost exclusively sourced from Germany. The dyeing process for textiles had itself spawned a service industry in the West Riding and amongst the products widely used was picric acid, whose high sulphur content was used to produce a yellow dye but also had another property. Picric acid could be used to produce explosives and for years dyeworks had also held licences to produce 'lyddite' – a picric acid explosive named after the town of Lydd in Kent where ordnance experiments had been carried out. Later, the dyeing properties of picric acid meant that munitions workers could easily be identified in a crowd by the yellowing of skin, hair and eyes that earned them the nickname of 'canaries'. With full and profitable employment to be had, especially employment contributing to the war effort, many men decided not to enlist, assuming that 'shirkers' (a term already in use by September 1914) should go first. As is human nature, the exact definition of a shirker varied from individual to individual but could generally be taken as meaning anyone regarded by the speaker as less valuable at home than the speaker himself. Indeed, the view was reinforced when some occupations, such as railwaymen and agricultural workers, were given protection by the government and contractors precisely to avoid having to enlist. A special Docks Battalion of the Liverpool Regiment, for example, was created offering special terms for volunteers:

> 1. He will engage to serve His Majesty as a soldier in a Dock Battalion of the Liverpool Regiment in the United Kingdom for the duration of the war, at the end of which he will be discharged with all convenient speed.

2. When attested by the Justice he will be liable to all the provisions of the Army Act for the time being in force, that is to say he will be subject to Military Law and Discipline, and so far as they are applicable, to Army Orders and Regulations.

3. He may be required to work any reasonable hours by day or night, and at any job that may be required.

4. Any complaint or difference of opinion regarding rate of transport pay, conditions of work, or other matter connected with Dock Labour, must be referred through the usual channels to the Commanding Officer, who will consult the Joint Labour Committee of the Port of Liverpool if necessary.

5. Men serving in a Dock Battalion, Liverpool Regiment, will be paid the Infantry pay of their rank, and in addition will receive transport pay at the rates recognised by the Joint Labour Committee of the Port of Liverpool, such transport pay to be in no case less than 35/- a week, unless on any day they have failed to parade in accordance with Regimental Orders. The following are the Infantry rates of daily pay:-

Company Serjeant-Major – 4s.
Serjeant – 2s. 4d.
Corporal – 1s. 8d.
Private – 1s.

6. Under no circumstances will men belonging to a Dock Battalion be entitled to either Lodging Allowance, Separation, Ration, or any other allowance, to Army Pension for themselves or their dependents, or to a Gratuity on enlistment or discharge or otherwise. They will be insured as civilians under the National Health Insurance Acts and make the ordinary contribution of 4d. a week, and in case of injury will be dealt with in accordance with the provisions of the Workmen's Compensation Act. No medical attendance will be provided from Army sources, and all benefits under the National Health Insurance Act will be drawn from civil sources.[26]

The folk memory of egalitarian 'Pals' battalions made up of a wide cross-section of society serving happily alongside each other is at odds with the reality of the situation. Workers in the commercial sector and other 'professionals' joined battalions for men like themselves, the loss of income cushioned by private incomes and savings, with many destined for the thousands of new commissioned posts suddenly available and granted at the discretion of the newly appointed commanding officer. Skilled workers – and especially textile workers – were among the least represented in the ranks. Nevertheless, a massive influx of volunteers had flooded into the army with 462,901 men enlisting in September alone,[27] swamping the regimental depots and creating chaos as local authorities and the War Office attempted to establish camps, find uniforms, provide instructors and to find something constructive for the men to do. Dissatisfaction spread quickly and the total recruiting figures for October, November and December fell short of September's.

David Kennedy has written of what he terms 'coercive voluntarism' to describe the overall public response to the war. After the initial rush of volunteers, recruiting figures dropped significantly and for a time remained steady at around 100,000 per month, but fell far below this in the summer of 1915. Contemporary commentators found themselves trying to reconcile the belief in the truly voluntary 'volunteer' army with the increasing level of social pressure men out of uniform were facing. Recruiting drives at theatres, music halls and football grounds had worked on peer pressure to encourage young men – often under the influence of drink – to commit to enlisting. Recruiting sergeants paid a bounty of 2s 6d per man resorted to hard-sell techniques on the streets, where young women handed out white feathers to passing men in civilian clothes. Harry Cartmell, Mayor of Preston wrote that as 1915 wore on,

> the average recruiting speech became a mixture of abuse, cajolery and threats … the men secured by pressure of this kind could hardly be described as volunteers … the whole business has become manifestly unfair … men were induced to join whose business and family obligations ought to have secured them a respite, while insensitive people with no such responsibilities smiled and sat tight.[28]

In Charles Pickering's home town of Todmorden, the 1911 census indicated that there ought to have been around 5–6,000 men of military age but by late 1915 3,750 men were still at home where, as Adrian Gregory points out, a figure of around 30 per cent of men voluntarily enlisting was the average for the region.[29] In some places, the figures for enlistments had become an embarrassment, with one recruiting speech claiming that Leeds had seen only 5.2 per cent of eligible men volunteering for service whilst Bradford managed 4 per cent. Leicester could produce just 2.6 per cent.[30] There were enormous differences between trades, too. By July 1915, a survey showed that the coal industry had lost 21.8 per cent of its workforce, chemical and explosives 23.8 per cent, but the worsted and woollen mils had contributed just 12.5 per cent.[31] By then, the label of 'shirkers' was indiscriminately applied. The fitness issues highlighted by the Boer War had not been resolved and many thousands of men had attempted to enlist but had been rejected on various, sometimes seemingly trivial, grounds. Billy Harrison, for example, had tried to join up in 1914: 'At first, I wasn't fit for service because of an impediment in my speech; I had a terrible stammer and they told me that I would be no good at passing messages down the line.'[32] Even poor dental hygiene could be enough to disqualify a man from serving. As recruiting standards dropped, men who had been rejected or even discharged from the army as unfit found themselves reclassified and could be accepted, but in the climate of 1915 few made the distinction or paused to ask why a man was not in uniform, seeing only that there were a great many able-bodied men still at home. Just as today the media depicts anyone receiving state benefits as a 'scrounger' regardless of their actual circumstances, so too in 1915 the media railed against 'shirkers' no matter the reason. As early as December 1914, the Admiralty recognised the degree of pressure being applied to its civilian staff and began issuing special badges to vital dockyard staff to provide some measure of protection. Some government contractors followed suit and in response to angry complaints from former soldiers discharged because of age, wounds or sickness that they had been abused in the street as shirkers, in September 1916 the government introduced the Silver War Badge to be worn on civilian clothes to show that a man had already served and thus reduce the risk of his being targeted.

One unforeseen result of the policy of unrestricted enlistment began to be seen in early 1915. As it always had, Britain had responded to war by establishing a naval block-ade of its enemies, with the intention of fighting an attritional war that would break Germany's war economy. The war would be fought on the battlefield, but it would be won in the factories and men vital to war industries were instead being trained for use as front-line infantry. Humbert Wolfe, the Bradford-based son of a German Jewish father and Italian mother employed to help found the Ministry of Labour, later wrote:

> The patriotic impulse was not cautious. It did not select its men, saying to the skilled man 'stay' and to the unskilled 'come'. It knew nothing of key industries or pivotal workers. It chose, if not all, the best of all ranks and grades of industry. It took the skilled man equally with the unskilled, it took the strong man in preference to the weak, and, above all, it took those to whom the struggle meant the most.[33]

The British Army had been struggling to maintain its artillery supplies since autumn 1914, and the BEF's Commander-in-Chief, Field Marshal Sir John French, gave an interview to *The Times* published on 27 March 1915 calling for more ammunition. On the basis of an assurance from Kitchener, Asquith stated in April that the army had sufficient ammunition but the failure of the Battle of Aubers Ridge in early May was attributed by *The Times* correspondent Charles Repington to a shortage of high explosive shells based on information leaked to him by French, who also sent officers to London to meet with senior Conservative figures. Keen to discredit Kitchener, Lord Northcliffe used his *Times* and *Daily Mail* papers to attack the government's handling of the various civilian contractors supplying munitions to the army.

That the British Army was experiencing a shell shortage was not in doubt, nor was the fact that British munitions production was not operating at anything like full efficiency. As Liberal Chancellor, David Lloyd George encouraged Northcliffe to publish details of the scandal and the resulting coverage, whilst unpopular with readers and leading to a dip in circulation, laid the blame at Kitchener's door. The

'Shell Scandal', as it became popularly and widely known, set in train a political upheaval which ultimately led to the downfall of Asquith's Liberal government and the creation of a coalition (albeit still under Asquith) on 25 May, but also ultimately to French's replacement later that year by Sir Douglas Haig.

The following month Lloyd George introduced into Parliament the first Munitions of War Act, which called for the setting up of a central department of state to oversee war production and when as a result the new Ministry of Munitions was created, its responsibility was handed to him. The aim of the new department was to rationalise war production and it was to be staffed at the highest levels by businessmen loaned by their companies for the duration of the war. These men were tasked to reconcile the needs of big business with those of the state, and to reach a compromise on price and profit that was acceptable to both sides. Government agents would buy essential supplies from abroad and the Ministry would control their distribution in order to prevent speculative price rises and to enable normal marketing to continue. Steel, wool, leather, jute, flax and other materials all came under similar controls. One of the first decisions at Whitehall Gardens, headquarters of the Ministry, was to undertake an industrial census of the workshops of the nation, and some 65,000 forms were distributed inquiring about the staffs, contracts, machinery and output of factories throughout Great Britain; more than 45,000 were returned to the Ministry within a month.[34]

The census highlighted the significant losses of manpower suffered by some vital industries and began to identify those workers more valuable at home than in the army. Some were obvious – farmers, skilled engineers, miners and so on. Others less so. It was not until the manpower crisis of 1918 that War Office Circular 27/Exemptions/362 was rescinded. Previously, employees of racing stables and hunt servants had been protected as 'vital' on the grounds that both helped maintain high quality horses for potential use as remounts for the cavalry, but hunt servants responsible for looking after the hounds were also excluded. The census also highlighted roles that could be taken by women to release men for service as women began to enter the workplace in increasing numbers. For chronic shortages, a 'Release from Colours' scheme was introduced to allow companies to apply for skilled men to be returned to civilian life (with the right to continue to wear their uniforms) and slowly these men trickled back into the factories. The competing needs of British industry for a workforce and the army for soldiers were by now becoming critical. Having highlighted those professions deemed of national importance, the census showed that there were a great many more men whose presence in the factories was not necessary to maintain production levels and whose place could be taken by women and school leavers too young to enlist. Despite centuries of opposition, the campaign to introduce not just National Service in industry but to take the politically dangerous step of bringing in compulsory military service became central to Britain's war effort.

The ancient *Posse comitatus* had given the shire reeve (or sheriff) of a county the power to embody any group of men for the defence of their local area (in 1871, *Posse comitatus* passed into Texan state law, creating the Sheriff's Posse of western fame), but the power had been abused by both sides during the Civil Wars of the seventeenth century and had been widely condemned by the writers of the history readers familiar to all schoolchildren. Since then, despite active campaigning by men like Wellington, Britain had steadfastly refused to follow the European model of universal conscription. In the wake of the Boer experience, supporters of conscription had again been active, but had never achieved popular support. The coalition government was faced by hostile opposition to the principle of compulsory military service by men who argued that such a policy – requiring as it did a dilution of the existing male workforce – would leave Britain bankrupt if not totally defeated. Nevertheless, many regarded it as inevitable. As early as 1914, employers in Manchester had offered to support volunteers enlisting in the forces if they joined as private soldiers, but the offer was 'for voluntary service only, and should the Government decide on compulsory training later, the offer will not apply to those affected by such compulsion'.

Following the industrial census, and with military and industrial needs in mind, a new proposal was put forward to ensure that the government was able to make best use of the skills and talents of its population by ordering that every individual's suitability for war work be registered. Despite recognition that this was just a step away from conscription, the National Registration Act passed its third reading with only token opposition in July. Sunday 15 August was designated as Registration Day when all citizens, male and female, between the ages of 15 and 65 were required under penalty of law to report to canvassers their names, occupations, current employment, family circumstances and any skills useful to war work.[35] The information gathered from male respondents between the ages of 18 and 41 was copied onto pink forms (white forms were used for females and blue denoted males not of military age or fitness), with those of men employed in necessary occupations marked with black stars – thereafter referred to as 'starred' occupations. By the end of October, the information gathered had been analysed and revealed that there were 5,158,211 men recorded on pink forms, with only 1,519,432 starred. Further reducing the number available by the accepted average of 25 per cent for medical rejection, this left a manpower pool of approximately 2.7 million available for the military.[36]

Now armed with concrete evidence, Lloyd George and the Munitions Ministry could show that the country could not afford to lose any more skilled men to voluntary enlistment, but that there was a significant pool of available manpower that could be used to reinforce the army. The main problem was one of how to introduce the scheme against opposition from powerful trade unions, who had already shown themselves willing to take strike action that harmed the war effort, and widespread hostility from the general public. The response, made public on 19 October, was the compromise 'Derby Scheme'. Under the control of Lord Derby, the newly appointed head of the Joint Recruiting Committee of the War Office, all males listed by the National Registration Act as being between the ages of 19 to 41 in England, Wales and Scotland were banded into one of forty-six age classifications, twenty-three each for married and unmarried men. Each was to be offered the chance either to enlist directly or to attest their willingness to serve in the army when called at a later date, in a kind of 'fall or be pushed' final opportunity to join up as a volunteer. The scheme stressed that workers in relevant trades deemed to be of national importance would be attested but would not actually be called up as long as they carried on working in those trades and that unmarried men would be called up first. All males who attested, regardless of skills, received 2*s* 6*d* and a special armband signifying their new status to provide protection against the growing hostility towards shirkers. Skilled men in key trades also received special armbands declaring their work to be a special contribution to the war effort. Tribunals would be set up to hear individual appeals for exemption or deferment.

Few saw the scheme as anything but a stepping stone to wide-scale compulsory military service and the results were disappointing. Half the unmarried men and around 40 per cent of married men failed to attest. Men in starred jobs, those least likely to be called, came forward in the highest numbers, with around 45 per cent of single and 48 per cent of married men attesting with just 38 per cent and 54 per cent respectively among those in unstarred jobs. Married men attested in greater numbers largely because they had been led to believe that they would not be called up for a considerable time, if at all, and that young single men would be called up first. In all, around 215,000 men joined the army under the Derby Scheme but recruiting figures continued to fall. The scheme was widely judged to have failed but, as R.Q.J. Adams and Philip Poirier have suggested, the question is really whether it was ever intended to succeed. Derby, a supporter of conscription, considered himself 'somewhat in a position of a receiver who was put in to wind up a bankrupt concern'. (*The Star*, 6 October 1915. Following a speech in Rossendale, Lancashire.) While Derby clearly worked hard to oversee the last stage of voluntary enlistment, the fact that a Military Service Act introducing conscription was already working its way through Parliament suggests that this was more a means of proving to the public that Britain could no longer rely on volunteers to fill the ranks. The first draft of the new act went before the Cabinet on 1 January 1916, just two weeks after the closing date for registration under the Derby Scheme, and on 27 January 1916 the new act introduced compulsory military service for every male who:

– on 15 August 1915 was ordinarily resident in Great Britain and who had attained the age of 19 but was not yet 41 and - on 2 November 1915 was unmarried or a widower without dependent children.

Under the terms of the 'Bachelor's Bill', as it became known, unless he met certain exceptions or had reached the age of 41 before the appointed date, from 2 March 1916 every unmarried male citizen was deemed to have enlisted for general service with the colours or in the reserve and was, for the time being, regarded as being in the reserve. Those with a preference for service in the navy could state it and would be offered to the Admiralty. Tribunals would be put in place to hear appeals or requests for exemptions and deferments where service would cause severe hardship to a family or business or where a man had a conscientious objection to the military. Each man was allocated into a class relating to the year of his birth, ranging from Class 1 (1896) to Class 23 (1875), and would be called forward according to that class, with the youngest not expected to be called until they reached their nineteenth birthday. A public proclamation would be posted announcing the call up of each class and each man would receive an individual call-up notice.

By March 1916, Sir William Robertson, Chief of the Imperial General Staff, complained that of 'the 193,891 men called up under the Military Service Act, no fewer than 57,146 have failed to appear'.[37] Part of the problem lay in the registration process. Based on similar work by insurance companies, the government had ignored the advice that this was a highly mobile population with one large London based company alone reporting that of an insured population of 1,450,000 policyholders, 600,000 moved address in 1913 alone.[38] Failures to notify the government of a change of address meant that call-up notices were simply not reaching the relevant men. By the summer of 1916, Ian Dewhirst writes:

> vociferous public opinion was raising the search for reluctant recruits to the tempo of a witch hunt. Words had been coined to fit the occasion. There were 'comb outs' of workers in exempted occupations, 'roundups' of those deemed to be 'shirkers'. The authorities were even reduced to raiding common lodging-houses and sweeping up any sorry serviceable flotsam they found there.[39]

Everywhere, 'the military authorities began taking strong action against the supposedly large numbers of unexempted men who were evading the net. Parties of soldiers swooped on the exits from railway stations, parks, football fields, cinemas, theatres and prize fights. All males who looked of military age and were not in uniform were apprehended.'[40] One such round up took place in Harold Wiseman's home town of Keighley:

> It speaks volumes for entertainment trends of 1916 that the authorities' first Keighley 'Roundup' took place at the Cosy Corner Picture House where a 'two act drama of the slums' called 'Little Marie' was raided and its male audience of military age examined. This operation netted 150 men who 'had not their papers with them', most of whom turned out to be, not shirkers but exempted

munitions workers not yet accustomed to carrying their documentation about with them.[41]

Frustratingly small numbers of men were found this way and the practice was eventually abandoned, but not before an amendment to the Military Service Act was introduced bringing with it conscription for married men. Universal military conscription now affected every man in Britain.

Across the country, around 1,800 tribunals sat in long sessions listening to appeals for exemption. In most cases, records were destroyed after the war so details are difficult to establish, but Adrian Gregory notes that the Birmingham Tribunal sat no fewer than 1,765 times between 1916 and 1918 to hand down 90,721 decisions. In Leeds, 435 sessions heard 55,101 appeals relating to 27,000 individual applicants.[42] Appeals came in many forms. Some were made on the grounds of the genuine hardship a family might face in losing its breadwinner, some from local businessmen who stood to lose everything if they were to enlist. Others, though, were chancers. In early 1917, Harold Wiseman would have read in the *Keighley News* of a man seeking exemption on the grounds that he was the only man in the village able to cut hair. Others had to stay at home to care for elderly mothers or widowed men to care for their children. The number of appeals from the sons of local businessmen needing exemptions to allow them to take over the family firms from frail fathers led one Lancashire observer to note drily that 'senile decay sets in at a very early age in Preston'.[43]

The tribunals have been described as being made up of the sort of local people one might approach to have a passport application countersigned – local councillors, magistrates, businessmen, solicitors and the like – and there was active encouragement to include trade union representatives on the panels. As such, they provided a representation of local feeling about conscription and the numbers of tribunal members involved seem to be huge – Gregory estimates that as many as 40,000 people is a realistic figure. Although tribunals sat solely to hear appeals against conscription, it wasn't unknown for them to find themselves in receipt of letters from disgruntled wives asking for their menfolk to be taken away on the grounds that they were sick of them being at home and felt a spell in the army would be good for them, or from angry neighbours demanding that a nearby 'shirker' be taken. But whilst attitudes for and against military service were represented, tribunals are most well known today for their treatment of those who objected to fighting on moral grounds. A great deal has been written about those men who sought exemption as conscientious objectors, but these never made up more than a tiny minority of those seeking to escape conscription. Even in Harold Whitwam's home town of Huddersfield, noted for its anti-war politics and described as 'a hotbed of pacifism', where the local tribunal heard 12,543 initial appeals in 1916 alone, only 1 per cent were on the basis of conscientious objection and these tended to be treated sympathetically with the majority of genuine cases granted exemptions. It was only the extremist objectors who refused to undertake any form of service whatsoever – even non-combatant service in the UK logging or agricultural industries – who faced imprisonment and punishment, and these objections tended to be political rather than religious or moral.

As the war drew on, the casualty lists steadily grew and the demand for more and more men became pressing. Once-sympathetic tribunals had to apply the rules ever more carefully to balance the demands of the military with justice for those left behind. Families of those who had been killed or maimed became ever more bitter that some served whilst others avoided their duty. While anti-war meetings were openly tolerated in Huddersfield without restrictions throughout the war and those who had been exempted from service as conscientious objectors continued to be employed as school teachers, other towns clamped down on meetings and as early as 1916 Leeds City Council refused to employ known objectors.

Opinion at home was sharply divided. The idea of compulsory military service had been strongly opposed just a few years earlier, but now that it was here people recognised that whilst some were shouldering their share of the burden of national defence, many were not. Businesses were seen as profiteering and the opposition of trade unionists was starting to be seen as self-interest, with skilled workers hanging onto their starred status whilst doing nothing to protect unskilled men. Against this background of unequal sacrifice, all conscripts came to be tarred with the same brush as 'wheelbarrows' (because they had to be pushed) and, as one bitter compiler of a trench dictionary defined them: 'Conscript. A man who tried to wait until the war was over before volunteering for the army, but was balked by the Government.'[44]

The insult was felt perhaps most keenly by those, like Ambler, Wiseman and the others, who fell between the stools. Having left school they were no longer children but, aged just 15 when recruiting was at its height, they were far too young to enlist. Much has been written about the boy soldiers of the Great War and in *Kitchener's Lost Boys*, John Oakes tells us that there 'were well over 250,000 underage soldiers in Kitchener's new armies during the First World War'. Put another way, one in ten of the 2.5 million men joining the army – and by extension serving in the trenches – by the end of 1915 were 'underage', but the subject is so deeply ingrained into the popular mythology that stories of underage enlistment are accepted without question. In his study of the memorialisation of the Somme, Geoff Dyer reports:

Like many young men, my grandfather was under age when he turned up to enlist. The recruiting sergeant told him to come back in a couple of days when he was two years older. My grandfather duly returned, added a couple of years to his age and was accepted into the army … Similar episodes are fairly common in the repertoire of recruitment anecdotes, but I never doubted the veracity of this particular version of it, which my mother told me several times over the years. It came as a surprise, then, to discover from his death certificate that my grandfather was born in November 1893 … and so was twenty when the war broke out. One of the commonly circulating stories of the 1914 generation had been so thoroughly absorbed by my family that it had become part of my grandfather's biography.[45]

According to the Commonwealth War Graves Commission, the youngest British soldier killed in action during the First World War was an Irishman from Waterford, 6322 Private John Condon of the Royal Irish Regiment, killed on 24 May 1915, who had, according to the *Waterford News & Star* of 7 November 2003, 'not yet reached his 14th birthday when he was killed on the fields of Flanders in Southern Belgium'. The controversy surrounding Condon has sparked acrimonious debate among historians, but the service records of 6322 John Condon survive and show that he enlisted as an adult, giving his age as 18 on 24 October 1913, almost a year before the war started. If, as the legend has it, he was still 13 years old when he was killed in the trenches, he must have been about 12 when he convinced a recruiting officer, medical officer, the entire regimental depot training staff and the officers and NCOs of his battalion that he was old enough to serve and six years older than his actual age. In fact, records for the Waterford area show that Condon was born in October 1896 and was almost 19 at the time of death. Underage, certainly, by the legal minimum age for overseas service at the time, but not the child soldier he is presented as.[46] Stories such as these have become an accepted part of the mythology of the Great War but ignore the simple fact that 'enlistment' is not the same as 'service'. We need to consider what 'underage' actually means. A boy soldier could join the army at the age of 14, a young man could enlist in the Territorial Force at 17 or enter the Regular Army at 18, but none were legally of an age to serve overseas until they reached the age of 19. Some, undeniably, slipped through. Frederick Gaines' brother James left home and travelled to Birmingham in order to find a place in the King's Royal Rifle Corps and was aged just 17 and a half when he died of wounds on 20 September 1915. Most, though, did not get far beyond the recruiting office.

The bombing of the army records office in the blitz of 1940 destroyed around 65 per cent of service records for the Great War army, among them all records for Gaines, Pickering, Whitwam and Wiseman, leaving only pension records for Ambler and Carr. Of the 135 men who formed the draft the six would join in 1918, only eighteen partial sets of records survive relating to sixteen individuals. Of these, ten relate to attempts to enlist at the age of 15 by boys who would later join the draft. John Warwick alone, a young man living near the Leeds home of Frederick Gaines, accounts for two pension records and a service record, having enlisted in September 1915 only to be discharged shortly afterwards when his true age was discovered. By January 1916 he was back in a different regiment of the army with the same result. In August 1917, John Warwick, a young munitions worker from Leeds who would eventually join the draft in France, wrote to the War Office asking for a badge to show he had been discharged from the army because 'every time I go out in civilian clothes shits [sic] are thrown out to you, go list, it's time you were in ... for I have nothing to show I have been discharged'. Now in possession of 'a protection certificate from the Munitions Area Recruiting Office Leeds to say I have not got to be called up for service with the colours so long as the certificate is in force',[47] his letter gives a sense of the local feeling towards men not in uniform and his own sense of shame, though in his case it was not from lack of trying. Warwick had first enlisted in October 1915 into the West Riding Divisional Cyclist Company after lying about his age, serving almost a month before being tracked down by his mother and being discharged at the age of 16 years and 40 days when his birth certificate was produced. Determined to try again, he had re-enlisted by 4 January 1916, this time into the Yorkshire Regiment, serving four months before again being found out.

On 11 January 1916, 16-year-old Arnold Ambler went with his brother William to the Halifax recruiting office to sign on together into the Duke of Wellington's Regiment; Arnold lasted just twelve days before being discharged when his mother tracked him down. William was killed on 3 September that year at Thiepval. Harold Wiseman's friend Ben Crawshaw managed ninety-six days in the Notts and Derby Regiment in 1915 and Charles Pickering's neighbour Wilf Landale spent a few weeks in the Lincolnshires. Anecdotal evidence suggests that, as Oakes claimed, as many as one in ten of the boys who would later make up the draft had enlisted successfully but had not been able to maintain the pretence long enough to serve. Under military law, giving a false statement as to age could result in criminal action including a severe fine but, in a time when literacy was relatively poor and documentation scarce, one expert explained, 'It is recommended that as a rule a man should not be tried for making a false answer as to age, as it is considered that his age is not a fact within his own knowledge, and therefore it could not be proved that the answer was wilfully false'.[48] In other words, many may quite genuinely not have known they were under the age of 19 when they enlisted.

In an interesting variation on the usual recruiting story, in 1985 Arnold Ambler recorded an interview about his life in which he says he went to the recruiting office where 'you were supposed to be 5'4". I'm only 5'1" you know. So [the sergeant] says ... take a walk out of that room, so I took a walk out of that room, and I came back he says 5'4" now. I was in the army.'[49] His memory is of joining at the age of 17 and being in France before his eighteenth birthday but, in fact, Arnold's record of his enlistment as Private 4757 in the 3/4th Battalion of the Duke of Wellington's Regiment in January 1916 shows he was accepted with a measured height of 5ft 1¾in before being discharged as underage. He then spent his eighteenth birthday at home before being called up in October 1917. Interviewed so many years after the event, some confusion about details is to be expected but, combined with Geoff Dyer's account of his grandfather, these stories demonstrate just how pervasive the myths of the Great War have become. Perhaps for Arnold, as with so many others of his draft, the stigma of conscription was so great that there was a need to prove that he had not been forced into the army but had overcome barriers in order to enlist. Certainly within the army itself, there was a clear distinction to be made between conscripts and 'real' soldiers. Percy Wilson, enlisting into the Manchester Regiment a few weeks before Arnold and the others arrived for their training, later recalled that his sergeant 'was having a swipe at the conscripts, as he'd found them a lot of rotters, and he was right. They had all been called up and they weren't relishing it. Only a few of us were volunteers. We all knew what the war was about by then.'[50] Volunteer or conscript, there was no outward difference, only a very personal self-image.

We can never know for certain how the six young men responded to their impending call up. In Harold Whitwam's home town, the tribunal figures 'strongly suggest that appeal was the automatic response to being called up in Huddersfield'.[51] Whether he appealed and was rejected is not known, but he joined the army, as required, at the age of 18 years and 1 month. In Keighley, Harold Wiseman was one of five young men, all known to each other, who found their way to basic training at Brocton Camp together. In Frederick Gaines' home, as we have seen, peer pressure was still strong, abuse being hurled at the hapless John Warwick despite his repeated attempts to serve. Hoping to join particular regiments or with an eye to promotion chances, several of the draft enlisted before their birthdays. One, Leeds-born John Cameron, attested under a special extension of the Derby Scheme on 1 September 1916, three weeks before his seventeenth birthday and waited to be called up. Others joined during 1917 as they approached their birthdays. Most, though, simply bided their time and waited for the call.

6

'The war was becoming impersonal'

For Harold Wiseman and the others, the first step on the journey to France took place shortly before their seventeenth birthdays. On 24 June 1916, under the terms of the Military Service Act, they were 'deemed as from the appointed date to have been enlisted in His Majesty's regular forces for general service with the Colours or in the Reserve for the Period of the war, and have been forthwith transferred to the Reserve'.[1] From that day, they were officially regarded as having enlisted into the army and would be called up in groups when they came of age. With the legal minimum age for overseas service set at 19, they would join one month after their eighteenth birthday and undergo almost a year of training before being sent to France.

Not all waited for their papers. Some, like Frederick Hodges, enlisted at the age of 17 years and 8 months in the hope that a voluntary enlistment would increase his chances of gaining a commission.[2] Likewise, F.A.J. Taylor 'had no desire to be conscripted into the infantry when I was eighteen, having a strong desire to be an airman' and so he, too, volunteered at the age of 17, as did many who wanted to serve in particular regiments. The protagonist of R.H. Kiernan's semi-autobiographical *Little Brother Goes Soldiering* was also prompted by the belief that by volunteering he would be a candidate for a commission, but others were prompted more by fear of the stigma of conscription and by peer pressure which, even late in the war, seems to have remained a powerful motivator, as the families of those already serving demanded the same of young men not in uniform.

Whether he volunteered early or not, the process for every recruit was the same. Soon after his eighteenth birthday, a summons would arrive requiring the young man to attend at the local recruiting office on a given day to complete an attestation form detailing his name, address, occupation, willingness to be vaccinated and any previous service. He would also be required to swear an oath of allegiance witnessed by either a local magistrate or a recruiting officer:

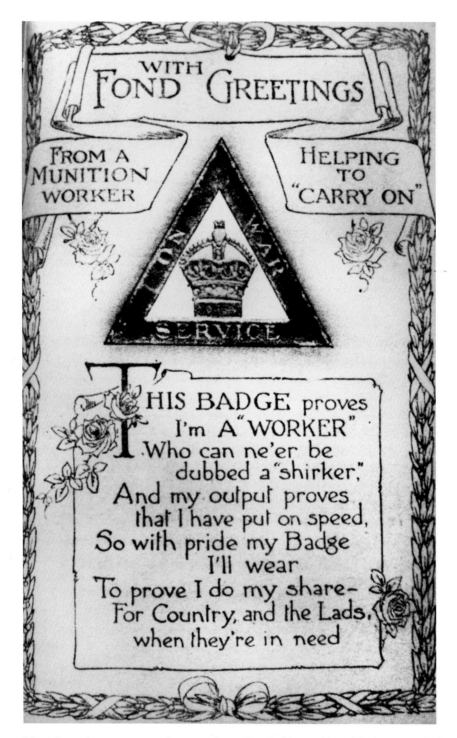

Many deemed too young or unfit to serve instead worked in munitions. Vital to the war effort, it nevertheless left them open to accusations of 'shirking'.

I, [Name] swear by Almighty God, that I will be faithful and bear true Allegiance to His Majesty King George the Fifth, His Heirs, and Successors, and that I will, as in duty bound, honestly and faithfully defend His Majesty, His Heirs, and Successors, in Person, Crown, and Dignity against all enemies, and will observe and obey all orders of His Majesty, His Heirs and Successors, and of the Generals and Officers set over me. So help me God.

Once sworn in, he received the King's shilling (5 pence) as his first day's pay and from that moment became subject to military discipline. He then moved on to the next stage of the process – the medical, which would determine in which capacity he would serve.

At first, recruits had been classified as either 'fit' or 'unfit' for service and, in the early days when there were more volunteers than places, even the most minor ailment could lead to a man being classified as 'unfit'. When Billy Harrison attempted to volunteer, he was turned away on the grounds that his stammer would prevent him passing messages effectively.[3] In a time of poor dental hygiene, the British Expeditionary Force sent to France in 1914 did not include a single dentist and for an army supplied almost endlessly with hardtack biscuits, the inability to chew could be a significant problem. Rotten teeth could be enough to prevent a man being accepted. As demand for more and more troops increased, these standards began to drop. From a minimum of 5ft 3in, the height requirement dropped to 5ft, although the special 'Bantam' battalions created for these short soldiers could include men as small as 4ft 10in.[4] In sharp contrast to the claims that most recruits for the Boer War were rejected because of poor health, by the end of 1916, medical examinations had often become cursory, accounting for only 6.5 per cent of potential recruits being rejected, and 50 per cent of those accepted immediately being classified as Category A and fit for front-line infantry service.[5] Clearly, this was at odds with the findings of the various reports on the nation's health published less than ten years earlier. Captain J.C. Dunn, the medical officer for the 2nd Battalion of the Royal Welch Fusiliers, described the physical state of men arriving at the front in 1916, which included:

an astonishing number of men whose narrow or misshapen chests, and other deformities or defects, unfitted them to stay the more exacting requirements of service in the field. Permission to send back a very few was accompanied by a peremptory intimation that a complaint of any future draft passed by Base would not be listened to. Route-marching, not routine tours of trench duty, made recurring temporary casualties of these men.[6]

To tackle the problem and make more effective use of its manpower, by 1917, the army had developed a system of medical classification of a soldier's fitness for service in different capacities. As Sir Andrew MacPhail explained in his account of the Canadian Medical Services, a universal system was adopted in which 'five medical categories were created, A, B, C, D, E, to include, respectively, men who were fit for general service; fit for certain kinds of service; fit for service in England; temporarily unfit but likely to become fit after treatment; and all others who should be discharged'. According to MacPhail:

> Category A was divided into four classes 1, 2, 3, 4, which contained respectively: men who were fit for active service in respect of health and training; men who had not been in the field but only lacked training; casualties fit as soon as they were hardened by exercise; and boys who would be fit as soon as they reached 19 years of age.
>
> Category B was likewise subdivided into four groups, to include men who were fit for employment in labour, forestry, and railway units; men who were fit for base units of the medical service, garrison, or regimental outdoor duty; men capable of sedentary work as clerks; or skilled workmen at their trades. In Category C were placed men fit for service in England only.
>
> In Category D were all men discharged from hospital to the command depot, who would be fit for Category A after completion of remedial training; and there was a special group to include all other ranks of any unit under medical treatment, who on completion would rejoin their original category. Category E included men unfit for A, B or C, and not likely to become fit within six months. It was a general rule that a soldier could be raised in category by a medical officer but lowered only by a board.[7]

The system was far from perfect, however. Civilian General Practitioners were used to carry out the medicals at a flat rate of £2 per session for the examination of thirty to forty men. If there were fewer, the rate would be set at 2 shillings and sixpence per man. Since the doctor would be paid the same no matter what the outcome, there was little incentive to create the extra work that reporting a physically unfit soldier would bring. As a result, men who had been rejected previously as totally unfit for active service now found themselves classified A1 – fit for front-line duty.

As a result, Billy Harrison, the 19-year-old previously rejected for army service because of his stammer, found himself called up in February 1917 and sent for his medical:

> It was cold and frosty that morning and there were no fires in the room where we went. There were about forty or fifty of us there, all wearing nothing but our socks and we went in two by two to be examined by two doctors. When it came for our turn, they tested our chests and then we had to bend down. They tapped our

Duplicate
Army Form E. 501.

(8889) WL·6086—1246—250 m. 11-14 J. T. & S., Ltd.

Gen. No. 8886

TERRITORIAL FORCE.
Duration of War.
~~4 years~~ Service in the United Kingdom.

ATTESTATION OF

No. 4754 Name *Arnold Ambler* Corps *3/4th W. R. R.*

Questions to be put to the Recruit before Enlistment.

iron-moulder

1. What is your Name and Address?
   1. *Arnold Ambler, 22 Skroggs View Terr. Bellon Lane Halifax*

2. Are you willing to be attested for service in the Territorial Force for the term of 4 years (provided His Majesty should so long require your services) for the County of *Yorkshire* to serve in the 3/4th Bn. Duke of Wellington's (W. R.) Regt.
   2. *Yes*

3. Have you received a notice stating the liabilities you are incurring by enlisting, and do you understand them?
   3. *Yes*

4. Do you now belong to, or have you ever served in the Royal Navy, the Army, the Royal Marines, the Militia, the Special Reserve, the Territorial Force, the Imperial Yeomanry, the Volunteers, the Army Reserve, the Militia Reserve, or any Naval Reserve Force? If so, state which unit, and, if discharged, cause of discharge
   4. *No*

5. Are you a British Subject?
   5. *Yes*

Under the provisions of Sections 13 and 99 of the Army Act, if a person knowingly makes a false answer to any question contained in the attestation paper, he renders himself liable to punishment.

I, *Arnold Ambler* do solemnly declare that the above answers made by me to the above questions are true, and that I am willing to fulfil the engagements made.

Arnold Ambler SIGNATURE OF RECRUIT.
Pte. H. Patrick Signature of Witness.

OATH TO BE TAKEN BY RECRUIT ON ATTESTATION.
I, *Arnold Ambler* swear by Almighty God, that I will be faithful and bear true Allegiance to His Majesty King George the Fifth, His Heirs, and Successors, and that I will, as in duty bound, honestly and faithfully defend His Majesty, His Heirs, and Successors, in Person, Crown, and Dignity against all enemies, according to the conditions of my service.

CERTIFICATE OF MAGISTRATE OR ATTESTING OFFICER.
I, *Captain R. W. Flanagan* do hereby certify, that, in my presence, all the foregoing Questions were put to the Recruit, above named, that the Answers written opposite to them are those which he gave to me, and that he has made and signed the Declaration, and taken the oath at *Halifax* on this *11* day of *Jan.* 1916. *Richard W. Flanagan Captain Recruiting Officer* Signature of Justice of the Peace, Officer, or other person authorised to attest Recruits.

If any alteration is required on this ADMINISTRATIVE CENTRE be requested to make it and initial the alteration under Section 80 (6), Army Act. The Recruit should, if required, insert a copy of his Declaration on Army Form E. 501A. DRILL HALL, HALIFAX Corps.

Arnold Ambler's first attempt to enlist with his brother failed after just a few days. His brother was later killed on the Somme.

private parts with a pencil and told us to cough, looked to see if we had piles and then we got dressed. We all had to report to an office where we were given the King's shilling and signed our names. Now we were soldiers.[8]

On 29 October 1917, Harold Wiseman duly presented himself at the Keighley office. Although his home straddled the border and most men joined the Lancashire Fusiliers, Charles Pickering was ordered to report to Halifax, as was Arnold Ambler. John Carr, Frederick Gaines and Harold Whitwam reported to Bradford, Leeds and Huddersfield, respectively; all underwent the same process and were classified as A4 'Under 19 years of age who should become A1 once they reach that age'. Having been passed as fit and duly enlisted, the next step was to decide how and where a man would serve. For centuries, the individual regiment had been responsible for its own recruitment and training, but the demands of the massively expanded wartime army had quickly swamped the system. At the same time, the War Office was acutely aware of the effect on local communities of the heavy losses suffered by the New Army 'Pals' battalions and the Territorial Force units. In the wake of the first day of the Somme, many regiments struggled to supply reinforcements and so men with only a few weeks' training were rushed to France to fill the gaps, arriving with only scant knowledge of how to use their rifles.

Instead, a General Service pool was created in which men would be posted not to individual depots but to numbered Training Reserve Battalions without any regimental titles. At huge camps housing many thousands of recruits they would undergo fourteen weeks of basic training, after which they would be posted to an active division in the field. These battalions typically consisted of six companies, of which three were filled with new recruits, two with men recuperating from wounds or illness and in transit back to France, and a final company was made up of employable but unfit men.[9] Although the system sought to standardise training and make the process bureaucratically effective, it also undermined the army's regimental loyalties. 'A rumour,' wrote Captain Dunn, 'which time proved to be true, was dismissed as a silly joke. Some hairy eared theorist, in whom the new War Lord trusted, had told him that the way to win was to destroy the Regiment, the immemorial foundation of armies, and nationalize the Army.'[10] With conscription coming into force, men were being enlisted into an impersonal and alienating environment. H.E.L. Mellersh, posted as an instructor to the 5th Training Reserve Brigade at Rugeley where Harold and the others would soon be sent, noted in the summer of 1917 that 'in belonging to the 5th TRB one belonged to nothing. The war was becoming impersonal.'[11]

Recognising the effect this was having on unit cohesion and motivation, further attempts were under way to restructure the training system and in May 1917, Army Council Instruction 873 created a four-stream organisation. On enlistment, men of 18 years and 1 month who fitted into category A4, B1 or C1 would be sent to Young Soldiers battalions which were being formed at Training Reserve Battalions. Junior

Description of _Arnold Ambler_ on Enlistment.

MEDICAL INSPECTION REPORT.
(Applicable to all Ranks.)

Name _Arnold Ambler_

Apparent age _19_ years _—_ months.

Height _5_ feet _1¾_ inches.

*Chest Measurement { Girth when fully expanded _34_ inches.
{ Range of expansion _2_ inches.

Vision _Good_

Physical development _Good_

* Chest measurement will be obtained by adjusting the tape so that its posterior upper edge touches the inferior angles of the shoulder blades, and its anterior lower edge the upper part of the nipples, while the arms hang loosely by the side.

Certificate of Medical Examination.

I have examined the above-named Recruit and find that he does not present any of the causes of rejection specified in the Regulations. He can see at the required distance with either eye; his heart and lungs are healthy; he has the free use of his joints and limbs; he does not suffer from hernia; and declares that he is not subject to fits of any description.

I consider him* _Fit_ for the Territorial Force.

Date _11/1/16_ 1916.

Place _Halifax_   _Edward Ellis_ MD
                                        Medical Officer.

* Insert here "fit" or "unfit."

NOTE.—Should the Medical Officer consider the Recruit unfit, he will fill in the foregoing certificate only in the case of those who have been attested and will briefly state below the cause of unfitness.

Certificate of Primary Military Examination.

I hereby certify that the above-named Recruit was inspected by me, and I consider him* _Fit_ for service in the† _3/4 = W. R. Regiment_ and that due care has been exercised in his enlistment.

Date _Jan. 12/11_ 1916.   _Richard W. Flanagan_ Captain
Place _Halifax_   Recruiting Officer.

* Insert here "fit" or "unfit."   † Insert the "Regiment" or "Corps."

[stamp: ADMINISTRATIVE CENTRE * HALIFAX * 12 JAN 1916]

No. _G.115_

* Certificate of Approving Officer.

I certify that this Attestation of the above-named Recruit is correct and properly filled up, and that the required forms appear to have been complied with. I accordingly approve, and appoint him to the † _3/4th Bn. Duke of Wellington's (W. R.) Rgt._

If enlisted by special authority, Army Form B. 203 (or other authority for the enlistment) will be attached to the original attestation.

Date _15-1-_ 1916.   _major_
Place _Clipstone Camp_ ──── 3/4th Bn. Duke of Wellington's (W. R.) Rgt. Approving Officer.

ᵇ The signature of the Approving Officer is to be affixed in the presence of the Recruit.
† Here insert the "Corps" for which the Recruit has been enlisted.

In an unusual twist to the usual story of enlisting underage, Ambler later recalled having lied about his height, claiming he told a recruiting sergeant he was the minimum 5ft 4in. His record, however, shows otherwise. At just under 5ft 2in he was accepted anyway.

Training Reserve battalions would take any of the above who could not be fitted into a Young Soldiers unit, as well as B2, B3, C2 and C3 recruits under 18 years 8 months. Extra Reserve battalions would cater for those over 18 years 8 months who were A2, whilst Senior Training Reserve battalions would take B and C recruits over that age. A further instruction, ACI 925/17, was issued in June laying down that Young Soldiers battalions would provide four months of training and Junior Training Reserve units six months. Any recruit still under the age of 19 would then be sent in formed companies to a Graduated battalion for specialist training until they were old enough to be sent overseas.[12]

One last step remained. After attesting, the recruit was given the opportunity to request his assignment. One of the main incentives offered before the introduction of conscription was that the volunteer could pick and choose which regiment to serve in, although it was always made clear that no guarantee could be made that he might not be redeployed if necessary to another unit. By the time the six boys attested, the chances of anything other than an infantry regiment were not impossible, but certainly slim.

Historians of the Great War have tended to ignore the restructuring of the training system in 1917 and instead have looked only at the General Service pool in operation as a stopgap measure. As a result, the introduction of conscription is frequently presented as having corroded the traditional regiment. Evidence for this view comes from historian Charles Carrington, who served a period in early 1918 as an instructor at a Training Reserve unit in the UK, and recalled that 'by these days the regimental system had quite broken down. [Recruits] came from any part of England and might be sent to any regiment'.[13] As we have already seen, however, the system had been through rapid changes in a short space of time. The small-scale regimental training model was quickly overwhelmed in 1914–15 and had been replaced by a general service pool that had caused fears of the death of the regimental system, but by late 1917 the old ways were reasserting themselves. Training Reserve Battalions retained their numbers, but were very definitely regimental in character. Not surprisingly, on being offered their choice of regiments, many chose to remain together. For those attesting in the West Riding, the likely choices would be the West Riding Regiment, West Yorkshire Regiment or the King's Own Yorkshire Light Infantry. No doubt many would have preferred the first option – Harold Wiseman and Arnold Ambler had brothers in it and the regiment had Territorial Units in Keighley, Halifax and Huddersfield. Bradford and Leeds had both contributed 'Pals' battalions to the West Yorkshire Regiment and perhaps John Carr and Frederick Gaines may have been interested. All, however, would settle for the Yorkshire Light Infantry. Travel warrants were issued and the boys ordered to report to what was still designated the 8th Training Reserve Battalion but in fact had now become the 51st (Young Soldier) Battalion of the King's Own Yorkshire Light Infantry at Brocton Camp on Cannock Chase.

The great adventure

In 1914, barracks accommodation in the UK could house an army of up to 175,000, but by December of that year alone over 1 million men had enlisted, creating an urgent need to build new camps to house troops currently living under canvas or billeted in private homes, schools, halls and warehouses. Plans had been made at various sites around the country for hutted accommodation based on a design 60ft by 20ft in size built around a light steel frame mounted on a concrete base and intended initially to house fifteen men, although in practice the installation of bunk beds meant the number could be two or three times that.[1] By the summer of 1915, 850,000 men were accommodated in these types of huts as vast sites evolved around existing garrisons and training depots. Lord Lichfield had already given permission for troops to use part of his property on Cannock Chase and building began immediately on what was to become a sprawling complex spread 'like a vast eczema of hutments on the skin of Rugeley Plain'[2] that by 1917 encompassed two huge camps – Rugeley and Brocton – between them capable of housing 40,000 men. Commenting on the camp in 1915, one local paper noted how the landscape of Cannock Chase had changed:

> Its natural beauty did not appeal to many in days gone by, but now that it is spoiled, crowds flock up there to gaze on a few dozen empty, ugly finished and unfinished wooden buildings of a depressing uniformity in design, and arranged in irritating and parallel straight lines. It is difficult to believe that the sight of a huge wooden encampment set in the middle of the best part of Cannock Chase, and uglier than the mushroom towns that grow up almost in a day in the localities in which gold and diamonds are suddenly discovered, can give anyone pleasure.[3]

It was to Brocton Camp that Arnold, John, Frederick, Charles and the two Harolds were told to report on 5 November 1917, going first to the regimental depot at

Pontefract to be kitted out with at least a semblance of uniform consisting of two tunics, two pairs of trousers, one overcoat, cap, one pair of boots, three pairs of socks, two pairs of pants, three shirts, knife, fork and spoon along with mess tins and a razor, toothbrush and brushes for boots and buttons.[4] Most of the kit would be second-hand and of varying quality but these were the best items of clothing some new recruits had ever owned. The recruits would then be ordered to change into uniform. Civilian clothes would be parcelled up to be posted home and it was said that postmen could identify the recruit's location based on the type of paper provided. Belts were an integral part of the uniform, but often were not issued at this stage. Not wearing a belt would mean that a recruit would be improperly dressed and therefore not allowed to leave camp and the issue of the belt became a reward for completing the first steps through training, giving the recruits an incentive to identify themselves as 'real' soldiers. Further forms would be completed along with another medical exam before the recruits paraded for the next stage of the journey, marching to the local station and travelling by train via Sheffield to Brindley Heath, where they would disembark and march up the hill to the windswept camp that would be their home for the next four months.

For many members of the new intake this was all familiar stuff. Although most of their service records were later destroyed during the Second World War,

A group of new arrivals show off their vaccinations. Painful but potentially life-saving injections were always among the first experiences of army life.

enough survive to show that at least one in ten of the recruits arriving at Brocton in November 1917 had, during 1915, lied about their ages to enlist as volunteers and had previously served in the army for periods ranging from a matter of days to almost sixteen months in the experience of Herbert Dennison, a butcher's son from Wharfedale, who had managed to remain undetected for so long in the ranks of the 6th West Riding Regiment before his true age was discovered and he was discharged 'having made a misstatement as to age'. A 1915 British training manual had observed that 'the human being does not thrive well in solitude, and to many men there is no greater desert than a barrack-room or camp'.[5] Writing about his own experience of answering his call up papers, one man recalled:

> At the station I met, by previous arrangement, a young fellow of about my own age … I did not know him well, for I had only made his acquaintance a few days previously, on hearing that he was due to report for service on the same day as myself, but I think that we were both glad that we did not have to set out on the 'Great Adventure' alone.[6]

For the less adventurous, for whom this was all new, there was comfort in the presence of other recruits from the same towns. With very few exceptions, a recruit arriving in Brocton was accompanied by at least one other man from his home town and often by friends and close neighbours who had enlisted together.

This was no coincidence. The British Army's regimental system was founded on a strong sense of feeling part of a group. That, after all, had been the logic behind the Pals' Battalions. The faster a recruit came to identify with the other members of his unit, the greater the unit's cohesion. It was a system intended to create mates. 'What a world of meaning there is in the words "me and my mate",' wrote Brigadier-General Haking in 1915:

> so often heard in civil life but with hardly a counterpart in the Army. A soldier in the Army has many acquaintances, a few friends, but rarely has he got a 'mate'. It appears that if such a combination could be introduced the military value of every two men would be greatly increased.[7]

Recognising the importance of 'mateship', the newly streamlined enlistment and training system brought with it an inbuilt 'buddy' system, with the recruits arriving at Brocton in early November remarkably similar in age, origin and background. Arnold, John, Frederick, Charles and the two Harolds all shared the same birth-date of 28 September and no fewer than seven other young men shared the 29th. Over half the intake had been born in the last week of September or first week of October 1899 and almost all came from the same six towns of the West Riding, so that often their birth records appeared on the same pages of the local register.

Civilian clothes were bundled up and sent home. Each man was issued with everything he needed, from toothbrush (albeit second-hand) to a brand new rifle. The next few weeks would be about learning to look after it all.

RIFLE

KNAPSACK

BAYONET

HAVERSACK

WATER-
-BOTTLE

ENTRENCHING
TOOLS

ENTRENCHING
TOOL HANDLE

Some vaguely knew each other from growing up in the same part of town or had mutual acquaintances whilst others, like George Spencer and Irvin Darlington, were near neighbours – in their case living respectively at 629 and 635 New Hey Road in Huddersfield. Harold Wiseman enlisted with three other local lads – Ben Crawshaw, John Meeking and Ernest Carter – all of whom lived within a few hundred yards of each other. Ernest was an only child, but all three of the others had elder brothers who had served together in the local Territorial unit of the West Riding Regiment before the war. Harry Meeking had emigrated to Canada and was killed serving with the Canadian Army, but Clayton Crawshaw and Jimmy Wiseman had been mobilised together in August 1914 and both went to France in 1915. Even those from the smaller villages appear to have arrived with at least one other local lad. With very few exceptions they were the sons of working-class families and many showed the signs of poverty – records show several with a height of just 5ft 2in and weight around 8 stones (50kg).

With so much in common, the process of adapting to their new comrades was made easier, but for middle-class recruits the introduction to army life could be harsh. In the class and status-conscious Edwardian period, contact with those of a different social order was limited. For those raised in the more genteel households the first – and perhaps greatest – culture shock of joining up was the company one was expected to keep. The priggish protagonist of **R.H.** Kiernan's *Little Brother Goes Soldiering* describes his arrival at a similar camp at Catterick:

> There were some horrible strange fellows in the Training Reserve Battalion. There was a slaughterer's boy from the Leeds Market. He had a smooth, shiny pink and white face, with hardly a chin at all, as though his face had been pressed up under his nether lip; he was very tall and sagged in the middle, and his neck was scraggy and curved forward. He described in the train from York to Catterick how he had contracted a filthy disease from a woman when he was fifteen, and had to wear cotton wool on his shirt. There was a Sheffield boy with a yellow face like an old man, and grey hair, who shouted filth at the top of his voice all the time. There were some pit-boys from Brierly Hill, but I could not understand what they said. They spoke in a quiet sing-song voice. Another boy had the Leeds whine in his voice, and looked sideways at anyone he spoke to. One side of his face was vivid red and purple with a skin disease, and the other side was dirty grey …
> I felt sorry at first that I'd joined before my time, as a private. But I'll stick it, as my brothers did, till I get a commission.[8]

Perhaps not surprisingly, after complaining that he felt as if he 'had been landed in a cage of apes', Kiernan next complains of being bullied by the others throughout his training – seemingly on the grounds that they did not share his views on his innate moral and intellectual superiority. His disapproval of those he was to serve with was not unusual for those meeting the working class for the first time on an equal foot-ing. Frederick Hodges describes being joined on his journey to camp by nine men under the command of a sergeant: 'three of them, Harvey, House and Wenderleish (a Jew), were refined, well educated boys; three were of the rough tough type … and three were harder to classify on sight.'[9] Elsewhere, another recruit wrote to his mother that 'I came up in company with 20 other weird blighters whose native haunts seem to be Stratford and Bow! … poor me, amongst twenty Eastenders!'[10] Worse was to come. 'Some of our food,' wrote F.A.J. Taylor:

> to me and some others, was disgusting and uneatable … Table manners were non-existent and one mid-day an elderly general came along to the dining room on a tour of benevolent inspection. He stopped at our table and with a look of utter astonishment on his face, gazed at the youth on my left, who was performing the incredible feat only used by the working classes, of eating peas with a knife.[11]

Frederick Hodges described meals at his camp:

> We took our places at rough wooden trestle tables … On each table were four large white basins and a basket with sixteen pieces of bread. Table manners were non-existent; each soldier immediately grabbed a piece of bread and an orderly filled the large basins with hot tea from a bucket. Each basin was for the use of four; two to each side of the table, and when they were empty we shouted the orderly to fill them again. Lifting the heavy basins filled with a couple of pints of hot tea was quite a balancing act as well as a feat of strength.[12]

Breakfast, according to Kiernan, was usually 'an inch or two of bacon swimming in dirty grease, and a big mug of weak tea' whilst dinner, at lunchtime, was 'black meat, again swimming in grease, and the pale yellow water of custard and apple skins'.[13] Frederick Voigt, a conscript 'combed out' in one of the periodic police and army sweeps, wrote of mealtimes:

> We filed slowly in and passed by a trestle on which three foot-baths were standing. We held out our plates while a soldier in a grimy uniform ladled cabbage, meat and a greasy liquid on to them. We sat down on benches in front of tables that were littered with potato-peel, bits of fat, and other refuse. We were packed so closely together that we could hardly move our elbows. The rowdy conversation, the foul language, and the smacking of lips and the loud noise of guzzling added to the horror of the meal.

> I was so repelled that I felt sick and could not eat. I sat back on the bench and waited. I observed that the man sitting opposite was watching me intently.

Suddenly he asked: 'Don't yer want it, mate?' I said 'No,' whereupon he exclaimed eagerly, 'Giss it.' A bestial, gloating look came into his face as he seized my plate and splashed the contents on to his own, so that the gravy overflowed and ran along the table in a thin stream. He took the piece of meat between his thumb and his fork and, tearing off big shreds with his teeth, gobbled them greedily down.

We washed our plates outside the mess-room in a metal bath that held two or three inches of warm water. Others had used it before us, and it was thick with grease and little fragments of cabbage and fat were floating about in it. From a nail in the wall a torn shred of a disused woollen pant was hanging. It was black and glistening, for it had already been used times without number. Some of the men wiped their plates on it, but others preferred to rub them with earth and then clean them with a bunch of fresh grass from a patch of lawn near by.[14]

Tea, served at the end of the day, was usually bread and margarine or jam with the ubiquitous tea. The problem was twofold; at a time when strict rationing was in force, civilian contractors sought to profit by providing the army with the cheapest and poorest quality supplies – sometimes food that was virtually rotten. The second problem was one created by the army itself, as Captain Leslie Vickers, an American volunteer serving with the Seaforth Highlanders in 1917, noted:

It has been my experience that the laziest and dirtiest men volunteer for the task of cook. The reason is that they are able to get the choicest portions for themselves, be free from the bore of attending drills and parades, and get a little higher pay, besides what they can get from the soldiers on the side for little favours. In an army such as was formed in England at the beginning of the war it was impossible to get enough trained cooks for the work, and all sorts of men were run in for the job. Many of them were thoroughly lazy and incompetent. There was, of course, a rooted objection to calling in the aid of women – though few of us ever think of employing men to do our cooking in private life – and when we suggested it for the purpose of improving the grade of our food in the Officers' Mess, we were met with the reply that it had never been done. That was the reason for keeping out a good many reforms in Dear Old England.[15]

But while middle-class recruits like Taylor, Hodges, Voigt and Kiernan found themselves revolted by both the food served up and by their fellow diners, the recruits were given, as Kiernan admitted, 'double rations, being "boy soldiers", and the men admitted they were better off than in "civil life"'.[16] This was undoubtedly true at a time when the food shortages at home had become so acute that it was reported to be having a serious impact on the morale of men at the front and suggestions were made by the soldiers themselves that rations for the BEF should be cut to feed families at home.[17] Harold Wiseman's home town of Keighley had been feted by the national press for its thriftiness, with the tale of a shop window display showing the daily ration for one man. The story had circulated of a visitor staring for a while at the six small sausages, half a loaf of bread and small saucer of sugar: 'By gum, we eat as much as that at Barnsley while we're waiting for dinner. If that's what they're doing at Keighley I'm off home by the next train!' For many, though, it was no joke. The *Times* observed that 'by effective organisation the average consumption of the whole population has been brought down well below the standard'.[18] That standard had not been high to begin with. Despite the shortages at home, thousands of tons of food were being wasted in France because men preferred the treats sent in food parcels from their own hungry families.

Even F.A.J. Taylor, despite his claim to have been constantly hungry, admits that during training he 'had filled out, put on weight and looked disgustingly fit and well'.[19] Brocton Camp also provided ample opportunities for the recruits to use their pay to buy extra meals and treats in the evenings. A large YMCA hut (one of three eventually built on the site) containing a concert room, billiards room and snack bar did brisk trade, as did a soldier's club provided by Lord Lichfield and various tea rooms and canteens in the surrounding neighbourhood, one of which was reported to have room for 400 men at a time. A measure of the popularity of such places

Even in the depths of winter, washing facilities were often very basic.

comes in the reported sale of 12,000 cakes per day in the Catterick YMCA hut at its peak.[20] On Sundays, off-duty recruits found many local churches and societies offering free tea, coffee and cakes to passing soldiers and took full advantage.

On arrival at Brocton, the recruits had eaten and were then allocated to their hut, one of thirty-three identical buildings making up each set of lines. Inside, beds consisted of a straw *palliasse* covered by three blankets spread over three bed boards across wooden trestles, with sometimes as little as 1ft between the beds. A slow combustion coal-fired stove stood in the centre of the room with a metal coal scuttle alongside it. A 6ft table with two wooden benches completed the furniture and the whole hut was lit by just three 25w electric bulbs. In each hut was an 'old sweat' usually recuperating from wounds or sickness assigned to act as mentor to the recruits, helping them to settle in and showing them the tricks of the trade – the first trick often being to charge for every piece of assistance. These men passed on tips to the youngsters – how to wear their uniforms correctly, how to pass inspections, how to soften the leather of their boots by urinating into them at night, to rub thick layers of soap on to their feet before long route marches and the dozens of other tricks picked up and passed on by generations of old soldiers.

Nearby, an open-sided ablutions hut contained a central bench with circular zinc bowls set into it, each one often having to serve up to twelve men. Perhaps for the

Army dining provided a massive culture shock to the more genteel recruits.

first time in their lives, men were required to wash daily and standing orders in some camps stated that they should have a bath at least once a week (although the rule was not universal and in other camps men had to wait until given permission to bathe). Facilities for this were provided in the then novel form of a shallow trough 18in deep with a shower fitting placed over it and water of varying temperature. In these cramped conditions with limited washing facilities disease was rife and spread rapidly. Young men brought up in slum conditions had never developed the habit of keeping their environment clean. It was necessary to carry out frequent cleanups of food scraps and other rubbish from around the huts to prevent infestations of rats around the living quarters, especially since outbreaks of spotted fever (or spinal meningitis), measles and other contagious diseases meant meals would have to be taken in the huts to prevent their spread. It was common for entire huts to be placed in quarantine for a fortnight at a time and for sections of camps to be placed out of bounds because of diseases brought in by new intakes. In one case, spotted fever caused an entire camp to be quarantined for three months, during which eighty recruits died and which was followed almost immediately by an outbreak of scarlet fever.[21] With diseases such as these potentially fatal, a further problem came from families anxious to visit, so when flu broke out at Catterick Camp, the YMCA spent £1,700 building accommodation for visiting relatives[22] and similar facilities were erected around Brocton.

Within a few days, John Carr had become 5/93631 Private Carr, J., and Harold Wiseman was now 5/93672 Private Wiseman, H. Everything was to be done alphabetically and so men got to know their comrades by their place in the line as they queued for a haircut, pay and the first of many vaccinations. At first, inoculation had not been compulsory for the New Army volunteers since the 1907 Vaccination Act had allowed for conscientious objection to the practice, but the British experience in South Africa had shown that preventable diseases had killed more men than the Boers had and arguments both for and against vaccinations were put forward. In 1876 Harold's home town of Keighley had become the centre of a political storm over the issue of compulsory vaccination against smallpox when seven of its Board of Guardians were imprisoned for refusing to implement the policy of free inoculations for all infants under three months despite a reported 42,200 deaths between 1870 and 1872 alone.[23] Opponents came from a wide variety of backgrounds and included such notables as George Bernard Shaw, who regarded it as 'a particularly filthy piece of witchcraft', and the doctor and medical writer Charles Creighton, who rejected outright the germ theory of disease. When, in 1914, the army had tried to introduce inoculations for new recruits:

Most men gladly accepted this medical boon and subjected themselves to this simple and painless operation. But there were others who objected, sometimes through fear of the pain, and sometimes through what they termed 'conscientious objections'. Anti-Inoculation Societies got busy and spread their wretched literature throughout the camps and made men thoroughly afraid, both of the operation and of its results.[24]

To counter this, the War Office began an information campaign of papers, pamphlets and posters explaining the need for inoculations and by 1917 the benefits were obvious. As a result, inoculations for the new arrivals, with the exception of diehard conscientious objectors, began within the first few days at camp. As one recruit later explained:

> our arms were jabbed with hypodermic needles to give us an injection of anti-tetanus, and anti-typhoid vaccine. Here and there, a faint hearted one would suddenly keel over and be dragged to one side by an orderly to recover but not escape the ordeal. One or two enterprising youngsters, thinking to delay any unpleasant reaction, sucked at each other's jabbed arms, but learned later that this was all to no avail. I considered it a waste of time and we all suffered in varying degrees some painful but temporary after-effects.[25]

Not noted for its sympathy, the army nevertheless allowed the men up to forty-eight hours to recover before training could really start.

Throughout history, the process of training a soldier has remained fundamentally the same. The aim is to create a soldier who is willing and able to offer the enemy the maximum opportunity to die for his country and this requires not only the teaching of specific skills to use weapons and tactics, but also what military theorists term the 'moral landscape' of war – the attitudes and beliefs that will take a man forward to engage with the enemy. According to Napoleon, 'in war the moral is to the material as three is to one'[26] and current British Army doctrine places great emphasis on the development of the motivation of individual soldiers, defining it as 'the enthusiasm to fight' that comes as 'a product of training, confidence in equipment, effective leadership and management, firm and fair discipline, self and mutual-respect ... and a clear understanding of what is going on and what is required'. While at the tactical level most soldiers will fight for the soldier beside them, they also need a clear view of the cause, and knowledge that this perspective is shared by those at home. This motivation, the doctrine continues, stems from 'ethical foundations':

> [S]ome of the most barbarous armies in history have had tremendous morale and will to fight and have been successful. This may suggest that victory is what counts, regardless of the methods used to achieve it. But the British armed forces are, in their modern origins, rooted in the spirit of democracy. This has created a clear necessity to act within the bounds of popular understanding of what is thought to be right.

This belief in the cause is supported by 'moral cohesion' – derived from an organisational culture which, the doctrine says, 'gives a group or organisation a distinctive character and identity – its ethos. The British Army has certain enduring characteristics which are part of this, embodied in its regimental system.'[27] Founded on the principles of cognitive-behaviourism, this simply means that the way one thinks about a situation will affect the course of action one adopts. If a soldier believes he is doing the right thing for the right reason with the support of his comrades, he will attack. If these elements are missing, he will not. Although the product of extensive research into military effectiveness in the late twentieth century, the same principles were already well established by the time the boys arrived at Brocton Camp. In 1915, Brigadier-General R.C.B. Haking, commanding the 5th Infantry Brigade, had published *Company Training*, which opens with the clear statement that:

> In modern war we are dependent for success upon the individual action of the infantry soldier. This action is greatly influenced by his state of mind at the moment, and by the power that can be exercised over his mind by his comrades and those who are leading him.[28]

The basic training the boys were about to undergo was intended, first and foremost, to provide them with the skills, attitudes and beliefs they would need not only to survive as infantry soldiers but to be aggressive enough to eventually break the trench stalemate and take the war to the Germans. John Hockey, studying the training of the British Army in the 1980s, described its training course as comprising two distinct phases: civilian role dispossession followed by what he terms 'the phase of adaptation and adjustment'.[29] The transformation from civilian to soldier requires that the recruit must first shed his civilian identity and stop thinking of himself as an individual, because the battlefield is no place for a committee. For the rapidly expanding volunteer citizen army of the early war, the letting go of their civilian identity had been a particular problem. Territorial Force and New Army 'Pals' battalions resolutely remained civilians in uniform, with an often strong trade union mentality. Whilst in training in the UK, a company of the 2/4 KOYLI (to which Pickering, Whitwam and Wiseman would eventually be sent) performed badly during a drill parade and provoked a torrent of abuse from Captain Humphrey Smith, a veteran of the South African campaign. A normal enough experience in the military, but in this case the response was to lodge a formal complaint that 'we, the freemen and volunteers of Ossett are not, and object to being designated as, blasted lop-eared baboons'. As Malcolm Johnson, historian of the KOYLI, noted, 'Captain Smith's previous experience in colonial Africa was going to be of little use when dealing with these independent minded Yorkshiremen',[30] but it was incidents such as this that had created a distrust of the discipline and effectiveness of such units among senior staff and, arguably, had contributed to the heavy losses suffered on the Somme. The New Army units, some suggested, could not be trusted to attack on their own initiative and needed to be closely watched – by ordering them to move at the same pace the unit could be kept together but presented an easier target for the enemy.

'The change from civilian to soldier is produced in one way only,' argued Leslie Vickers:

> The Learning of Obedience. This is the first and last lesson. The civilian is only obedient in certain ways and to a limited extent. The soldier is obedient in every way and to any extent, even to death … It is the heart of the system. Obedience is given to some one by every rank in the army, from the highest general to the humblest private.[31]

As soon as they arrived at Brocton, the boys had entered stage one. Civilian clothing had been replaced by baggy, often ill-fitting military uniforms. All had received the regulation haircut and their individual outward appearance had blended into

Orderly Officer. "WHAT WAS THE EXCITEMENT IN NO. 1 DINING-HUT TO-DAY, SERGEANT?"

Orderly Sergeant. "LANCE-CORPORAL SMITH FOUND A PIECE OF KIDNEY IN THE STEAK-AN'-KIDNEY PUDD'N, SIR."

Food quality was a major issue. Meat was often either rotten or had been sold on by cookhouse staff.

a khaki crowd. The boys had not been issued with belts and so could not leave the camp in whatever free time was available to them, creating what sociologist Erving Goffman termed a 'total institution' in which every waking moment was spent in the army. The recruit was no longer in control of how he looked, where he went or what he did. His day began at 5.45 a.m. with Reveille and ended at 9.30 p.m. with Lights Out and each hour in between was spent on drill, physical training, route marches and learning to keep his uniform and equipment clean. F.E. Noakes, a Guards recruit in 1917, later recalled that whilst formal training finished at around 4 or 5 p.m., his evenings were spent preparing for the next day's parades:

> Every bit of metal on uniform or equipment had to be polished, bayonets burnished, scabbards and chin straps heel-balled, boots blacked or dubbined, and webbing blancoed. There were nearly seventy pieces of brass alone – buttons, buckles, cap-badge, numerals, studs etc – which had to shine like the sun every day on pain of punishment drill; for not only the articles in actual use were included, but also the metal 'adornments' of spare uniform and greatcoat, and even the duplicate pair of boots must be kept polished, even the insteps of the soles! … We were also expected to keep a knife-like crease in our slacks, which we did by soaping the insides of the folds and sleeping on them.[32]

At first glance, and certainly to the recruits exposed to it, this 'bull' had nothing to do with killing Germans and seemed to many to be a waste of time, but it served two important functions: firstly, it kept the recruits busy and focused on the fact that they were under the complete control of the camp staff and subject to strict discipline, a constant reminder that they were no longer civilians; secondly, it instilled a habit of maintaining the equipment they would need when they reached the front.

Leslie Vickers wrote:

> Moderation is the word. It is possible to be too enthusiastic and do the men more harm than good with hasty training. Exercises should be graduated. It must be remembered that many of the men who will constitute civilian armies are not used to out-of-door life and their training must be gentle. It is not fair for an officer to expect his men to be able to march twelve or twenty miles on a hike while he rides comfortably with them on a horse! It is a good thing for him to share the fatigue of his men that he may be the better able to direct their training. I have found that a good many of these hikes were planned by the higher officers who never walked and never understood when men began to fall out from fatigue.[33]

Even if the army were carrying out their training in moderation, the first few weeks were marked by long route marches and exhausting drill instruction which built stamina but left feet blistered and sore. Many, of course, had some experience of drill from school days or, like Arnold Ambler, from their short periods of enlistment earlier in the war, but this was a new level of drill demanding instant obedience and bringing down a terrible wrath on those who faltered. R.H. Kiernan, describing drill instruction at Catterick, found that some of the instructors were:

> … really funny, and they are not personal or abusive to any particular recruit. They are all old Regulars. 'Come orn, come orn, leftright-leftright – Yer broke yer mother's heart but you won't break mine – Gor blimey-soldiers – I've passed better – tike yer eyes orf the grahnd, yer won't find no money there – I was out before reveille – habout turn'. They run it off mechanically – they've been doing it for years.[34]

Writing in 1986, Hockey noted that whilst drill had been essential for the deployment of troops on the Napoleonic battlefield, by the twentieth century it had 'no place in an operational context, and its sole value for the organisation lies in its socialising potential, and it remains a central means by which recruits are conditioned to respond obediently to commands'.[35] A measure of the importance in this role can perhaps be taken from Army Order 324, published in 1914, which laid down the syllabus for basic training. On his first day, the recruit could expect to undergo four hours of drill instruction and one of physical training, interspersed with introductory training with the rifle. By week two, no less than twenty-eight of the allotted forty-eight hours of instruction per week were devoted to drill – ten hours without rifles, eighteen with. Even as late as the tenth week of training, route marching, drill and physical training accounted for thirty of the forty-eight hours. The drudgery of constant drill did, however, come with rewards. Once a certain level of competence was achieved, belts could be issued and those who had 'passed off the square' were allowed the leave camp in their free time – creating an incentive to comply and a small rite of passage marking the recruit's transition from civilian to someone accepted as a soldier. For Hockey, this also marks the move to the 'adaptation and adjustment' phase. Life became easier as the recruits gained the basic skills needed to gain at least the outward appearance of soldiers. Drill became instinctive and, with the help of 'old sweats' acting as mentors in each hut, the boys began to learn the shortcuts that meant they could maintain their equipment with less effort and to scrounge or otherwise obtain additional items where necessary. They also began to adapt to an identity not just as a soldier, but as a KOYLI soldier. This was a crucial element in developing the soldier's motivation to fight and an area much neglected in the history of the Great War. A great deal has been written about the sudden transfer of men from one regiment to another before reaching an operational unit in France, often seemingly on a whim. Widely quoted, Taylor describes how:

Route marches – usually planned by officers on horseback – formed a major part of every recruit's training in preparation for the long hours they would spend marching across France.

THE RECRUIT WHO TOOK TO IT KINDLY

Bayonet training. An acquired taste.

... we were regrouped and parted with our insignia identifying us with the 19th City of London Regiment or St Pancras Rifles for ever. Our cap badges, shoulder names, fancy buttons we all discarded to be replaced by insignia linking us now to the 2nd Battalion Worcestershire Regiment. As I had never developed any particular loyalty for the London Regiment, into which I had been unceremoniously thrust a few months previously, and no one had taken time or trouble to tell us anything about the traditions or battle honours of the regiment it was not difficult to transfer to a new regiment equally unknown.[36]

Certainly many found themselves in a similar situation when the demands for reinforcements at the front were at their peak, but Taylor's comments about his lack of loyalty to his regiment need to be read with a note of caution. From the outset, his account makes it clear that he enlisted in order to join the Flying Corps specifically to avoid infantry service and it was only due to a physical problem that he had been forced into that role. As a very reluctant recruit, it is perhaps not surprising that he chose not to identify with the regiment. The surviving records for men like John Carr show that he enlisted into the KOYLI training battalion, then moved into the KOYLI graduated battalion before being sent to an infantry base depot in France that supplied the KOYLI with reinforcements, and finally he was posted to a KOYLI battalion in the field. Given that path, it seems unlikely that he did not see himself as a KOYLI soldier. This in itself was another element of the hidden agenda of basic training. By identifying himself as a KOYLI, the recruit would begin to create for himself a part in the culture or *esprit de corps* of the regiment. As Haking put it:

it is customary to select an anniversary of one of the greatest battles in which the regiment has taken part and to celebrate the victory in the time honoured manner of holding regimental sports &C ... What we desire to teach is a spirit of emulation; if our forefathers could do these things, it is quite certain that we ought to be able to do the same.[37]

Or, as the current doctrine puts it, quoting Sir Edward Bruce Hamley:

A moth eaten rag on a worm-eaten pole,
It does not look likely to stir a man's soul,
'Tis the deeds that were done 'neath the moth-eaten rag,
When the pole was a staff and the rag was a flag.[38]

Having just missed the August celebrations of Minden Day, the boys instead learned from their instructors and mentors about the exploits of the regiment in the war so far. It quickly became apparent that there were two types of instructor at the camp.

A typical 1917 recruit. He has acquired a swagger stick and belt and so has completed his first few weeks of training.

Some were men who had secured a safe and comfortable job at home and who believed that the way to maintain their position was to give every appearance of efficiency by doing things by the book. Writing about the staff at one training camp to which he was temporarily posted, Captain Charles Carrington recalled that the 'dominant note in conversation at a reserve battalion was determination to stay there. You could hear good men almost boasting that they were still category B and admitting concern that the next medical board might pass them as fit.'[39] Others, though, were men who had served overseas and who would provide the role models for what real soldiers were like. Typical of the latter type was Lieutenant Gilbert Hall, another new arrival at Brocton that November after being commissioned into the regiment a few weeks earlier. Hall had originally joined the 13th (Service) Battalion (1st Barnsley Pals) of the York and Lancaster Regiment in September 1914 (when the regiment had shared its depot at Pontefract with the KOYLI) and had served throughout the Somme battles, returning to Pontefract a dirty and mud-covered corporal straight from the front lines on 3 July 1917, en route for officer training. It was during this training that Hall had also learned about the difference between the types of instructors. After a lecture on the use of hand grenades as part of his bombing course, Hall and the other cadets had been taken to the ranges. Having used them in anger many times, Hall had paid little attention to the 'correct' way to do it and had pulled the pin, allowed the spoon to fly off and counted to two before throwing it down the range. With surprise, he noticed his instructor had jumped out of the practice bay and into a nearby safety trench in panic. Hall had to explain that there had been occasions when a bomb thrown too early had simply been picked up and thrown back – a fact his instructors were unaware of.[40] Now posted as an instructor to the Young Soldiers Battalion, Hall would be directly involved in the training of the new boys and set about ensuring that they learned not just what was in the book, but what had been learned by hard and sometimes bitter experience. As a former private, Hall fell out of favour with the sergeant major of the battalion at Brocton after intervening to help a young soldier nearing exhaustion and in tears as he struggled up the hill to camp under the weight of almost 70lb of equipment. The sergeant major was about to send the boy back down the hill when Hall moved in and ordered the punishment stopped. The next day Hall was given a dressing down by the colonel for undermining the sergeant major's authority and knew it was time to get back to France. In April 1918, he took charge of a new draft as they left for France and was himself posted to the 2/4th battalion.

As the recruits learned about becoming 'real' soldiers, they learned to use their essential tools – the rifle and bayonet. Starting slowly with short lessons on naming the parts and how to clean and care for it, the boys were taught the theory and practice of rifle shooting. Hours were spent learning to strip the weapon, how to pour boiling water down the barrel after firing, how to measure out the right amount of cloth and how to oil it so that it would not get stuck in the barrel as they pulled it through with long cords to oil the inside of the weapon. They were taught to recognise the difference between the sound of the bullet they had fired and one fired at them, how to pick out targets at a distance and how to identify that target to others. They learned to judge range by using the rifle's foresight to measure the appearance of the head and shoulders of men at various distances and how to allow for wind speed and direction. They spent hours on physical exercises designed to build strength and stamina-carrying the rifle and holding it at arm's length. Only after all these things had been learned did they progress to firing their rifle for the first time on a miniature range. It had been the British infantry's skill with the Lee-Enfield rifle that had saved the BEF in the retreat from Mons when fast, accurate rifle fire had held back the German Army, and skill at arms was still considered essential. After a three-week intensive course on the ranges, men undertook a classification test that could mean an extra 3*d* per day 'Proficiency Pay' if they could prove themselves as marksmen.

They also needed to learn what their weapon was capable of and, in turn, how to protect themselves from the enemy's fire. They were taught that at short-range a rifle bullet would penetrate about 40in of earth so that nothing less than 36in could be considered as giving any kind of protection from ordinary bullets.

Bayonet training.

Where sand could be found around 26in would be enough, but it would take almost 5ft of ordinary turf to provide any real cover. Bricks, they were told, were effective if they could be placed in such a way that they formed a wall at least 9in thick. Thirty inches of hardwood or forty-five of softwood could be considered fairly safe. Out on the ranges, the lessons were rammed home by firing at dummy positions built of various materials to show how effective – or not – different types of cover could be.

Alongside musketry training ran courses on the use of the bayonet, a weapon that had become the focus of the British Army's attention to an almost obsessive degree. 'The spirit of the bayonet,' states the manual of 1918, 'must be inculcated into all ranks so that they go forward with that aggressive determination and confidence of superiority born of continual practice without which a bayonet assault will not be effective.'[41] Chillingly blunt, it describes the range of the bayonet as 5ft 'measured from the opponent's eyes' but states that 'killing is at close quarters, at a range of two feet or less'. Men needed to be trained, it said, to use the bayonet 'with enthusiasm'. According to Vickers, 'the object of all troops must be to get into touch with the enemy and drive him out with the bayonet':[42]

[A]ll infantry work leads up to the use of the bayonet, and so, if a man is to be ready for this final test, his bayonet must be in good shape. Of course there is not much to get out of order, but there are a few movable parts that must be kept oiled, and the blade itself which must be kept clean. It is a slight courtesy that you can pay your enemy, that you give him clean, instead of rusty, steel.[43]

The recruit bayonet course consisted of five lessons and a final assault practice with the syllabus divided so as to allow daily practice of at least half an hour every day for five days per week. Lesson one covered the correct stance for 'on guard' – the point directed at the base of the opponent's throat and the rifle 'held easily and naturally with both hands'. Standing in lines, and taking turns to be the attacker, recruits were taught to aim for the throat and eyes and that:

other vulnerable and usually exposed parts are the face, chest, lower abdomen and thighs and the region of the kidneys when the back is turned. Four to six inches' penetration is sufficient to incapacitate and allow for a quick withdrawal, whereas if the bayonet is driven home too far it is often impossible to withdraw it. In such cases a round should be fired to break up the obstruction.[44]

Lesson two moved on to learning to thrust and parry, with bayonets fixed but covered by scabbards as lines of recruits hacked away at each other. Lesson three introduced the 'short point' stab and four the 'jab' or 'upward point' into the throat or chin, and finally lesson five covered the various means of using the rifle butt to disable opponents. Robert Graves recalled his time as an instructor in France:

In bayonet practice, the men had to make horrible grimaces and utter blood-curdling yells as they charged. The instructors' faces were set in a permanent ghastly grin. 'Hurt him now!' 'In the belly! Tear his guts out!' they would scream, as the men charged the dummies. 'Now that upper swing at his privates with the butt. Ruin his chances for life! No more little Fritzes! … Naaoh! Anyone would think that you loved the bloody swine, patting and stroking 'em like that! *Bite him, I say! Stick your teeth in him and worry him! Eat his heart out!*'[45]

Like so many other aspects of their training, though, the recruits knew that much of the knowledge being passed to them was entirely theoretical. When Lieutenant C.P. Blacker asked another officer how many of the instructors had actually bayoneted anyone he was told, 'very few. But we don't insist on their telling the strict truth when asked that question.'[46] Key to the bayonet was aggression and key to aggression was its link to masculinity. Being a 'real' soldier meant being a 'real' man, evidenced by R.H. Kiernan's recollections of the abuse poured on recruits by one of his instructors:

Yo, yo' bastard. Yo' in the end file. Christ. What was your father, a cab horse? Tried for a stable I'll bet. Your mother – Gawd, wouldn't she be glad to see you ne-ouw? To see what she dropped in the straw. She'd cry 'er eyes out and wish she'd let a soldier with go 'er – a real man. No, you never came from a woman – if you did, what a woman. You came from a de-ouse o' castor oil, you did.[47]

The bayonet course culminated in the final assault, a mock attack on an enemy trench. It began from a trench around 6 or 7ft deep and involved a charge across an open area intended to bring the recruits to the lip of the enemy trench system 'in a comparatively exhausted condition' in order to test the accuracy and power of the stabs made to discs attached to straw dummies set at various points around the trench. Competitions were set for times to clear the enemy, number of discs gathered on each bayonet and, according to the manual, for 'style' when carrying out the assault. 'This consisted,' recalled a graduate of the course:

of some of the chaps holding the trench and the remainder charging like hell. The men in the trench used to duck when the attackers arrived because they used to jump over the trench and stick a dummy that was supposed to be a German soldier. We found it was different when we got into action in France.[48]

Gradually, step by step, the raw recruits turned into soldiers. Christmas came and went. Those who were lucky or could afford to bribe the orderly room clerks went home on leave, but most stayed in camp to enjoy a treat of chicken for Christmas lunch. As winter drew in some fell victim to colds and chest infections and others whose physical ill health had not been picked up by the medical examiners were finally discharged. On 5 February, John Gledhill, an 18-year-old from Huddersfield who had arrived with the others, was discharged on the grounds of 'hereditary imbecility' which the examiners felt 'requires institutional life and constant care' despite having passed through three medical examinations and three months of service. He would be followed a month later by Joshua Howson from Ingleton, whose long-standing stomach condition caused him to vomit after meals. The condition had now deteriorated to the point where he was discharged completely as unfit for service.

By March, the boys who had arrived at the beginning of November had turned into soldiers. Proficient with rifle and bayonet and veterans of countless section and platoon attacks on the practice trench systems built around the camp, they had also begun training in their specialist roles. Marksmen like Harold Wiseman were singled out for training on the Lewis gun, learning how to provide covering fire for the platoon with the heavy, 28lb weapon and carrying out timed tests on his ability to load and change the forty-seven round magazines, each weighing 4.5lb, clearing stoppages, firing from the ground and from the hip and the difference between targets suitable for the Lewis gun and those that should be left for the riflemen. Others with strong arms had been selected as bombers, starting by throwing cricket balls and cans filled with stones, then moving on to dummy hand grenades before undergoing a specialist course that would teach them about the use of all Allied and

Barrack accommodation on Cannock Chase. Outbreaks of disease frequently meant putting entire huts into quarantine for weeks at a time.

After basic training, recruits went on to more specialist skills. For Harold Wiseman, this meant becoming a Lewis gunner.

enemy hand grenades, rifle grenades and improvised explosive devices. They would learn to build and dismantle booby traps and to demolish obstacles. Still others would specialise as bayonet men, leading the charge into the enemy trenches, or as scouts pushing ahead of the rest to locate the enemy. By 1918, the infantry platoon had become the main fighting unit on the Western Front. In 1914, companies and battalions had attacked under the direction of officers in slow, deliberate attacks, but now corporals commanded and initiative drove home individual sections to support each other – the scout section to patrol and reconnoitre, the Lewis gun section to provide covering fire, rifle bombers to provide local artillery and the bombers and bayonet men to clear the enemy trenches.

'The skinny, sallow, shambling, frightened victims of our industrial system,' wrote Charles Carrington:

> suffering from the effect of wartime shortages, who were given into our hands, were unrecognisable after six months of good food, fresh air, and physical training. They looked twice the size and, as we weighed and measured them, I am able to say that they put on an average of one inch in height and one stone in weight during their time with us. One boy's mother wrote to me complaining that her Johnny was half-starved in the army and what was I going to do about it. I was able to convince her that Johnny had put on two stone of weight and two inches

of height and had never had so good an appetite before. Beyond statistical measurement was their change in character to ruddy, handsome, clear-eyed young men with square shoulders who stood up straight and feared no one, not even the Sergeant Major.[49]

Charles Wilson, later Churchill's private physician, had served as a medical officer in the Great War and had complained that men broke down in combat, at least in part, because they were, as he put it, 'miserable creatures from the towns'. Having watched his recruits develop, Carrington recalled that the effect was to make him a socialist when he thought of how their home lives had stunted them and a militarist when he saw what soldiering had done for them. 'I shall never think of the lower classes again in the same way after the war,' he concluded.

In the bleak days of 1916, men had arrived in France barely trained but the system had recovered. After four months of basic training, at the end of March 1918 the November intake were fit, strong and trained to undertake a variety of specialist roles using their own initiative. They had become, as one recruit put it, 'much harder, in body and soul'. Now they would be posted to the Graduated Battalion to hone their skills until they reached the age of 19 and became eligible to be sent overseas. It should have meant another six months of camp life, but the Germans had other ideas …

Eat apples

By late 1917, the situation on the Western Front was becoming ever more desperate for the German Army as the British blockade starved the German population and the United States prepared to enter the war. Erich Ludendorff, the Chief Quartermaster General, had accepted that the strength of the Allied naval blockades meant Germany and its allies could no longer win a war of attrition and the tide would soon turn against them. The Bolshevik Revolution had effectively removed the Russian Army from the war and around half a million additional German troops were now available for use in the west. Although unsure whether the Americans intended to field a strong combat-ready army, at a meeting of the Chiefs of Staff of the German armies on the Western Front on 11 November 1917 Ludendorff proposed an offensive aimed at knocking the British out of the war before they could be reinforced. Operation Michael would strike, on ground that was well drained and which would dry quickly after the winter, near St Quentin, where the British and French Army boundary was situated. After breaking through this relatively weak sector, they would strike north to Arras, rolling up the British flank as they did so and pushing it back towards the Channel ports. Operations Georgette and Mars would be directed at ports in Belgium and northern France to divert attention away from Michael and the whole would serve to effectively destroy the British Expeditionary Force as a fighting formation. It would be launched in the spring.

As Ludendorff put forward his plan, Britain was in the process of once again restructuring its wartime organisation with the newly formed Ministry of National Service now taking over responsibility for the recruitment and deployment of both civilian and military labour. In December, a Cabinet Committee on Manpower sat for the first time, chaired by the Prime Minister, Lloyd George, and comprising Lord Curzon, Mr George Nicoll Barnes of the Labour Party, Sir Edward Carson and General Smuts – but with the notable absence of any representative of the British Army. The task of the committee was to determine manpower priorities for the coming year and it was decided that the army should be given lowest priority after the navy and air forces, agriculture, tree-felling and the building of cold storage facilities in the UK. On the basis of its experience and expectations for the coming year, the army had requested 615,000 men, having lost some 900,000 in the 1917 offensives. It was given just 100,000 category A men and another 100,000 of lower medical grades, as 50,000 more category A men were diverted instead to the navy. 'The British Army,' said Lloyd George, 'had, of course been fighting hard on the offensive all through 1917; but as it was to stand on the defensive for the early part of 1918, the committee considered that the military estimate was likely to prove unduly large.'[1] Instead of bringing the army up to strength, the decision was made to 're-tailor' the existing force to fit that conclusion. As both France and Germany had by this stage reduced the size of their divisions, the BEF would be asked to do the same – overlooking the fact that the French and Germans had reduced the size of their divisions to create new formations while Britain would simply be trying to maintain the ones it already had. In January 1918, Haig was ordered to disband two of his five cavalry divisions and allowed to select just four battalions to save from a list of 145 that would otherwise be broken up and their men redistributed. Lloyd George, ever a critic of Haig, later wrote that far from reducing the British Army to a skeleton, in March 1918 it stood at its highest ever level, but chose to ignore the fact that the numbers reflected the overall strength of the BEF, not its fighting strength. There had been, as historian John Terraine explains, some 1,949,000 men

The notorious Bull Ring at Etaples, where new recruits and seasoned veterans alike were put through a punishing period of training before being sent to the front.

serving in the BEF in January 1918 and a further 1,560,862 at home in the United Kingdom, but whilst it was true that the BEF total was higher than a year before, the vast majority of these men were labour and transport troops and infantry strength was down by 126,000. As the war became more technical, the numbers of men working behind the lines had increased but the number of front-line infantry had fallen dramatically when losses had not been replaced.

In March 1918 the Allies anticipated that there would be a major German attack, but not exactly where or when it would come. The British reinforced their positions near the coast while the French strengthened their positions to the south of the boundary at St Quentin, but these preparations left a weak spot in the line to the west of Cambrai where the British defences were still either incomplete or inadequate. Commanding the Fifth Army, Sir Hubert Gough was well aware of the predicament and even more conscious of the lack of reserves available to him if the Germans did attack his sector. In addition, in mid-March, there were around 88,000 men of the BEF on leave in Britain and a further 30,000 on courses or in various depots, further depleting the troops available to Gough should the attack come. Then, on 21 March 1918, around 1 million artillery shells – more than fifty per second – poured onto Fifth Army positions in a five-hour barrage followed immediately by stormtrooper units of the most experienced men available to the Germans. Travelling light, they launched fast, hard hitting attacks on vulnerable

Sketches of Tommy's life In Training. — Nº 9

It was a thrilling moment that day, at tea time, when our lot were told off for the Overseas draft.

Once training was completed, recruits waited until placed on a draft for France. Names would be read out in the barracks shortly before departure.

points, bypassing strongpoints and moving quickly to cover as much ground as possible, creating panic in rear areas with the use of flamethrowers and machine guns. By the end of the first day of the offensive, around 21,000 British soldiers had been taken prisoner and the Germans had made huge advances through the lines of the Fifth Army. After three years of static warfare, senior British officers struggled to react to this new, mobile battle. As Gough and his neighbour, General Byng, attempted to contain the breakthrough with their meagre reserves and any forces Haig could send them, it became clear that they would need help from the French. With fifty German divisions in action on the first day alone, Haig sought out his French counterpart, General Pétain and asked him to attend Haig's Advanced Headquarters. Previously the two men had agreed a mutual aid pact to cover just such an emergency and Haig now needed Pétain to honour the agreement. Explaining the situation, it soon became clear that Pétain was more concerned by a potential attack through the Champagne region towards Paris (which materialised in June) and was, for the moment, quite prepared to pull his men back to cover Paris, thus leaving an even bigger gap for the Germans to exploit. Frantic diplomatic and military efforts led to the appointment on 26 March of Marshal Foch to oversee French and British strategy in a move that at last created a unified Allied command structure. So successful was the initial attack that Kaiser William II declared 24 March to be a national holiday in Germany where rumours quickly spread that the war was all but over. This optimism was misplaced. After years of near starvation, German stormtroopers became distracted by the stockpiles of food behind the British lines and in many places the offensive broke down into an orgy of looting. The offensive had created a crisis in Allied High Command, but it had also been costly in terms of the heavy losses in stormtrooper units, removing many of Germany's best and most experienced soldiers in one blow.

By early April, the German offensives had run out of steam and had been halted but although the immediate crisis was over, the German Army was still a formidable force and Britain needed to rebuild the shattered divisions that had borne the brunt of the fighting. Training depots across the country were stripped of trained men over 19 and, in France, men previously deemed unfit for front-line service found themselves hurriedly regraded to category A and posted to fill the gaps. At the same time, though, large numbers of fit and able troops remained stationed in the eastern counties of England against the perceived threat of a German seaborne invasion while another 62,000 men were tied down in Ireland where General Sir John French, commanding Home Forces, warned that they were needed because the 'situation in future may involve a general strike throughout the country, accompanied by general sabotage'.[2] Discussions about the possible introduction of compulsory conscription in Ireland had been met by a one-day general strike on 23 April in which work was stopped in railways, docks, factories, mills, theatres, cinemas, trams, public services, shipyards, newspapers, shops, and even government munitions factories.[3] Fears of uprising in Ireland and invasion by sea meant that although some 600,000 trained category A men were available, the committee only considered 449,000 as available for reinforcement drafts to France but preferred not to use them.[4] Instead, it took the politically risky step of reducing the minimum age for military service overseas by six months. As the Under Secretary of State for War explained in June:

> the minimum age at which lads are being sent to France for service in the Infantry is eighteen and a half years, and the minimum period of training for such lads is four months. I can assure my hon. Friend that no lads have been sent to France unless they are sufficiently trained to take their place in the firing line.[5]

After six months of intensive training, Ambler, Wiseman and the others were granted embarkation leave. It was time to go home in uniforms that some had had tailored to fit, but all had learned to wear well. Over the Whitsun Bank Holiday they allowed themselves to be displayed to friends and neighbours by proud but anxious parents in churches and parks and showed themselves off to younger friends, awestruck by the tales of heroism yet to come. John Warwick, the young man who had twice volunteered and who had written of the abuse he suffered when walking home, could show his neighbours that he was in uniform at last. In Huddersfield, where anti-war sentiment was still openly expressed, Harold Whitwam could read about the increasingly desperate pleas to be excused from call up but know that his uniform earned him respect. Photographs of the young men in uniform were taken to be given pride of place on the mantelpieces at home. For the families, this could mean more than just a memento of his days in uniform. Only a few weeks earlier Mary Jane Ambler had learned of the death of her son George, the second son to die so far in a war that was far from over. In Leeds, at 18 Frederick Gaines had already outlived his elder brother, killed in 1915 just weeks after his seventeenth birthday. In Keighley, Harold Wiseman met his brother Jimmy, who was on convalescent leave after his third wounding. The recent Spring Offensive had caused havoc and neighbours and friends anxiously awaited any news at all of men still missing since the German onslaught. One of Frederick's Leeds chums went home to see his mother and learned that his father was listed as missing. The few soldiers home from the front found themselves besieged by requests for news of lost loved ones.

When their embarkation leave was over, the boys began the trip back to camp knowing that they would soon be heading for France. One veteran later described his departure from home:

> I could not, or rather did not want, to show emotion or to be affected by other people's feelings … My mother had clung to me and begun to weep. I remember

it was her 53rd birthday, and she said, 'If you don't come back …' I just squeezed her and kissed her and broke away saying 'Don't worry mum, I shall come back.' Then I hurriedly left the station.[6]

Making the most of his last days of freedom, Tom Hall, the son of a church officer from Baildon, near Bradford, chose to overstay his leave and lost eight days' pay as a result when he was picked up by Military Policemen at the Midland Railway station in Sheffield, but most returned on time. The next few days would be spent waiting for orders and listening to rumours and counter-rumours. More medical inspections, the issuing of Active Service pay books, the completion of a wide range of forms including wills, the checking of kit and the myriad final preparations for the move which could come at any time. Finally, at the end of the month, the publication on orders of the names of the men who would make up the next draft.

In all, 135 names appeared on the list. The vast majority had been together since November, but a few were men who had missed earlier drafts because they had been sick or on a course and who now found themselves attached to the KOYLI group. In keeping with the 'buddy' system, though, almost every man was posted to the draft with at least one other from the same area or Training Reserve regiment. Most of the additional men were from Durham and Middlesbrough and had been slated for the Durham Light Infantry. Others were from Sheffield and had been intended for the York and Lancasters. Two, Joseph Turley and Harold Wakelin, had been Staffords and two more, Gilbert Henthorn and William Fay, had been destined for the Lancashire Fusiliers.

All drafts were given a parade to mark their departure.

Then came the day. The draft paraded. 'The boys suddenly looked much younger,' recalled Carrington, 'loaded down with their marching order, their new steel helmets and gas-masks, their pouches stocked with live ammunition, and their iron rations tied to their packs at the last moment in white linen bags – the unmistakable sign by which you recognised a new draft in France.'[7] The end of training and the move to finally being 'real' soldiers was marked by a change in attitude from even the most hardened of training staff which meant that for all who joined a draft, this last day as a recruit left a marked impression. 'It was clearly "Our Day",' wrote one, 'for officers and NCOs alike made a most unaccustomed fuss of us, and to the rest of the battalion we were already almost heroes!'[8] Elsewhere, another veteran later wrote, 'The roll was called & then the Regimental Sergeant Major came & shook hands with each one & wished us all "good luck."'[9] The commander of the camp or some other high ranking officer then gave a parting speech, such as the one recorded by Frederick Hodges:

'You men', he began, and then paused as he surveyed our eager young faces, 'I know, of course, that you are only boys of eighteen ... I trust, indeed I am sure that the training you have had in this Division will stand you in good stead. You have all fired your course with the rifle, and some of you have learned to use the Lewis gun. What we have taught you on the ranges, you have now to put into practice at the Front, and, from what I hear, there is no lack of targets there! Good luck to you all.'[10]

With a band leading the way and laden down with last-minute gifts of cigarettes and sweets, the draft marched out of camp and down to the local railway station. Part of a draft leaving in April 1918, Alfred Abraham later described how many of his contingent 'had bought small union jacks with which to brighten our march through the streets ... When we paraded that day, ready to march off, we had attached these little flags to our rifles'.[11] In some places, the sight of drafts marching away had become so commonplace that the local civilians paid no attention but, for the most part, it seems that the mothers, wives and sweethearts of men already at the front made an effort to turn out so they could cheer and wave as the boys marched through town, leaving the lads feeling an odd mix of patriotism and embarrassment. 'As the long train drew out of the station,' wrote one, 'the massed bands played "Auld Lang Syne" and the roof re-echoed to the sounds of cheers and singing.'[12] Then the long journey to the Channel ports began.

Troop trains were long, slow-moving beasts and the lads soon became bored. It was not unknown for some to start taking pot shots at cows and sheep as the train trundled southwards until darkness fell and in 'the yellow light in the carriages the men sprawled in all sorts of queer, curved positions. They lay curled against each other, asleep. Some were curled up on the floor, their heads on their new packs. They snored and slavered and broke wind. They were exhausted with singing and excitement.' Passing through London late at night, 'children and women came on to the verandahs of the slum tenements and cheered us. Their cheers sounded shrill and faint over the noise of the train. Many were in nightclothes, and we could see them dimly, and their little rooms, by the light of their tiny gas jets.'[13] The day of departure for all drafts was long, often starting as early as 3 a.m. and ending late that night, with journey's end the port of Folkestone and another long wait to board ship for France. By now they were officially on active service. Billeted in either requisitioned houses or in a transit camp outside town, the warning was issued that any absence from parade now was a far more serious matter. This would be the last chance for the men to go absent without leave while the offence was still relatively minor. Once across the Channel, the offence became desertion and potentially carried the death penalty.

This would be the longest journey most had ever made. For many it would be the longest journey they would ever have the chance to make and they knew that it was one from which some would never return. It was with mixed feelings that they took the offered lifebelt and walked up the gangplank of a variety of ships from old paddle steamers to Manx packet boats and freighters. Crammed with new drafts, men returning from leave or convalescence, possibly with horses and supplies too, the boats could be extremely uncomfortable places. Crossing took place at night in convoys escorted by warships to lessen the risk of torpedo attacks. Smoking was absolutely forbidden to prevent lit cigarettes being seen by German submarines and bombers and guards were posted to prevent anyone striking a match. Rations were

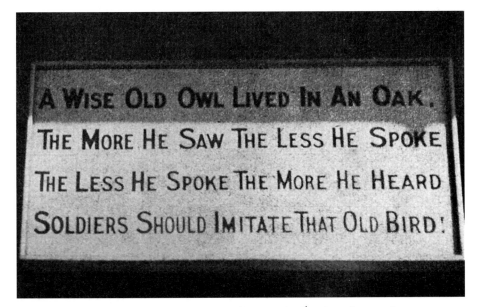

Every man leaving for the front line passed this sign posted at Étaples railway station.

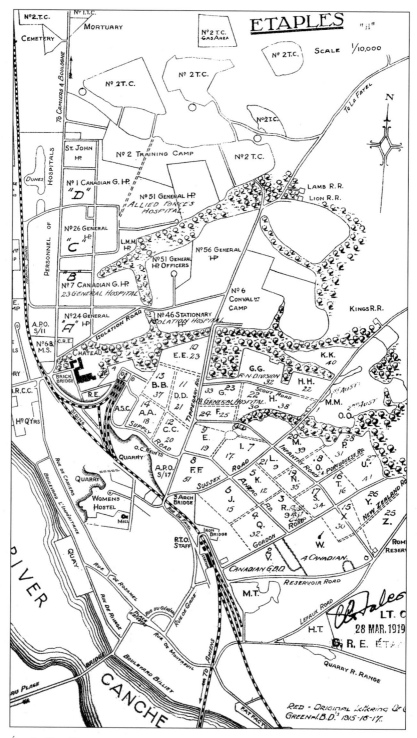

Étaples Base Depot.

handed out by officers and NCOs and interminable games of Housey Housey were set up to relieve the boredom. On a good crossing, it might only take two hours to reach France. More often, men were aboard for ten hours or more. Sleep was often difficult with little or no room to stretch out and, when sea conditions were rough, seasickness added pools of vomit to the misery of the crossing. Once across, the next delay was in getting off. Night crossings meant long waits for the tide to change; one man later recalled arriving off the port of Le Havre at 5 a.m., but waiting until 11 p.m. to actually leave the boat.[14]

Arrival in France was usually a disappointment. The docks, crowded with British and Allied troops coming and going and staffed by British labour units, looked identical to those the men had just left behind in England and it was only by searching for signs written in French that the new arrivals could tell they had reached another country. Lined up on the quayside at Boulogne on 2 June 1918, Tom Hall, the church officer's son from Baildon, had obviously spent the time aboard playing Housey Housey. As a long list of regimental numbers was being read, he called out 'House!' earning a laugh from the draft but three days' loss of pay when Regimental Sergeant Major Thew failed to see the funny side.[15]

Next began the 15-mile journey from Boulogne to the sprawling base depot at Étaples. Once clear of the chaos of the docks, the boys were able to get their first view of France. Few were impressed. Children gathered around the new arrivals demanding 'beeskeets' or pimping their sisters. With no time to sample the latter, the troops were only too pleased to hand out hardtack biscuits to children who seemed to appreciate them far more than the average Tommy did. It was also a chance for the draft to experience for the first time the difficulties of marching on French *pavés*. Badly maintained cobbled roads and heavy hob-nailed boots were a painful combination that took some time to get used to but it was only a taste of what was to come.

Étaples in 1918 gave one new arrival the impression of bees swarming in and out of hives, with thousands of men in constant transit through the huge camp's port facilities, railway yards, stores, hospitals, prisons, training areas and all the administrative facilities of an army at war. It was also home to a series of Infantry Base Depots (IBDs), gathered on the rising ground to the east of the railway which runs north–south beside the town. Drafts from England destined for infantry divisions at the front passed through the IBDs where they were regrouped according to unit, put through a period of training, and sent forward, but the base also housed men transferring to other theatres of the war or classed as 'Temporary Base' after hospital or convalescence and those returning from periods of leave in the UK. By late 1917, Étaples, or 'Eat Apples', had become notorious as an oppressive place run by 'base wallahs' known as 'canaries' because of the yellow armbands they wore. Like their counterparts in England, these men were often keen to remain out of the firing line and tried to ensure that they did by appearing as efficient as possible, gaining a poor reputation as officious bullies from

Despite several medical checks, 'immatures' deemed unsuited to the front lines still reached France. At the Étaples base camp, these young men were taken out and posted to No. 5 Convalescent Camp at Cayeux to be held until ready for service. This photo, taken in July 1918, may well include privates Tom Hall and Joseph McNulty, both of whom would later be posted to 10th Battalion Royal Fusiliers at the end of the war.

The ambulance park of the vast Étaples Base Depot.

whose often vicious abuse not even the most experienced soldiers were given respite. At the infamous 'Bull Ring' training grounds in the dunes near the camp, soldiers who had seen extensive service in the trenches and who were now returning from leave or hospital were put through the same training as the latest drafts from England and treated with the same casual scorn. One former officer remembered the training as 'demoralising beyond measure' whilst another found the Bull Ring to be 'like passing hell for 2 weeks'. A corporal encountered several men returning to the front with wounds which were far from healed: 'When I asked why they had returned in that condition they invariably replied: "To get away from the Bull Ring."'[16] Matters came to a head in September 1917 when a New Zealand soldier returning from a visit to the nearby resort of Le Touqet (which was officially out of bounds to other ranks) was arrested by Military Police as a deserter. A large crowd of angry men gathered near the Pont des Trois Arches on the way towards town. An anxious military policeman opened fire on the crowd, killing one man and wounding a French civilian. The police then fled, chased by around 1,000 soldiers and in the coming days the men mutinied and broke out of camp to protest against conditions there. The regime changed as a result, but still remained an unpleasant experience for those passing through.

As the draft arrived, they marched over the 'Three Arch Bridge' where the mutiny had started and along Tipperary Road to 'F' Infantry Base Depot, their

Étaples was used to ensure that every man was properly trained. Here machine-gunners are drilled in firing wearing their respirators.

home for the next two weeks. The atmosphere around Étaples at the time was tense. On the night of 31 May German planes had bombed the camp and hit almost all the base hospitals. A nurse had been killed and several others were wounded and at the 56 General Hospital the Operating Theatre, X-ray room and administrative block had been completely destroyed. At the Canadian hospital, the kitchens had received a direct hit and scattered damage had been done to accommodation

British soldiers back aboard a 'forty and eight'. This time, their journey would take them into captivity in Germany.

huts and wards. Fortunately, despite the scale of the damage done, there were relatively few casualties because the hospital wards had recently been emptied and most
patients sent back to the UK, leaving only the 'walking wounded' able to reach shelter in the trenches dug nearby. Dugouts were still being built for the hospital staff by
tunnelling into the nearby hills and the draft would take their turn labouring there,
but for the time being, staff were camping in the nearby forest each night to await
the 'all clear'.

Although Étaples was a permanent base camp, with many of the Salvation Army,
YMCA Huts and other amenities that camps like Brocton had developed, year-round
accommodation was still in tents. 'At the top end,' one man later recalled:

> was the sergeant's tent who was in charge of that particular line. The tents were
> crowded out. In mine there were 18 men & we had a rare job to put out kit & find
> room for ourselves. At night when all were in there were more feet to the pole than
> there was room for so that the feet had to pile on each other. It was a good job it
> was summertime as the door was left open & gave more air. I am sorry for the
> troops who came there in winter.[17]

Certainly for those passing through in winter Étaples was a grim place. The two
blankets issued to each man were barely enough and men woke to find water
bottles and boots frozen stiff, but this draft had luckily arrived in the relative comfort of late spring.

Just as at Brocton, meals remained a focal point of the day. One man claimed
that during his stay there the principal meal of the day consisted of two slices of
bully beef, two biscuits and an onion, but opinions varied:

> The meals were all taken in large mess-rooms of which there were several & large
> queues formed up in front of each about 5 deep & regulated by Military Police
> for all the world like lining up for the pictures or the theatre & each room had two
> sittings so that if you were not well to the fore you had a long wait for your meal.
> The food was good here and fairly served out …

Another complained: 'On many occasions after finishing my first meal I would
come out and again take my place in the queue for a further meal. On some
occasions it was necessary to do this three times in order to get a decent meal.'[18]
As before, when time allowed the men headed for the various civilian-run canteens
to slake their appetites. Those who could headed for *estaminet*, small cafés set up in
French homes where men could buy egg and chips washed down with 'plonk' –
cheap 'vin blanc' sometimes sweetened with sugar – all at vastly inflated prices.

The day after their arrival in France, the draft paraded to be issued with their
new regimental number and to be assigned to their units. As ever, they lined up

alphabetically – more or less – with Alfred Aspinall becoming 62479 and John Warwick 62615. Somewhere in the middle, the parade appears to have been disrupted so those men with names beginning with F, G and H became mixed up. Somehow, the number 62556 was missed altogether and, somewhere along the line, the number 62515 was issued to Harry Dennison from Leeds but also assigned to Private Harold Cope, a KOYLI soldier killed the previous May. Once given their numbers, the men were lined up. From Aspinall to 62548 John Kane would go to the 5th Battalion of the KOYLI; the remainder to the 2/4th. Separation from friends was cushioned by the fact that after so many months of lining up alphabetically, most knew at least some of the men around them and in any case both battalions were part of the 187th Infantry Brigade of the 62nd (West Riding) Division so they would be serving close by each other with a chance of staying in touch. This process was followed by yet another medical in which two men, Tom Hall and Joseph McNulty, were assessed as being 'immature', a term used to cover both those too young for service and those deemed physically unfit for the trenches. The two lads were despatched a few days later to No. 5 Convalescent Camp at Cayeux, a special depot for 'Immatures' where they would be kept until they were assessed as ready. The camp itself was split into regionally based companies so that when, in November, Hall and McNulty were finally posted to the 10th Royal Fusiliers, they were part of a draft of similar young men from Yorkshire regiments and the two lads could continue to serve together.

Before they could finally join their units at the front, though, the rest of the draft would undergo two weeks of intensive training. The Recruit Syllabus in the UK, though standardised by the War Office, varied greatly in quality. Étaples was intended to make sure every soldier was ready for the job ahead of him and that each man had learned the same way. Every day, they marched to the infamous Bull Ring, a large open space in the sand dunes where, under the intense scrutiny of the permanent staff of the 'blood on the bayonet' school of instruction, they would march and double march across the dunes to build fitness and stamina, practice assaults, trench routines, weapons drill and always, always, bayonet fighting. They would also undergo gas training to ensure that their respirators (as gas masks are more accurately known or 'exasperators', as many troops knew them) worked properly. The poison gas test was sometimes held in a sealed tent, but more usually in a wooden hut, with notices up at either end warning the men to ensure their mask fitted properly and the word 'dangerous' in large letters on a notice board close to the entrance. It was essentially a long corridor with a few windows to allow light in. Every soldier was supposed to be put through a standard course which included an hour immersed in a cloud of gas to give him, as the manual put it, 'confidence in his respirator' and half a minute exposed to tear gas to teach him to take anti-gas precautions seriously. Masks had to be put on in a regulation six seconds – but before being allowed to do so, and while still exposed to the tear gas, men had to repeat their name, number and battalion to ensure they caught an unforgettable dose of gas.[19]

The regime was harsh. Frank Sumpter, passing through Étaples in late 1917 after convalescing from wounds, described watching 'two Canaries, one each side of a man, and both of them were shouting in his ear and when he put his hand up to stop the noise they knocked him down. This brutality was going on all over the place and people would apply to go back to their regiments, they'd had enough.'[20] In some ways it helped as a kind of inoculation against the stress that the newcomers would face in the trenches, but few saw it that way at the time. After two weeks of endless fatigue and brutal training, it came as a relief when the draft was finally declared ready. In separate groups, they marched back across the Three Arches bridge to the railway station where on the platform hung a final piece of advice:

A wise old owl lived in an oak,
The more he saw, the less he spoke;
The less he spoke, the more he heard;
Soldiers should imitate that old bird.[21]

On 11 June 1918, Privates Pickering, Whitwam and Wiseman arrived to find the 2/4th Battalion out of the line near Bucquoy, south of Arras. Two days later, Ambler, Carr and Gaines reached the 5th. Their war was about to begin.

'The witches' sabbath'

The two KOYLI battalions the draft joined had first arrived in France in January 1917 after two years of preparation. As part of the expansion of the Territorial Force on the outbreak of war the 4th Battalion, recruiting from around Wakefield, and the 5th Battalion, covering the area between Doncaster and Goole, had formed the 1/4th and 1/5th and their 'duplicate' 2/4th and 2/5th Battalions. Designated 'first line' units, the 1/4th and 1/5th battalions had taken priority for men, equipment and training and had sailed to France in April 1915 as part of the 49th Division. The 2/4th and 2/5th formed part of the 49th Division's duplicate 62nd (West Riding) Division. Initially spread throughout South and East Yorkshire and North Nottinghamshire, the 62nd had finally come together for training on Salisbury Plain in January 1916 but, as the official history put it:

> Repeated orders to hold themselves in readiness for active service were becoming monotonous until the men were suddenly fitted out with steel helmets, and then, and not till then, did they really believe that they would see France. The actual date of their departure for France was the 15th January 1917.[1]

On arrival, the 62nd Division came under the control of V Corps, Fifth Army for their introduction to the war. The winter was severe and the freezing conditions of the early months of 1918 took their toll on officers and men as they struggled to adjust to the demands of active service, with sickness picking off the old, the unfit and the frail as often as wounds affected the fitter men. The 2/4th Battalion commander was gone by April and his replacement, a colonel of the East Kent Regiment, immediately set about reorganising the battalion's officers. The second most senior officer, Major Walker, was relieved of his duties as adjutant and instead given the less demanding job of town major – responsible for discipline in garrisons behind the lines. It became clear that Walker was not really cut out for active service after a series of incidents that demonstrated how out of touch he was with events. On one occasion, after the officers had finished a meal in their temporary mess, a servant had taken the tablecloth outside and shaken it. An angry Walker had berated the man, insisting that such an action, even this far behind the lines and out of sight of even the most advanced German observers, could attract enemy shelling or worse, might be taken as an attempt by the KOYLI to surrender.[2]

Slowly, the two battalions, fighting alongside each other as part of the 187th Infantry Brigade, gained experience, but at a heavy price. On 3 May they took part in their first offensive operation in the attack on Bullecourt, where poor planning and inexperience led to heavy casualties. Working alongside the plan devised by the more experienced Australians, the 187th Brigade accepted a plan of attack that left a 600-yard gap between the two forces and failed to engage enemy guns a short distance away. Junior officers underestimated the difficulty involved in moving heavily laden men forward in darkness under fire and were 300 yards further back than intended when the barrage lifted, allowing the Germans time to recover. The result was chaos in which the brigade lost 55 per cent of its officers and 48 per cent of its men in a single day. Alongside them, in the 186th Brigade, the 2/6th West Yorkshires lost all their officers and 287 of the 393 men sent forward.[3] In all, the 62nd Division lost 191 officers and 4,042 men in its first real battle and failed to dislodge the enemy from the strongly fortified village that defeated even the battle-hardened 7th Division. The 62nd Division's commander, General Walter Braithwaite, had previously acted as Chief of Staff for the Mediterranean Expedition under Hamilton and had been regarded by many of the Australians involved as 'arrogant and incompetent', and there was little chance

PLAYER'S CIGARETTES.

62ND DIVISION.

The 62nd (West Riding) Division's Pelican insignia, widely referred to as the 'bloody duck'. The origin is obscure but it was said that it would put both feet on the ground when Germany was defeated. When the division became the only Territorial Force formation to enter Germany, the insignia changed and the Pelican stood on both feet.

German stormtrooper. The success of the German offensive in March 1918 depended on small groups of heavily armed and experienced infantrymen like this man who were able to infiltrate the British lines.

that they would accept any responsibility for their part in the failed operation. In truth, a new and untried second-line Territorial Force formation would have needed extraordinary luck to have achieved the goals set for them under the circumstances, but High Command had little sympathy for their situation, and General Gough joined the Australians in accusing the 62nd of 'lack of fighting spirit' and 'ill discipline', claiming that initial success had been let down by poor discipline that failed to press home the advantage.[4]

Although angered by the comments, privately, many officers recognised that the attitudes that had held the Territorials together in England would not help them here in France. At the end of May they were transferred from Fifth Army to Third Army control and began a period of officer reorganisation and intensive training to bring them up to standard. In June they moved to the rear and a number of officers and men from the KOYLI Battalions were sent for training at various schools covering everything from instruction on the Lewis gun to bayonet work and even cookery before moving to a new sector and a return to the usual round of trench work. In between tours of duty in the front line they underwent intensive training in company and battalion strength attacks and the art of forming up at night ready for the next big operation. A series of old German trenches south of Arras had been taken over to make the training as realistic as possible so that by November, when the Brigade was included in an attack at Havrincourt near Cambrai, the 62nd Division and the rest of the British Third Army achieved an advance of over 4 miles – a record for any army on the Western Front at that stage of the war. Following its initial success, though, the attack failed to such a degree that questions were raised in Parliament and an official inquiry launched, the results of which were seen by politicians and soldiers alike as a whitewash of the High Command. In his statement to the inquiry, the commander of the Third Army, Sir Julian Byng, blamed 'lack of training on the part of junior officers and NCOs and men'.[5] A neat piece of buck passing from the man whose responsibility it was to ensure that the men under his command were adequately trained.

After leaving the Battle of Cambrai, the division was sent to training areas west of Arras for the whole of December and speculation grew about the proposed restructuring of the army as a result of the findings of the Cabinet Committee formed to determine military priorities for the coming year. On 10 January, the changes began. Among those affected were the 1/5th and 2/5th KOYLI, which would now be reduced to a single 5th Battalion, with some ten officers and 216 men from the 1/5th going to the 1/4th and the remainder sent to join the amalgamated 5th Battalion, which would remain with the 62nd Division. Having lost its 1/ and 2/ prefixes, the 5th took over as the 187th Brigade's senior battalion, much to the annoyance of the previous holders of the title, the 2/4th KOYLI, but the injection of a draft of highly experienced men who had been in France with the 1/5th since 1915 brought with it a new boost of confidence to the brigade. As a result of the reorganisation, February and early March saw the roads of France filled with British units seeking their new homes and the disruption was still evident when Luddendorff's *Kaiserschlacht* (Emperor's Battle) opened on 21 March. Warned as early as 12 March that something was coming, the 62nd Division were in position around Arras as the German onslaught smashed into the British lines. On 26 March, the two KOYLI battalions moved into position around the village of Bucquoy, where large numbers of German troops were reported to be massing in the sunken road between Hébuterne and Rossignol Wood nearby. As they prepared for the attack, the 2/4th asked for more grenades but were told none were available and when the Germans attacked in strength along old trench lines, the shortage proved critical in preventing the defenders from being able to hold them back – a situation made worse by the discovery that among the few grenades that had been supplied were a number of dummy bombs intended to be used only for training.[6] Forced back, a gap opened in the British lines. A counter-attack and vicious fighting over the next two days cost the 5th Battalion the equivalent of three companies and the 2/4th one, with a total casualty list of 22 officers and 716 men between the two units. The survivors were relieved on 1 April and made their way to the rear but, by then, the 2/4th had been reduced to just seven officers and around 200 men still fit to fight. The German offensive around Bucquoy had been halted but with the continued threat of further attacks, the men found themselves back in the front lines by 6 April, reinforced by whatever men could be found to make up the numbers. The defence of Bucquoy earned them an official mention in despatches and finally established the division as an effective fighting force, but as they slowly tried to bring the battalions back to full strength, April and May saw a return to trench duties with the steady haemorrhaging of men on an almost daily basis. Without engaging in any major attacks, the 62nd Division lost nineteen officers killed, wounded or missing, sixty-two men killed, 392 wounded and fourteen missing in the last two weeks of May alone. It was these men the draft would need to replace.

Gilbert Hall, the young lieutenant who had been their instructor at Brocton, arrived with a draft in late April to join 'A' Company of the 2/4th KOYLI and found a battalion struggling to rebuild itself after the chaos of recent weeks and unsettled by changes in leadership. The 2/4th's commanding officer, Lt Colonel Barton, had qualified for six months' leave and handed over the battalion to Major Beaumont, who eagerly anticipated the chance to show higher command that he was fit to run the battalion. The day after he wrote to his wife with the good news, Beaumont heard that his command would be a short one and that the new CO was to be Lt Colonel Kaye, former adjutant of the 1/4th Battalion. No sooner had he adjusted to this news than he heard that yet another candidate was to take over, again an outsider. The new man, Lt Colonel Chaytor, arrived at the end of June, just as Beaumont left for a Senior Officer's Course at Aldershot. Such changes unsettled the battalion because each unit took its unique culture from its commanding officer's approach to leadership, but despite this Hall found what appeared to be a relaxed but effective unit. When a young soldier desperate to escape the trenches shot off his own toe, he failed to eject the empty case from his rifle and it was clear to all that it was a self-inflicted wound. Such wounds were treated very seriously by the army and, if court-martialled, the man faced at best a period of imprisonment or potentially the death penalty (although almost 4,000 such cases were tried during the war, none were executed). Instead, his company commander took a more pragmatic approach. The battalion's rest area was plagued by packs of dogs, some suspected of carrying rabies. The young man was sentenced to spend his days hobbling around the area hunting down the dogs and shooting them. It not only served a practical purpose, but was also a useful reminder to the other men that a self-inflicted wound did not mean an escape to a safe prison cell behind the lines.[7]

The 2/4th's share of the new draft, with Pickering, Whitwham and Wiseman among them, arrived on 11 June; the 5th's group arrived two days later. Where possible, such drafts arrived when the unit was out of the line so that they had a chance to meet the men they would serve with and learn to recognise their officers and NCOs, for a great deal depended on fitting in quickly. As unknown quantities, the newcomers could expect to be given the bulk of the work and the riskiest tasks by men who had already 'done their bit' and so proved themselves. From day one, being accepted as part of the group could mean the difference between life and death. Men who had won medals for rescuing comrades under fire were rarely short of a smoke or a bit of cake from home, in part from men who hoped that if they were ever hit, he'd come for them, too, but also from new arrivals who hoped to gain some reflected glory in befriending a proven hero. The first lesson for the new men was that the world of the front-line infantryman was a small one, limited by what he could see and hear, his social contact reduced to the men in his section, then platoon, but rarely wider than the men of his company. As one veteran later put it:

> We tolerated and understood each other. Men would swear at one another, swear about each other, but the true fact was there was always that other bond … Your pals are almost family, a very rough family, mind. Everybody had their own pals, teetotallers got together, and those who liked a drink.

Comradeship, he believed, 'was a necessity'.[8] Any sentimental feelings of affection towards one's 'band of brothers', though, would come later. There has been a tendency among historians to romanticise the complex web of alliances and bonds that supported men in the trenches to a point far beyond the reality most of those men encountered. For some, the army was a strange and lonely place, whilst others, officers and men alike, speak unashamedly of bonds of love between the members

German troops during the March offensive.

of a unit. Many likened their relationships with their comrades to those of a family and it is worth taking time to consider what this actually means.

In the field of social sciences, researchers sometimes speak of 'reconstituted families'. Imagine a stereotypical nuclear family of two parents and two children. Now imagine that the parents divorce and each marries another divorcee who also has children. After a year or so one partnership has another child together. The parents now have to negotiate relationships with their biological children, their step-children and their joint biological child whilst the children themselves have to develop a relationship with their half-sibling, both parents and both step-parents. To continue the analogy, on the Western Front, the regimental family saw the arrival and integration of a long procession of stepfathers (officers) and stepbrothers (replacements of other rank), each new draft needing to assert his position in the regimental family but also needing to know his place.

Whilst popular officers and NCOs inspired loyalty and dedication in their men, they were also aware that in the front lines, whatever military law might say, any perceived abuse of the power they wielded could be a dangerous thing. Throughout history, bullying men have gone to war fearing their own men as much as the enemy. As Richard Holmes points out, before the Battle of Blenheim in 1704, the unpopular commander of the 15th Foot took the extraordinary step of publicly apologising to his men and asking that he be allowed to die by an enemy bullet. One replied that with the enemy in sight the men had more to think about than him. At the end of the fight, he turned to his men to raise a cheer – and was killed by a single shot from an unknown marksman. Writing about his experiences in a Territorial Force artillery battery from the West Riding, P.J. Campbell describes an incident in late 1917 when an experienced sergeant's advice to an officer was taken as a sign of insubordination. Trying to calm the situation, Campbell spoke to both men. After discussing the matter with Captain Garnett, Campbell next spoke to Sergeant Denmark:

> I told him Garnett was a very brave man with a very high sense of duty. 'He's got an unfortunate way of talking', I said. 'That's all.'
>
> 'He'll get a bullet in the back one of these days', Denmark said, 'Unless he learns to talk civil.'
>
> He was so angry that I was alarmed. 'Don't be a fool', I said. 'You would never do anything so daft.'
>
> 'I didn't say *I* would', was his answer.
>
> I was very upset. Garnett was even more unpopular than I had supposed.[9]

Tucked away in the memoirs of First World War soldiers are references to what would later become known as 'fragging' after the use of fragmentation hand grenades to kill unpopular officers and, as Richard Holmes has explained, 'Brigadier-General Crozier knew of "the bullying NCO who was blown to pieces by a bomb, with the pin extracted, being placed between his shirt and trousers"'. Robert Graves' poem 'Sergeant Major Money' in which two young Welsh soldiers bayonet a hard-driving sergeant major, is founded on fact, and in *Goodbye to All That* Graves describes how two men in his battalion shot their company sergeant major having mistaken him for their platoon sergeant. Two British soldiers were executed in April 1918:

> One had shot his platoon sergeant, the other a lieutenant. The Australians were sharp with unpopular officers … One Australian recalled throwing a lump of clay at an engineer officer who reprimanded him: 'He cleared off without a word, fearing worse treatment, for our rifles were handy, and a shot more or less is never noticed among the incessant firing during darkness.'[10]

Historian Gregory A. Daddis has considered relationships within US Army units in the Second World War and argues that if these truly were family-like then officers, like parents, had the power to punish or reward behaviour, whilst soldiers, like children, competed with one another, vying for status and attention in their respective family units. The idea that sibling rivalry and inexperienced or poor parenting can be a dangerous combination has, he claims, 'been conveniently lost in the established band of brothers thesis. The brotherhood, much like a loving family, is an idealized institution ... and oftentimes masks the fact that relationships between brothers can be a complicated emotional issue.' Drawing on examples from writings of Second World War veterans, Daddis shows that the 'brotherhood of arms' image has been so attractive to such a wide range of writers that contradictory evidence has received very little attention, meaning that few scholars and even fewer readers have ever asked whether it truly reflected life in the harsh environment of the front line at the time. As he shows:

> Cliques of more seasoned veterans often viewed replacements as little more than freshmen outsiders undeserving of admission into the squad or platoon level fraternity. Sergeant Hadden, serving in the 28th Infantry Division, insinuated that replacements could pass virtually unnoticed through his unit without any consideration of their worthiness to assimilate into the group. 'There must ... have been well over a dozen men, both young and some in their thirties, who joined my squad as replacements, were there for a time, and then disappeared ... [I]n some cases, they were with us so briefly that I hardly had time to learn what they looked like.'[11]

Similar comments appear from time to time in British memoirs, too. The accounts that survive, from both wars, tend to come from men who viewed the military positively and who were predisposed to accept the 'family' analogy but who, even then, show that the definition of 'friends' and 'family' could stretch quite far. Writing of the experiences of the 5th Seaforth Highlanders in the Second World War, for example, Alistair Borthwick admitted that, at the end of the war, 'we remembered friends who were dead. It had been a long time. *Sometimes we could not remember their names ...*' (author's emphasis).[12] That one could simultaneously claim a close emotional relationship without remembering the name of the individual – even in wartime – demonstrates how flexible the perception of close bonds could be.

Recognising the difficulties involved in integrating newcomers into established units, practice dictated that each member of the draft was paired up with a more experienced man who would act as his mentor. Trench foot, a circulatory condition that could lead to swelling of the feet and legs, temporary paralysis or even gangrene, remained endemic. To counter it, daily foot inspections would be carried out by the officers but alongside this, men would be assigned to work together to check each other's feet, creating a situation in which each would have to get to know the other and so aid the process of creating a bond between the men of the unit. In his memoir *Taught to Kill*, John Babcock, an American who served in the Second World War, described his relationship with the men with whom he shared a foxhole:

> Foxhole mates learned to share body warmth, even rubbing each other's chilled feet to ward off trench foot. We drank from the same canteens, shared ration

bars, canned spam, and smokes. It was the kind of closeness you associated with mouth-to-mouth resuscitation, driven by desperate need; it was intimate, for sure, but involved no interplay of personal feelings.

Faced with the need to check his trenchmate's feet during the winter of 1944, he wrote that whilst 'rubbing someone else's stinky feet might be distasteful [it] was overridden by sheer necessity, and the hard fact that you desperately needed the same personal care for your own feet'.[13] Bonding and sharing, then, was often less about a family relationship than about the simple practicalities of survival – a lesson the new boys needed to learn quickly. For the new arrivals, in many ways it helped that the battalions they were joining were themselves filled with recent replacements and so the cliques were less entrenched in their attitudes to newcomers as each man now joined a section within a platoon.

Arriving at his first unit in France, one man later recalled that:

we paraded for inspection, and were closely questioned about our training. As we stood in line, a young soldier questioned each boy in turn. As he neared me I wondered what his rank was, as I could see no stripes on the sleeve of his tunic. When he reached me I saw the single pip on the epaulettes of a private soldier's tunic, and I realised that he was an experienced active service officer, which was a new type of officer to me.[14]

By 1918, the platoon was firmly established as the main tactical formation, described as 'the smallest unit in the field which comprises all the weapons with which the Infantry Soldier is armed'. After the heavy fighting in March and early April, many platoons had fallen below the twenty-eight-man minimum and had been amalgamated on a temporary basis. The new draft allowed the rebuilding of the battalion to an average platoon of a Headquarters group of an officer and four men with thirty-six men in four specialist sections:

One section of bombers – 1 NCO and 8 men including 2 bayonet men and 2 throwers. The bomb grenade was the secondary weapon of every rifleman but specialist bombers trained to clear trenches and dugouts with the best throwers surrounded by a bodyguard of bayonet men to kill any of the less seriously wounded.

One section of Lewis gunners – 1 NCO and 8 including the Number 1 (the Lewis gunner) and 2 (who acted as loader) with the rest acting as ammunition carriers.

According to the Instructions for the training of Platoons issued in 1917:

The Lewis gun is the weapon of opportunity. Its chief uses are to kill the enemy above ground and to obtain superiority of fire. Its mobility and the small target it and its team present render it peculiarly suitable for working round an enemy's flank or for guarding one's own flank.

One section of riflemen – 1 NCO and 8 men made up of the best shots, scouts and bayonet men.

One section of rifle bombers – 1 NCO and 8 men including four bomb firers.

'The rifle bomb,' the instructions continued, 'is the "howitzer" of the infantry and used to dislodge the enemy from behind cover and to obtain superiority of fire by driving him underground.'[15]

In the 2/4th, Harold Wiseman's 'LG' badge on his tunic sleeve marked him out as a qualified Lewis gunner and he was sent to join a Lewis gun section as their new gunner. The Lewis gun, with its 47-round circular magazine, was a vital element of the platoon's firepower and needed a gunner, a loader and five men to carry its ammunition. On the march, the Lewis gunners were issued a cart to transport the ammunition and spare parts needed to keep the gun in action, but in battle the whole section would be needed just to maintain its rate of fire. As a gunner, Harold would be the centre of the team. Within the platoon, each section had its own speciality and with it, its own subculture. Some, according to their particular skills, could be almost a law unto themselves and scout and sniper teams particularly relished the independence their job could bring. Others, like William Holmes from Wharfedale, had trained for 'the suicide club' as bombers and found themselves marked out as special men, flanked by riflemen whose job it was to provide protection as they did their work.

With the battalion out of the line, the draft had a little time to start to adjust. As West Riding men in a West Riding Division, they found they had things in common. They knew the same towns, had worked in the same mills and factories and visited the same cinemas. It broke down barriers. Few things, though, broke down barriers more than 'chatting'. 'The first night in the candle lit barn,' wrote a veteran:

I could not restrain my curiosity at the sight of the old hands performing mysterious rites with their shirts off. So I went across and asked one of them what he was doing. 'Chatting up', he replied. 'What do you think I'm bloody doing?' he added. He introduced me into the process of reducing the population of those slow crawling, grey, loathsome, filthy creatures called lice. His method and that of the troops whose clothing they infested and on whose bodies they lived, was to hunt and pick one from their clothing and one at a time squeezing it between his thumb nails until it cracked. Its blood would be smeared over the nails and with an extra fat specimen might spurt into the face of the chatter up. After all, it was really his own blood. The he showed me lying snugly in their thousands, along the seams of his trousers and shirts, glistening, whitish, translucent eggs, which he proceeded to destroy by running the lighted candle flame smartly along the egg-laden seam, just stopping before singeing the garment.

It would not be long before the new arrival felt the itching of his own batch, 'and I knew then that I was well and truly loused up and could now join that happy band of regular chatters-up, whenever the opportunity arose'.[16]

Chatting was a constant, and vital, occupation. Trained and prepared to face the Germans, the dangers brought by smaller enemies had not occurred to most men. On 15 June, only days after its arrival, the draft suffered its first casualty when Private Harry Robinson, newly assigned to 'B' Company 2/4th KOYLI ,was admitted to the West Riding Field Ambulance suffering 'Pyrexia of unknown origin' (or PUO). Passing quickly down the line, he moved from the Field Ambulance to 29 Casualty Clearing Station and on to 1 Australian Hospital at Rouen. By 20 June he was on his way back to Britain, his war over. (Robinson later made a claim for injuries sustained on 18 July 1918 near Rheims, but his records show he was not discharged from hospital in the UK until 2 August. He was invalided out of the army in September 1919 and awarded the Silver War Badge on the grounds of sickness.) In mid-1915, a medical officer named Major J.H.P. Graham had reported a new illness on the Western Front: 'A private belonging to an infantry regiment was admitted to a casualty clearing station from a field ambulance where he had been detained suffering from a febrile illness of three days' duration and of sudden onset.' It was unlike anything that he had previously encountered: 'the patient's condition on admission was marked by frontal headache, dizziness, severe lumbago, a feeling of stiffness down the front of the thighs, and severe pains in the legs referred chiefly to the shins.' One of the most curious qualities of it was the relapsing fever it brought.[17] Initially diagnosed as PUO, the case was followed by others and sparked debate in the medical profession as to whether 'trench fever' was an entirely new illness or a mutation of something else, but after hundreds of cases had been found it was eventually classified as a new disease in the summer of 1916.

After observing cases in a stationary hospital, Captain T. Strethill Wright noted that the disease was especially prevalent during the winter, when mosquitoes and flies were absent from the trench environment, suggesting that the most likely cause was the body louse, and by the end of 1916 this was generally accepted. In the middle of 1917, a special British Expeditionary Force Pyrexia of Unknown Origin Enquiry Sub-committee was formed and a concerted campaign by the BEF's scientific advisors persuaded the War Office to fund a special research committee on trench fever in Britain. The War Office Trench Fever Investigation Commission was granted permission to use laboratories in the Medical Research Committee's hospital at Hampstead and to obtain civilian volunteers for human experimentation. With help from the American Red Cross, the BEF investigation was able to draw on American volunteers to prove that the disease stemmed from infected louse excreta being rubbed on to irritated skin, and at the end of 1917 the War Office agreed to recognise the disease as 'trench fever'. According to one *Lancet* article: 'Trench fever

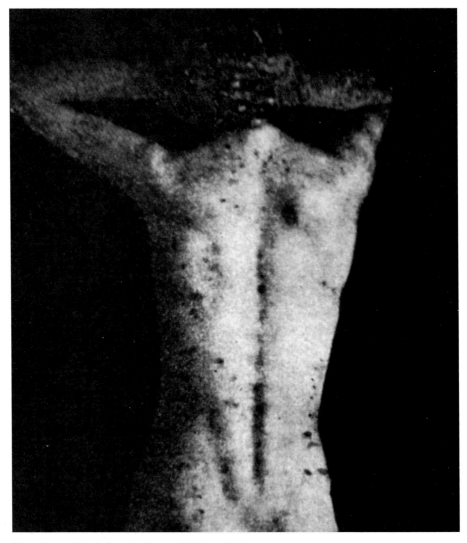

The effects of lice infestation from a 1917 medical report

is a matter of national importance ... and it merits the attention of every physician and pathologist who has the opportunity of working among the troops.'[18]

Specific cures, such as the quinine used to treat malaria, proved ineffective so doctors turned their attention to attempts to prevent it by eliminating the parasitic cause. In the Department of Government Circular Memorandum No. 16, the War Office published a list of recommendations designed to minimise louse infestation. In theory, men were to be stripped and their clothing rigorously examined at least weekly, but, as the *Official History of the War – Medical Services* admitted, 'adequate routine medical inspection of healthy troops was an impossibility'.[19] The army also established divisional baths, the aim being to wash every man at least once every two weeks and a visit to an army bath house left vivid impressions:

> We queued up to enter, and in the first compartment we rapidly undressed, throwing our underclothes into large wooden crates. We bundled our tunics, trousers, puttees and boots and handed them through a trapdoor into another compartment. Naked, we passed into the bath section, which had a concrete floor with a drain in the centre and overhead a number of one inch diameter pipes with holes drilled in them.[20]

Twenty or thirty men at a time would scrub frantically under a thin stream of lukewarm water, but were seldom allowed the luxury of a full wash before the little hot water available ran out. They would then find new underclothes waiting for them – often dirtier than those they had just discarded – and would have their uniforms returned with the lice eggs still nestled in the seams. Insecticide began to appear only in the last year of the war and so seriously was the potential threat of a trench fever outbreak in Britain taken that elaborate disinfestation stations were established at Boulogne, Calais, Rouen, Le Havre, Dunkirk and Dieppe where men were stripped and had their kit thoroughly disinfested.[21]

After their first introduction to the irritations of life on the Western Front, the draft turned to the other great discomfort – how to cope with the burden they had to carry. They had arrived laden with equipment. To what they had brought from Britain had been added various other items at Étaples, including a groundsheet and cape, gas mask, a sandbag from which to make a helmet cover and various other bits of kit. They had also been given 120 rounds of SAA or small arms ammunition. 'This personal possession of such a large quantity of ammo excited us,' wrote one:

> we were used to having SAA doled out to us by our sergeants as we lay in the firing position on the firing ranges, where there had always been the strictest discipline. There, every round had to be accounted for but now, we all had 120 rounds, and so, as soon as the train moved well away from Etaples, there was some rather reckless firing by some of the boys at various objects in the fields or at doors of farm buildings.[22]

By the time they reached their units, the new arrivals were carrying around 100lb (45kg) of clothing and equipment and working out what would be needed on a tour of front-line duty was a daunting task. The more experienced soldiers offered advice on what would be useful and what should be left behind, but it would still be a formidable load to take forward into the trenches when the time came.

The system in operation was that each company would take its turn in a front-line trench for a period (usually a matter of days) before handing over and withdrawing to support trenches where they would be held in reserve in case of an attack. From there they would withdraw into what was optimistically called 'rest' but which usually consisted of fatigues and training that left little time for any real relaxation. For each of the new arrivals preparing to go forward for the first time, the procedure would be very similar. At dusk they would parade and make ready to move up the line when darkness fell. The first journey to the trenches was one that no soldier ever forgot, the final leg of his journey from a civilian child to real soldier. One man remembered it as 'an eerie and unforgettable experience' as he set out in darkness lit only by flares and distant explosions.

By day the Western Front was relatively quiet, but as darkness fell the trenches came to life with patrols and working parties climbing out into no-man's-land and ration parties, reliefs and signallers filling the communications trenches as they worked their way to the front lines or repaired damaged trenches and telephone lines. In the rear areas, convoys of supplies, artillery and other traffic filled the roads. For Frederick Hodges, heading for the trenches in another sector at about this time, the moment he realised he was now at war came when a friend's rifle was struck by a passing artillery limber and broken:

> We lads were shocked to see a rifle broken; in England an incident like this would have been the subject of an official enquiry. It would probably have resulted in

British troops 'chatting' – the endless battle against lice.

punishment, but here, in a forward area, Corporal Hobson merely said, 'Don't worry lad, you can easily get another rifle when we get to the trenches!'[23]

Still some distance behind the lines, the men going forward entered the communication trenches running at right angles to the reserve and fire trenches at the front. Attempts to organise traffic control by designating some as leading to and others as returning from the front helped a little, but as trenches were hit by shell fire or flooded, it frequently became a scramble for men to move forward against the flow of stretcher bearers, ration parties and others all trying to make their way back. It was a disorienting place:

> [T]he trenches are a veritable wonderland. From a road swept by shellfire, and showing the sort of desolation it might have done the day after the Flood, you enter the communication trenches and commence the most remarkable tour it is possible to imagine. Winding in and out, twisting and turning like round the edges of a jigsaw puzzle, you walk on and on through trench after trench, and seem to be going miles and miles ahead, when in reality you may have advanced only a few hundred yards.[24]

Along trenches named after streets back home, the men stumbled and slid forward until they reached their home for the next few days – the front line.

British doctrine always regarded trenches as temporary positions and discouraged the men from making them too comfortable. They were to be used as the starting point of attacks and not to be seen as 'home'. In sharp contrast, the French and Germans settled into defensive wars, creating huge, deep dugouts capable of housing entire platoons in conditions British soldiers considered palatial. Accounts of the capture of German trenches are filled with stories of wood-panelled dugouts filled with chairs, tables and beds far below ground and almost impervious to shelling in which the Germans could win simply by letting the Allies wear themselves out in repeated failed attacks. By contrast, in the British trenches, four men might be forced to share a dugout measuring just 9ft x 4ft x 2ft 6in carved into the wall of the trench and even company HQs might only measure 12ft x 5ft. In such cramped conditions, it is scarcely surprising that for every man who served there, the abiding memory of front-line trenches was the smell. Outside, putrefying human and animal flesh, rotting vegetation, the chemical stink of old gas and high explosives and the stench of latrines mingled with the smell of newly turned earth and flowers blooming in no-man's-land. In the dugouts, smoke from wood fires, candles and cigarettes mixed with the powerful odour of unwashed bodies. Men brewed strong tea made from chlorinated water brought forward in old – and often uncleaned – petrol tins over cans containing a mix marked 'Tommy's Cooker' whose peculiar aroma added to the funk. As one man put it, 'those famous roses of Picardy seemed a long way away, and probably stank'.[25] Alongside the stench came other irritations. In summer, flies were everywhere, attracted by the decay and corruption all around. Rats feasted on the living and dead alike and plagued men by eating any rations left unattended. Even men from British slums, for whom rats were a familiar domestic annoyance, became fixated with the sport of rat killing after a while. Gas attacks were sometimes welcomed: for the most part, they caused few serious casualties among the men but helped reduce the vermin.

For many new arrivals, it was the mundanity of trench life that came as the greatest shock. This was the time of the 'empty battlefield' when men could spend several tours in the front lines within hailing distance of the enemy without once seeing a live German, only the shattered terrain of no-man's-land between the two forces. 'I was surprised at the peacefulness of the scene,' wrote one:

> Everything was very quiet in the sunlight, and it was difficult to believe that this was the actual frontier between two great nations locked in the greatest war in history! … It seemed almost incredible that the enemy was only a few score yards away. I don't know what I had vaguely imagined it would be like – attacks, bayonet-charges, constant rifle fire, hand-to-hand fighting, shouting, excitement? Probably I had had no very definite picture in my mind. But this silence! … The general atmosphere seemed to be one of bored indifference.[26]

Unofficial truces were a frequent occurrence as both sides chose to live and let live. From time to time token firing would take place, but it was not unknown for either side to warn its counterparts first so that no real harm was done. Even in areas where both sides were willing to fight, daytime was usually quiet. Eager newcomers were warned about upsetting the peace and it seemed to some that the dangers of the front had been vastly overrated.

Far from cowering under constant fire, life in the trenches was, for the most part, monotonous. While nervous newcomers slowly adapted, old hands looked for ways to relieve the boredom:

> During dusk stand to I was fooling about behind the trench where I found a dump of German stick bombs, close to where a hole in the ground acted as a ventilator to our dugout. I was prompted to perpetrate a little joke, and later, when Johnny Teague entered the dugout to talk to Ewing, I unscrewed the canister of the bomb, removed the detonator, then pulled the fuse and dropped the stick just inside the ventilator shaft. With a fizz the fuse burnt for five seconds, growing louder and ending in a sharp dull spurt … Putting my ear to the hole I heard Ewing say 'Good God! That was a near one!' 'Blinking good job it was a dud,' replied Johnny, whereupon I chuckled hugely and prepared half a dozen more. I waited a few minutes until they settled down, then I dropped them in rapid succession. There

was a faint groan from Ewing and I heard Johnny say in a puzzled tone, 'They can't all be duds.' Then I pictured Ewing's horrified face as he yelled 'They're GAS! Can ye no smell them?' I heard the rustle of their gas masks and thought it was time to end the comedy, so I jumped into the trench just in time to meet them as they rushed out to warn the company … I was quite at a loss as to how I should persuade them to unmask when Chalk came along and stared in blank amazement at the sight of the masked figures. 'Are the officers testing their masks sir?' He asked, 'because I wanted to speak to the captain if I might.'[27]

A favourite pastime for all ranks, and for both old and new men alike, was the gathering of mementos. As one veteran put it, 'those in the battle-line were very swift in the pursuit of the so-called souvenir'. Every opportunity was taken. One officer wrote:

yesterday broke very misty and, as I went along the reserve trench where I live, it occurred to me that the enemy could not see me. So I climbed into the field, which consists of shell holes, and had a look round … along by the high banks of the trenches thousands of tins are lying, bully beef, jam, soup, cigarette, sausage etc. Bits of iron and bits of shells are everywhere, and here and there are the conical fuses, our own and the enemy's since this ground was once in German hands. Well I collected some fuses and went off across the top to my men. I told them that the misty day would give us good opportunities for finding new gun emplacements, and that they were to clean all the guns, and not to go a-souvenir-ing on top. Then I went off and souvenired all day.[28]

Souvenirs could take many forms: for some they were proof of having been there, for others they were trophies. Some collected for personal interest, some for the lucrative trade in battlefield relics among rear area troops. Sometimes the dead were robbed by necessity. Rations, ammunition, boots (German officer jackboots were highly prized in the mud of the trenches) and other useful military items were taken from British and German dead alike under official orders to retrieve as much 'salvage' as possible. One man sent home the shoulder titles of a British soldier killed 'in a famous action' as a way of linking himself to that piece of history. Others collected out of professional interest. The father of one officer received a parcel of his son's latest collection: 'I've got some more things for you: a ball bomb, a light friction bomb, nose cap of a 77-millimetre field gun shell, aluminium, and a complete 77-millimetre shell.' A short description of each followed with the confident claim that '[t]hey can't possibly go off'.[29] But some did. Sometimes they killed the collector in the fields where they lay; others went off later, in billets or even back at home, because over familiarity at the front led to unrealistic assessments of the risk involved.

Apart from rare opportunities for daytime 'souveniring' and taking turns at two-hour 'sentry-go', there was little that could be done in daylight without attracting enemy fire and so it became a largely nocturnal war. As dusk fell, every man put on his equipment for 'stand-to'. Last light was a good time to attack, allowing men to move forward in the failing light while the coming darkness would hamper any attempt to reinforce the defenders. It was after darkness had fallen that the trenches came alive. Repairs and general maintenance took up a great deal of time and effort, along with seemingly endless wiring parties out into no-man's-land to replace damaged sections of the wire. Faces were blackened with soot or mud and balaclavas replaced steel helmets since the sound of even a breeze blowing over the rim of a helmet echoed inside it and could mask the tell-tale approach of a shell or enemy patrol. Men wore gloves and wrapped mallets in hessian sacking to muffle the sound of hammering the picket posts that supported the wire. Both sides needed to go out and check the wire and frequently British and German work parties encountered one another in the darkness. Stories abounded of each borrowing tools from the other but, for the most part, both kept a wary distance and bombers would accompany a wiring party as protection against enemy patrols.

British doctrine called for the domination of no-man's-land and patrols were constantly sent out. Small, two- or three-man 'listening posts' were established in specific shell holes, their task to lie silently and listen for any sounds of movement by the enemy as an advanced warning for sentries in the trenches. Other men would be detailed for patrols which:

> used to crawl out into No Man's Land in a V-formation, each man close enough to be able to touch the legs of the man in front. We communicated solely by signals. If the Germans sent up flares we had to freeze. We were armed only

A group of volunteers for the 'Trench Fever' experiments.

with our bayonets which were wrapped in sacking or in a sock so as not to catch the light.[30]

Tasked with keeping trench maps up to date, the scout (Intelligence) section commander would be required to send out raiding parties to test German responses and to capture any documents, prisoners or even insignia from the dead that might help build a picture of the forces ranged against them. Men going out on patrol left all badges, identification and personal items behind in case they, too, provided the enemy with the same sort of information.

In some battalions, specialist raiding parties were formed from the unit's best men. Excused fatigues and given various incentives, these raiding teams became star players in the low-key battle for dominance over no-man's-land. Other units used raiding to 'blood' new arrivals:

They never asked for volunteers, they'd say, 'You, you, you and you', and you suddenly found yourself in a raiding party. They went over at night, in silence, and the parties always arranged in the same way. Number one was the rifleman, who carried a rifle, a bayonet and fifty rounds of ammunition and nothing else. The next man was a grenade thrower and he carried a haversack full of Mills hand bombs. The next man was also a bomb thrower, he helped the first man replace his stock when it was exhausted. And the last man was a rifle and bayonet man … The idea was to crawl under the German wire and jump into their front-line trench. Then you'd dispose of whoever was holding it, by bayonet if possible, without making any noise, or by clubbing over the head with the butt. Once you'd established yourself in a trench you'd wend your way round each bay. A rifleman would go first, and he'd stop at the next bay … The bomb-thrower would then throw a grenade towards the next bay, and when that exploded the rifleman who was leading would dash into the trench and dispose of any occupants … But the raiding parties were rarely successful because by the time we got half way across no-man's land and come up against the Jerry wire, the Germans had usually realised something was going on and opened up their machine guns on that area. So we'd have to scuttle back to our own lines before we all got killed.[31]

Even when successful, live prisoners could slow the group's return to their own trenches, especially if they had been hit over the head with a cosh or wounded by a bayonet. 'So if it were impossible to get a wounded enemy back without danger to oneself, he had to be stripped of his badges. To do that quickly and silently, it might be necessary first to cut his throat or beat in his skull.'[32]

Behind the lines, ration parties were sent back down the communications trenches to collect the next day's supplies. Carrying only their gas masks and rifles, the ration party placed the next day's rations into sandbags for the trip up the line so that men complained that the meat and bacon arrived 'so hairy it needed a shave' and in wet weather tea and sugar arrived as a sodden lump. 'The meals in the trenches,' one Halifax man wrote:

> consist of bacon, biscuits and tea for breakfast; meat and potatoes for dinner, and biscuits, cheese, and tea for tea. Bread is a rarity ... All sorts of dishes prevail – bacon and fried cheese; meat, potatoes and onions, tea containing broken biscuits, then there is what has been truly named 'trench pudding'. This consists of broken biscuit, boiled in water until reduced to a pulp, with the addition of jam, and it is very good. The food is excellent, but living in the trenches reminds me very forcibly of the old saying: 'God sends the food, but the devil sends the cooks.'[33]

Despite the standard complaints about army food, many men actually enjoyed the bully beef, biscuits and especially Macanochie's M and V (meat and vegetable stew) – 'God help any ration carrier who lost a parcel of that in the mud!'[34] In addition, when in the front line, men received 1oz of pea soup powder and a 1oz OXO cube per day, along with emergency rations of biscuit and beef to be used only when ordered. Rations were intended to provide 4,000 calories a day and were supplemented with food parcels from home along with, from time to time, special treats purchased by officers for the men of their platoon. It was common for men to actually gain weight whilst on active service. John Burnett, in his social history of diet, claimed that 'for millions of soldiers and civilians wartime rations represented a higher standard of feeding than they had ever known before'.[35]

Food was usually plentiful, if not thrilling, but it was thirst that made trench life most uncomfortable. Water parties carried old petrol tins filled from wells far behind the lines, but fresh clean water would always remain scarce at the front. Five or six men might need to share a mess tin full of tepid water for washing but despite water filled craters all around them, water supplies at the front were likely to be contaminated by bodies or by chemical residue from explosives and gas that made it toxic. Clambering back along narrow communication trenches with heavy and cumbersome loads, men were tempted to climb out of the trench and walk along the parapet instead. With so many men above ground at night, pre-registered machine-gun fire periodically swept areas men were likely to be and flares suddenly burst overhead. The newcomers learned to react by freezing rather than dropping into cover because movement would be spotted first.

In the trenches themselves, sentry duty sapped even the strongest men. The trick was to place the point of the bayonet under his chin so that if he began to fall asleep, a sharp stab would wake him and men with small scars under their chins were a common sight. Sleeping on sentry risked losing men unnecessarily to enemy raiders and was an offence punishable by death, but of 449 men court-martialled for the offence during the war, only two men (in Mesopotamia) were actually executed. No executions for this offence took place on the Western Front, where officers knew only too well how exhausted their men were. It was common for an officer to ensure he made enough noise during his rounds to alert men of his arrival. Staring out into the darkness for two hours at a time made men start to see movement everywhere as tree stumps or fence posts seemed to jump at the edge of their vision. New men, unsure what to expect, fired at imaginary patrols, triggering volleys of fire that rippled along the line and even artillery. Describing the experience of newly arrived Americans, Theodore Roosevelt noted that the biggest fear for most was a gas attack:

> The result was that everyone was thoroughly apprehensive of gas and afraid he would not be able to detect it. We had all sorts of nice little appliances in the trenches to give the alarm. They consisted of bells, gongs. Klaxon horns, and beautiful rockets that burst in a green flare. A nervous sentry would be pacing to and fro. It would be wet and lonely and he would think of what unpleasant things he had been told happened to the men who were gassed. A shell would burst near him. 'By George, that smells queer,' he would think. He would sniff again. 'No question about it, that must be gas!' and blam! would go the gas alarm. Then from one end of the line to the other gongs and horns would sound and green rockets would streak across the sky and platoon after platoon would wearily encase itself in gas masks. One night I stood in the reserve position and watched a celebration of this sort. It looked and sounded like a witches' sabbath.[36]

As dawn approached, the order to stand to would be given. Again every soldier manned his post ready for any attack. Only when it was fully light could he finally have the chance to have a tot of rum, some tea and whatever breakfast could be rustled up. Weapons were cleaned and checked, feet inspected and any problems reported. Only then could the lucky ones grab some sleep. For officers like Lt Gilbert Hall, though, there was still the paperwork to be completed. Reports of activities overnight, ration returns, stores to be checked and all the other administrative tasks needed to keep their men supplied. Even such tedious routine, though, was danger-ous, especially for new men who had not yet adjusted to the particular dangers of trench life. On 20 June Kenneth Ely Crosland, the only son of his widowed mother, became the first of the draft to be killed in action. The circumstances of his death were not recorded, but records show that both sides significantly stepped up their shelling in this period and it was probably this that killed the 18-year-old son of Amy Crosland from Huddersfield.

From time to time, the routine would be broken by some 'stunt' or other and the KOYLI role in the relatively quiet sector became increasingly aggressive towards the end of June. Raiding parties were a normal part of trench routine, but a week after the draft arrived, 'D' Company of the 5th KOYLI, along with a platoon of

Troops in a communication trench. The problems of trying to navigate a trench like this in darkness and with two-way traffic using it are obvious.

'B' Company, were tasked with a large-scale raid that would take place at 2330 hours on 22 June with support from five tanks of the 10th Tank Company. This was to be the first offensive action for most of the men involved and they found older soldiers happy to pass on advice:

> 'The second bayonet man kills the wounded,' says the bombing-instructor. 'You cannot afford to be encumbered by wounded enemies lying about your feet. Don't be squeamish. The army provides you with a good pair of boots; you know how to use them … Don't go wandering down deep dug-outs in search of spoil or enemies, but if you think there's any Bosche down below, just send them down a few Mills bombs to keep 'em quiet … At this point the Germans come out of the machine-gun nest holding up their hands, and the man with the Lewis gun forgets to take his fingers off the trigger.[37]

Fired up by this kind of advice, on a bright moonlit night the force moved off into Bucquoy, where it ran into stiff resistance and a firefight lasted until around 1.45 a.m. when the infantry broke contact and returned to their lines. No one was reported killed in the action but several were brought back wounded, among them 18-year-old Harry Verity Dennison, the son of widowed Louisa Dennison and a near neighbour of the Gaines family in Leeds. Harry died of his wounds on 4 July, the second member of the draft to die in their first two weeks. The exact purpose of the raid is unclear: the battalion war diary simply notes that 'no identification was obtained'.

Three days later, the brigade was pulled out of the line and sent back to the area around the Chateau de la Haie near Couin to rest and regroup. The next couple of weeks were spent in the luxury of huts:

> the Division not only set to work to train hard, but also to *play hard*. Comfortable billets and glorious summer weather, drill and parades in the morning, sports in the afternoon, performances by the, now famous, 'Pelican Troupe', which played to crowded houses in the evening, all combined to make this rest period one to live in the memory. And with death their constant grim companion in the front line trenches, how men lived and laughed away from them![38]

Sports events every afternoon not only helped let off steam and kept the men fit but also helped cement relationships as section sizes lent themselves to team sports, sections competing against one another to build cohesion.

The time, though, was also spent in intensive training for open warfare. By 1917, tactical doctrine had shifted towards the use of the platoon as the basic fighting formation and gone were the massed company- and battalion-sized attacks of 1914. Then, all sides had more or less assumed that having a large body of men fix bayonets and charge would eventually win the day, but effective use of firepower had

Daytime trench routine was, for the most part, boring.

An artist's impression of a successful raid. Things rarely went so smoothly.

shown that to be wrong. Now the emphasis was far more on a dispersed formation tasked with an objective, but without the usual prescriptions about how to go about the tasks – sometimes referred to as 'tell them what to do, but not how to do it'. This allowed junior officers or even NCOs to take the initiative in organising an attack using the platoon's mix of Lewis gunners, rifle bombers, bombers and bayonet men to best advantage. Fresh from training, the draft were already familiar with battle drills that minimised the need for orders since every man knew what to do in a given situation and this was an opportunity to fully integrate with the older members of the unit and show their skills.[39]

On 13 July, as bets were being taken on the Divisional Gymkhana, the rumours of a move proved to be accurate. For several days there had been speculation about a move to Italy or even to Russia in support of the 'white Russians'. It would be neither.

10

'A dainty breakfast'

'If bread is the staff of life', the joke went, 'then the life of the staff is one long loaf'. For soldiers in the front line, everyone not in the trenches was considered to be having an easy war and the idea that staff officers led a safe life far behind the lines in comfortable chateaux is a staple of Great War mythology. Divisional Headquarters were situated out of artillery range for obvious reasons and based in chateaux because they were the only self-contained buildings large enough to accommodate the myriad departments necessary to maintain a force in the field and to plan operations – close enough to the battle to be able to exercise control, but not so close that it became part of it. As Gordon Corrigan has shown, four lieutenant generals, twelve major generals and eighty-one brigadier generals were killed or died during the war, with another 146 wounded or taken prisoner.[1] Given that a general's job is to direct operations, not to take part in them, an average casualty rate of one per week suggests that whatever generals might be doing, skulking in safety was not their main priority. As the men of the 62nd rested, its divisional headquarters were set to work to prepare for its next move.

At the end of May, Operation Blücher had opened with another massive bombardment and, just as they had against the British, the Germans initially made great progress, reaching the town of Chateau-Thierry on the banks of the Marne within two days, but determined defensive actions by American and French forces prevented the development of the salient between Soissons and Reims. On 15 July, Luddendorf launched an attack with the aim of crossing the Marne, encircling Reims and gaining control of the Marne Valley. If successful, he would be in a position to threaten Paris itself. Two days earlier, Foch had requested the transfer of four British divisions to the Champagne region to counter the growing threat. Haig agreed and ordered General Sir Alexander Godley's XXII Corps of the 15th, 34th, 51st and 62nd Divisions south to join the French reserve. The latter two, both Territorial Force divisions, were to join the French Fourth Army on the Marne.

The 51st (Highland) Division, under Major General G.M. Harper, had arrived in France in 1915 but had been described by Haig as 'practically untrained and very green in all field duties'. Their 'HD' insignia had quickly earned them the nick-name 'Harper's Duds' but, like the 62nd, by 1918 they had become a professional fighting force and the two divisions would bear the brunt of the coming fight.

It says much about the work of the staff that, as the 187th Brigade was enjoying its sports day on 13 July, orders for the move came through and by the afternoon of the following day the brigade had completed a three-hour, 16km route march to entrain at Doullens North railway station while the 185th Brigade waited at Doullens South for its own transport. The movement of a British division was a major undertaking at the best of times; all the more so at such short notice. It would take a single division on the move around five hours to pass any given point, occupying 15 miles of road with each brigade alone taking up around 5,000 yards.[2] To reach its destination, the 62nd Division would require forty trains, of forty trucks each, to move its men. A timetable needed to be established to ensure that the men arrived in the right order, with administrative troops going first to set up billets, provide meals and transport and arrange guides to lead newly arrived troops to where they needed to be. Forty trains needed to be made available and a route around Paris agreed. In the early stages of the war, such an operation might take months of planning. By 1918, staff officers could achieve incredible results in days. At 4.42 p.m. on 14 July, the first train carrying the 187th Infantry set out, with

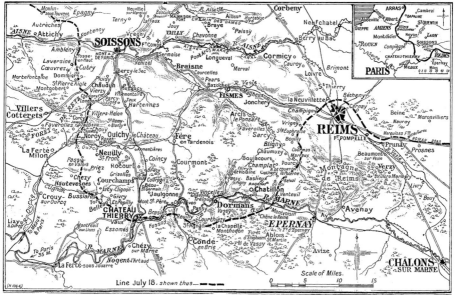

THE SECOND BATTLE OF THE MARNE.

The Marne Front, 1918.

the last elements of the division en route by 6.12 a.m. the next morning. The route would take them in a huge loop via Paris, Melun, Troyes and on to Sommesous south of Chalons-sur-Marne in a thirty-eight-hour, 250-mile journey.

For every soldier of the Great War, the abiding memory was of travelling by 'forty and eight'. A railway truck, it was decreed, could accommodate either forty men or eight horses and it mattered little to French railwaymen which load was put into which truck. As a result, already cramped men often had to find an area of floor that didn't bear evidence of its last occupants. With no toilet facilities, it was a blessing that the journey was usually slow enough for men to hop off, find a convenient bush and then run to catch up with the train a little way down the line – although with a few anxious moments whenever the train picked up speed whilst a man was mid-flow. Seated opposite the open door, the passing landscape seemed almost like a picture show framed by the dark interior of the truck. Far behind the lines, the countryside lit by the July sun, the trip took on the aspects of a tour which 'took us through some of the most beautiful parts of this country and past some historic places'.[3] Arnold Ambler recalled sitting gazing out of the truck during one of the many halts when a passing officer pointed out a landmark in the distance: '"Look, do you know what that is?" I says, "No." He says, "That's the Eiffel Tower." And that's all I saw of it. We kept going.'[4]

As they passed the city, men bought fresh newspapers:

> True, they were in French, but we were anxious to know what was on and he's a
> poor Britisher, indeed, who can't decipher a French newspaper headline, espe-
> cially when it relates to the war. The headlines told us that the expected Boche
> onslaught had begun and that explained much that had hitherto been Greek to us.

Alongside the trains, the men saw 'Union Jacks, generally in company with the tric-olour of France and the Stars and Stripes of USA floated from private houses, and at the few stations we pulled up, there were cries of "Vive les Anglais." Tommy had not been seen hereabouts before, certainly not since 1914, and the people gave him a right joyful welcome.'[5]

The journey, according to the 62nd Division's history, 'raised in all ranks an extraordinary degree of enthusiasm'.[6]

Detraining at Chalons, the men found themselves in the midst of a coalition army. French, American, Italian and Portuguese troops thronged the area making ready for the coming offensive. By truck and route march the brigades moved for-ward, greeted by French peasants bearing gifts of fresh fruit – a stark contrast to their first encounters with local children begging food from them just a few weeks earlier. After some confusion, with 'D' Company of the 2/4th becoming 'delayed' (and certainly not 'lost') on the way, the 187th Brigade reached Aulay-sur-Marne and the French Fourth Army area. As they did so, General Braithwaite visited

French HQ at Mailly-le-Camp to be told that plans had changed. Rather than supporting operations east of Reims, the division was now to move on the following day to the control of the French Fifth Army instead. Orders were issued to divert bus convoys and those men who had already reached billets had to be on the road again by 5 a.m. to reach their concentration areas with, in some cases, marches of up to 30 miles in the summer heat. The 187th Brigade would now be based around Bisseuil and Mareuil and it would take until the afternoon of 18 July for most to reach their correct areas, the last men not arriving until the morning of the 19th. It was fortunate that the weather remained warm and dry because the KOYLI arrived to find no tents available for them. Instead, the tired men simply slept in the open.

After the long journey, there was a chance to rest. On the 18th, the men were allowed to go down to the river to swim. Lieutenant Ralph Fox reported that 'swimming patrols' were established to collect the results of an incident in which 'a Mills bomb dropped into the water amongst Mr Trout and his family'. It caused 'a dull thud and half a dozen dazed and stunned fish floated downstream'. These, he said, provided a 'dainty breakfast for officer and Tommy alike'.[7] If a blind eye might be turned to such matters, a local French colonel protested angrily about the sight of the men swimming naked in view of the women of several of the big houses alongside the river. An order to wear underpants was quickly issued.

Grabbing their chance, troops enjoy a bath in a stream.

The respite was brief. That evening, orders arrived that they were to move forward that night to positions along the river Ardre. The 2/4th KOYLI set out at 10.30 p.m., the 5th a few minutes later on what would become a long, exhausting overnight trek. Neither unit would reach its destination until after 5 a.m., the 5th moving into the Bois de Pourcy, the 2/4th into the village of Sermiers, Brigade HQ setting up at the Ferme d'Écueil just outside the village of Chamery. At 2.45 a.m., new orders required the 185th and 186th Brigades to move at 5 a.m. to positions at St Imoges and Germaine and those two formations set out on yet another route march at short notice as the situation changed yet again.

The final plan was for the British divisions to reinforce the Italian Corps in its push to force the Germans out of the Ardre Valley and link up with the French offensive already under way on the other side of Reims. They would advance for about four miles along the banks of the Ardre with the 51st Division to the south, the 62nd to the north, supported by French troops with the Italians to their right. What was not known at that point was that the Italian Corps, a force of 24,000 men, had suffered over 9,000 casualties that day, and as a result the British would need to go into action immediately without any chance to reconnoitre their objectives first. The British artillery was not yet in position so fire support would have to come from French and Italian guns. At about 7.30 p.m., battalion commanders of the 185th Brigade were summoned to a conference which went on until 8.45 p.m.

Resting during the march.

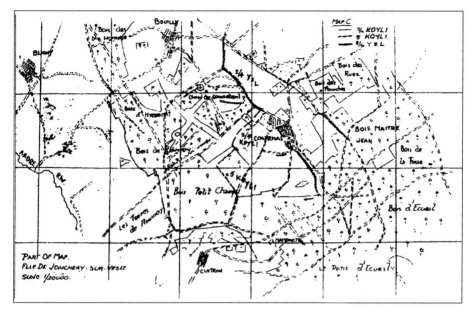

The Battle of Courmas, 20 July. By evening, 2/4th battalion was intermingled with 2/4th Y&L in the sunken road leading to Courmas village.

The units of the 187th Brigade were notified at about 8 p.m. that they would attack enemy positions at 8 a.m. the next day, but the delayed conference meant the units of the 185th Brigade heard slightly later. With the conference ending at 8.45 p.m. and the first units being expected to move at 9.30, there was little time in the fading light to give more than a brief explanation of what was to happen. General Braithwaite had decided to attack on a two-brigade front with the 187th on the right moving along a steep-sided valley through the Bois du Petit Champ and the wooded grounds of the Chateau de Commetreuil outside the village of Courmas. On their left, the 185th Brigade's first objective would be the village of Marfaux. After they reached their objectives, the 186th would pass through them and on to the final objectives between the villages of Bligny and Bouilly. By the time the plan had been finalised, it was too late for any detailed reconnaissance of the ground to be covered. They would need to improvise the details on the way.

Settling into the routine of 'hurry up and wait', the men of the KOYLI now slept and awaited their next set of orders. For Arthur Field, the son of Clifton and Annie Field from the village of Skelmanthorpe near Huddersfield, there were mixed emotions. His elder brother, 21-year-old Joseph, was already missing in action somewhere along the Marne. Several men took the opportunity to write a field postcard home, among them Fred Sutcliffe to his parents in Hebden Bridge. The official field postcard was a set form and was little more than a means of letting family know that one was still alive, but a real letter would have to wait.

Along the Marne front, British troops joined French, Italian and American forces. Here French tanks advance in support of US troops.

A church service before the battle.

Without the need for an officer to censor out any military information, the card could go straight to the Field Post Office and most mail could be delivered within days. Knowing that back home families had often been left without any information about the deaths of loved ones, Fred had agreed with his friend Clement Smith that each would get in touch with the other's mum and dad if need be. The two lads had grown up together and joined up together; their regimental numbers, both in training and in the battalion, were just one digit apart, as if to emphasise how close they were. Nearby, Lieutenant Gilbert Hall spoke quietly to his batman, Tom Rushworth to remind him that he, Hall, had a £5 note in his pocket left over from his last leave. In the event of Hall being killed, he wanted Rushworth to have it on the proviso that he would tell Hall's family that his death had been quick and painless. Like many junior officers, Hall had a genuine affection for his batman and felt that the former Huddersfield weaver looked after him more like a son than an officer. Having enlisted early in the war into the Duke of Wellington's Regiment and transferred to the KOYLI after being wounded, Hall felt Rushworth had done his share and approached the CO to ask if he could be left behind in the 'nucleus' – the small cadre of men kept out of a large attack in order to help reform the battalion if things went wrong. The request was denied. This was to be an all-out attack.

What lay ahead 'could hardly be called warfare in open country', the divisional history records, 'for the attack would, in places, have to go through thick forests … the troops, in moving up to their assembly positions, tramped through almost impenetrable woods'.[8] General Braithwaite would later claim he had seen nothing thicker since the Burma campaign thirty-five years earlier. Trench warfare was, for now, over. For all of them, veteran and newcomer alike, this was to be a very different kind of battle.

11

Stupefying shell fire

On the evening of the 19th, the 2/4th KOYLI was the first battalion of the brigade to move; by 12.20 a.m. the first groups had reached their destination at Écueil Farm, but at 3 a.m. others were still trying to reach the start line, having become lost on the way, angrily blaming their French guides since few in the French Army spoke English and communication depended on the schoolboy French of the British officers. Neither group spoke Italian, making contact with the Italian Corps to their right and the Italian artillery who would be firing in support a complex problem. To the difficulties of managing coalition warfare was added the sheer logistical problem of simply getting the British into position quickly in a night march through thick woods. For all the units moving forward it was, by any standard, a nightmare march. A short distance to their west, Lieutenant H.R. Burrows of 'D' Company, 8th West Yorkshire Regiment, described that night's journey to the assembly points in his personal diary:

> We now reached one of the worst stages of the journey. The track, hitherto quite respectable, now became a mere narrow space between trees, and later on, into a mere nothingness. This thick blackness was everywhere, excepting a faint illumination showing where the tops of the trees were. On and on and we stumbled in single file, colliding with trees and with our neighbours and plunging into deep holes full of sticky mud.

After emerging from one wood, the column found itself on a road leading to a crossroads crammed with dozens of units all making their way forward:

> The scene was awesome. French guides, interpreters, company commanders, vied with each other in apt description of the situation, and present and future state of the responsible authors. The men were feeling too done to comment

much beyond an occasional muttered curse. Again and again a kind of a raid had to be organized in order to rescue one of our men who had been whirled into the running stream of humanity and mules ... Once more we plunged into the horrors of those forest depths and, in the early hours of the morning these dark woods, with their muddy paths and their foul stenches of gas and decaying bodies of horses, began to tell on the energy and spirits of the men. I walked, or rather stumbled along in a kind of mental haze ... in a pestilential blackness with only a hazy moonlight above the trees we stumbled on and on and on, through trees, over trees, into trees. When I could think, it was about our attack at dawn ... There is no energy left for grim jokes or curses, and the only sounds are the sobs of some youngster who found his load of rifle, ammunition, pack, rations, bombs, equipment, one or two panniers and other impedimenta almost too much for his boyish strength ... It was some time before I could realise that my guide was informing me that we had finished the journey.[1]

As dawn approached, the last troops straggled into their allotted assembly areas and immediately dropped to the ground to grab what sleep they could whilst officers and senior NCOs went forward to get their first look at their objectives. Ahead they looked out over a natural amphitheatre nestled among low hills with their objectives

Troops await the signal to advance.

visible in the distance. A long slope covered with standing corn lay before them, surrounded by thick woods, broken here and there by a few hedges and vineyards. To their left was the river and the Bois du Petit Champ, directly ahead the Chateau de Commetreuil and the village of Courmas and beyond the final objectives of Bouilly and the hamlet of Saint-Euphraise-et-Clairizet. The brigade would attack with two battalions – the 5th KOYLI and 2/4th York and Lancaster Regiment (Y&L) with 2/4th KOYLI in support, ready to push through any initial break-through. Facing the British were at least four German divisions (identified later from prisoners taken as including men from the 50th, 86th, 103rd and 123rd Divisions) dug into strong defensive positions who could call on artillery support pre-registered to fire on the open ground in front of them and, as the troops soon learned, into the woods where the British were forming up. There was little they could do but endure the harassing fire. As shells struck the tops of the trees, shrapnel and shell fragments mingled with viciously sharp wood splinters. Even as the British now formed up under cover ready for the start of the assault, German artillery began taking its toll in casualties. Recalling his own experience under bombardment, West Riding gunner P.J. Campbell wrote:

> Then I stopped noticing the crying voices. I was conscious only of my own misery. I lost count of the shells and all count of time. There was no past to remember or

The advance across open ground.

future to think about. Only the present. The present agony of waiting, waiting for the shell that was coming to destroy us, waiting to die ... None of us spoke. I had shut my eyes, I saw nothing. But I could not shut my ears, I heard everything, the screaming of the shells, the screams of pain, the terrifying explosions, the vicious fragments of iron rushing downwards, biting deeply into the earth all round us. I could not move, I had lost all power over my limbs. My heart throbbed, my face was burning, my throat parched.[2]

It was by no means unusual for men, even men hardened in previous battles, to vomit or lose control of their bodily functions under bombardment and many began that day with dark, damp patches. If not during the initial bombardment, then sometime in the next few hours, fear would grip them all. For the young men going into their first real battle, it was often not fear of death that disturbed them, but fear of disgrace. Fear of letting down their friends, their families, their regiment, their country.

In all, the 2/4th KOYLI's forming-up area was under fire for about an hour and a half before they were due to cross the start line. Hidden under the trees, they were spared direct fire but lost a company commander and several men before

French troops advance through heavy undergrowth.

the battle even started. Everyone was now in position. As 8 a.m. approached, they checked their equipment one last time. Across the brigade front, the troops prepared for the signal:

> We stood there in dead silence … and the fellow next to you felt like your best friend, you loved him, although you probably didn't know him a day before. They were both the longest and shortest hours of my life. An infantryman in the front lines feels the coldest, deepest fear. Then it was just five minutes to go – then zero – and all hell let loose. There was our barrage, then the German barrage, and over the top we went. As soon as we [started] the fear and terror left us. You don't look, you see; you don't listen, you hear; your nose is filled with fumes and death and you taste the top of your mouth. You are one with your weapon, the veneer of civilisation has dropped away.[3]

Exactly on time, artillery from the French 120th Division crashed down 1,000 yards ahead of the waiting British and the attacking brigades stood and began to move forward in the bright sunshine. In front of them 'stretched a golden panorama of cornfields – a wonderful sight in the early morning light'.[4] 'Surely', as one officer put it, 'there was no war in this pleasant country'.

But war there was, and no battle can be won without attack:

> The enemy's troops, wherever they may be or whatever they may be doing, are the sole object of our attack … Ground comes into our operations to a very great extent, but it is never the ground that we are attacking, but always the enemy's soldiers, whom we must defeat and drive back wherever we find them. The only way in which we can defeat them and drive them back is to close up to them with the bayonet and compel them to break and run.[5]

Everything in their training had emphasised that. All the hours of bayonet practice had been towards that goal. This was finally the moment when the new draft would put their training to the test.

In 1914, all armies held the fervent belief that massed infantry attacks would win the day and training manuals insisted on the need for aggressive action. 'The main essential to success in battle,' stated a British Army manual of 1914, 'is to close with the enemy, cost what it may'[6] – a view shared in almost identical terms by the equivalent German manual. The French, in particular, considered enemy battle tactics irrelevant, requiring their men to simply fix bayonets and charge the enemy at any opportunity, usually without firing a shot themselves. At Charleroi in August 1914, the elite 2nd Zouaves attempted to stop the equally elite German Imperial Guards by bayonet alone. It cost them almost 700 casualties, but this was regarded as the price to be paid. If the Germans outnumbered the French, it was reasoned, then

British and French troops fought alongside each other in dense undergrowth one officer later compared to the Burmese jungle.

A Brigade HQ in action.

the only option was to attack first and to keep attacking repeatedly. Writing about the French Army of this period, Jean-Norton Cru, a veteran of the Great War, cited fellow veteran Henry Morel-Journel in his *Journal d'un Officier*:

> 'A bayonet charge,' an officer who has led several was telling me, 'is a band of frightened men who rush forward closing their eyes and pressing their weapons against their chests. That goes on for a bit, until a volley makes them crouch or a shell has scattered them or they reach the enemy. The real hand to hand encounter is extremely rare; that one of the two adversaries who has the less confidence in his strength surrenders or runs away several seconds before contact.'[7]

Although the Germans experimented with small-unit tactics as early as 1914, battalion- or company-sized attacks were the norm, with all elements directed by a single commander orchestrating what would happen where.

By 1917, the thinking had changed. Effective control of large formations on the battlefield could no longer be left to a central command. The emphasis now was to be on platoon-scale tactics led by junior officers or NCOs based on clearly defined battle drills that meant that any soldier from any regiment would know what was expected of him in a given situation. The basic tactics to be employed were simple:

A soldier of the 62nd division moving through the Bois de Rheims.

(i)   Push on to the objective at all costs and get in with the Bayonet.

(ii) If held up, obtain superiority of fire and envelop one or both flanks.

(iii) If reinforcing another platoon which is held up, help to obtain superiority of fire and envelop a flank.

(iv) Cooperate with platoons on either flank.

Each section within the platoon was given a role in how this would be achieved:

The section of riflemen should, without halting, gain a position on a flank from which to attack both with fire and with the bayonet.

The section of bombers should, without halting, gain a position on a flank and attack under cover of the bombardment of rifle bombs.

The section of rifle bombers should open a hurricane bombardment on the point of resistance from the nearest cover available.

The section of Lewis gunners should in the first instance open traversing fire on the point of resistance from the nearest cover available. At a later stage it may be desirable to work round a flank.

Camouflaged German troops. Hidden in the thick woods and standing crops, sniper teams like this took a heavy toll amongst the attackers.

Section commanders control and lead their sections, keeping touch with the platoon commander.[8]

Closing with the enemy was the first, and most difficult, problem. To reach the German positions in front of them, the British would first need to cross open country towards an enemy who knew they were coming. In basic training, infantrymen were told about how artillery would be used by comparing the artillery piece and the rifle, although as one manual explained, 'Every endeavour has been made to render the following explanation as simple as possible, but if it is considered too difficult for the recruit to understand, or that it is undesirable, at this stage of his training, to burden his brain with too much detail, it can be omitted'.[9] Statistically, it was argued, artillery was more a psychological weapon than an effective battle winner because of the sheer number of shells needed to cause real casualties – estimates vary from thirty to as many as 1,400 shells for every man killed.[10] Whilst the argument was valid, with hundreds of shells fired for each individual hit, the statistics were small comfort for the average infantryman. If, fatalists argued, there was no shelter from the shell with one's name on it, the real worry came from those many others addressed 'to whom it may concern'. Human nature has evolved the 'fight or flight' reflex, but artillery fire – indirect, impersonal – allowed neither response. In the trenches, especially, both sides had increasingly come to rely on the shock and awe created by enormous barrages as a preliminary to any attack or as a first response by defenders to any movement by the enemy, and all soldiers came to dread the feelings of helplessness that came from being under fire with no way to either escape or to actively fight back.

The gunner, recruits were told, needed to be able to time the shell to burst in exactly the right place to be effective. This would mean not only being able to set the right range and elevation, often without being able to see the fall of shot in order to adjust, but also setting a time fuse so sensitive to barometric pressure that even the smallest difference could significantly alter the point at which the shell burst, meaning that by the time the gunner had ranged properly, an advancing line would have moved on, creating a continuously moving target. The manual confidently advised its readers that it would take between five and fifteen minutes for accurate fire to be brought onto a locality unless the guns had already been registered onto selected targets. The problem for commanders was in crossing the open area in front of the German lines before their artillery support became effective, but at the same time getting the attackers across in organised groups still fit to fight. A sprint would leave them blown and too tired to press home the attack, whilst too slow would leave them vulnerable to the counter barrage. Theorists argued the relative merits of the extended lines so familiar from the opening day of the Somme against 'artillery formation', with scattered groups moving in concert towards the enemy, and about:

A wounded German. Both sides frequently killed prisoners but the wounded were usually cared for.

whether our attack is more likely to be hampered or damaged by the practical certainty of a few men in every part of an extended line being knocked over at intervals by the enemy's shrapnel, or by the extreme probability of ten or twenty men in one section being killed or wounded by a lucky shell here and there.[11]

For the coming attack, the 187th Brigade would deploy in artillery formation.

As they stepped out with their men, KOYLI officers like Gilbert Hall were thinking ahead, breaking down the coming attack into its distinct phases, at the same time knowing that 'the chances of surviving the next battle for us company commanders is four to one against!' First would come the advance to contact that would take them across no-man's-land under artillery fire from German guns attempting to disrupt the attack, but also from Allied guns firing to destroy the German defences and to silence their artillery. The Germans were organised for defence in depth and heavy machine guns positioned further back would be elevated to fire over their own front lines in an interlocking arc to rain their fire down into oval-shaped 'beaten zones'. With an effective range of 2,000 metres and capable of firing up to 3,500, second and even third-line guns could be brought into action this way. Only once they had crossed these beaten zones could the second stage of the Allied attack begin:

The commencement of this stage of the attack is clearly marked by the sound of the enemy's rifle bullets and by the desire on the part of the men to return their fire. The section commanders must now exert every effort to get their men forward, even if only for a hundred yards, without returning the fire. One of the few advantages the defence possesses over the attack is the facility for supplying almost unlimited rifle ammunition to the firing line.[12]

That was when fire discipline became vital. In training, every rifleman had learned how to fire fifteen shots a minute and now each carried 120 rounds of ammunition – enough for eight minutes at that rate – and two bombs. Men with other roles (as scouts, signallers, runners and Lewis gun teams) carried just fifty rounds. Between them, the Lewis gun section carried their own rifle ammunition and thirty loaded drum magazines in haversacks slung across their chests. Each bomber carried five bombs, the rest of the section taking ten each to resupply him with. Rifle bombers carried six bombs each. Flares and other munitions would also be carried, enough for a formidable weight of fire to be brought into action, but not sustained for more than a few minutes, and section commanders needed to guard against running out. Carrying parties would follow up later with supplies, but if the attacking force had managed to cross without taking too many casualties from defending artillery, by the time carrying parties began to make their way forward, they could expect the ground to be under heavy fire. The almost obsessive focus on the bayonet was based on the simple fact that, in the last instant, it might be the only weapon left available to the men going forward. Some historians have argued that, in reality, bayonet combat was rare – an assumption based on the relatively low numbers of bayonet wounds treated by medical staff. Historian and Second World War veteran John Laffin suggested otherwise:

> I think surgeons may be mistaken in their assumption that few wounds are made with the bayonet. Such an assumption ignores the frequent and early fatality of bayonet wounds: a man with a bayonet wound in the throat, stomach or chest does not live long enough to reach the surgeon. Again a bayonet wound is often a secondary one. That is, soldiers attacking forward after firing at an enemy often kill with the bayonet disabled troops who are nevertheless still firing their rifles or machine-guns. I can only say from experience … that bayonet fighting occurs more frequently than surgeons believe, although few soldiers would engage in it if they still had a bullet in their firearms.[13]

Every man needed to be able to make his shots count and that meant holding his fire for as long as possible as the sections deployed. In order to make the best use of the firepower available to them, every section needed to be able to work together to concentrate their fire at the same time. Once in position, the men would open with a fierce volley of all weapons to try to gain fire superiority over the defenders. Usually, this would lead to an equally fierce response followed by a slackening of the firing by both sides as the initial shock wore off, then by bursts from one side, then the other. It was up to the platoon commander to judge the level of fire coming from the defenders so that when he felt that their response was slackening (because of casualties or weapons failures, for example), he would order the riflemen into the final assault as the Lewis gunners and rifle bombers kept up covering fire. If the attack was successful, it would be necessary to regroup and make ready to defend against a possible counter-attack, and to be aware of what was happening to the platoons to either side and be prepared to assist them if necessary. After that, there would be the need to start to clear the wood …

At 8.10 a.m., a heavy enemy counter barrage fell. Experienced men noted the different types: 'coal boxes' or 'Jack Johnsons' (named after a famous African-American boxer) were high explosive shells that detonated in a cloud of black smoke; a 'whizz-bang' or a 'pip-squeak' came from a 77mm gun, often fired at such close range that the screech of the shell's arrival coincided with the explosion and, most feared of all in the open space, 'woolly bears' exploded 20ft in the air to blast 270 balls of shrapnel and thousands of shell splinters down into the advancing troops. The effects were both terrifying and random. A woolly bear

Troops of 5th KOYLI search captured German trenches about 22 July.

might explode directly above a group and harm no one or it might kill them all. A single shrapnel ball might hit just one man in a group crowded together or hundreds might riddle him, missing the others entirely. High explosives might turn a man into unidentifiable 'pink mist' whilst blast waves might leave another body completely intact but the internal organs smashed to jelly. A man could be left unharmed when the men either side of him were torn to shreds. As the men move forward, 'timed shells fall from the sky and explosives rise from the earth. They form a terrifying curtain that separates us from the world, separates us from the past and the future'.[14]

In front of the village of Courmas, 'D' Company of the Y&L were hit by a devastating barrage but their advance continued steadily and the village was taken before 'C' and 'D' Companies went on to reach the edge of the chateau's woods. 'The Chateau seemed to belch fire from every quarter,' the divisional history records, 'and to avoid being hung up and possibly endangering the flank of the left battalion [the 5th KOYLI], the two Companies of Hallamshires passed on towards Bouilly, which they cleared of the enemy, capturing several machine guns and twenty prisoners, including one officer.'[15] To their left, the 5th KOYLI also made good progress. Once across the open ground, the infantry became increasingly safe from enemy artillery fire since the Germans needed to allow a margin for the safety of their own infantry. By then, in theory, British artillery should have disabled the first line of defenders and moved on in a creeping barrage to the next line of objectives. 'Fall shorts' added friendly fire to the risk posed by enemy fire, but once the attackers closed with the defenders the artillery battle was effectively over. This was the start of the infantry battle and when things started to go wrong. Tasked with clearing the Bois du Petit Champ, the 5th Battalion made good progress until the centre company reached the edge of the woods around the Chateau de Commetreuil. Then the German machine guns opened up.

The Allied artillery barrage had only been agreed at 1 a.m. and, because of uncertainty about the positions of troops, had been arranged to allow for the possibility that some French units were in the area. As a result it was targeted 1,000 yards ahead of the 62nd Division's troops, which was to prove a fatal mistake. The men were attacking not one line of defences but a whole series of *points d'appui* – strongpoints surrounded by machine-gun nests hidden in the woods and fields of standing corn. Trained to aim low so as to either hit the enemy's legs or to kill him as he lay down to take cover, the machine guns now cut a swathe through the standing corn. 'Before we knew it,' Arnold Ambler recalled:

> machine guns on the top of the hill were peppering us … The sergeant was yelling 'Get down, get down'. So we got down. My pal was right next to me and he was killed. I was trying to crawl to him to get to him, I got it in the ear … the sergeant hollered, 'get down or you'll be next … he's gone.'[16]

Troops of 8th West Yorkshire return from the fighting in the Bois de Rheims.

All around, machine guns suddenly burst into life, firing into the flanks of the advancing troops, and 'it was very evident that the barrage had affected the enemy not at all, for everywhere his machine guns poured a perpetual hail of bullets into the waves of advancing Yorkshiremen'. And the worst of it was that the guns could not be located; they were very skilfully hidden among the trees and corn. 'It was an invisible foe which we were pitted against,' said an officer of the Battalion. 'And very few of us ever caught sight of a Boche.'[17] Pinned down, another burst swept Ambler's group, one bullet lodging in a can of bully beef in his pack as he began to crawl towards a water-filled ditch nearby. As he reached it, another burst hit him in both arms, breaking one of them. 'First battle,' he said later. 'I never even fired a shot. I never told anybody that but I'm awfully glad that I didn't. I didn't want to kill anybody.' Two and a half years after he first tried to enlist, Arnold's war was over.

Nearby, the rest of the 5th Battalion was in trouble. The artillery formation was effective for an advance under shell fire, but it also concentrated the men into small clumps that made them tempting targets for the machine-gunners and snipers left unscathed by the French barrage passing overhead. As the machine-gunners fired, the attackers were forced into an extended line. On the other side of the wood, the 185th Brigade were also finding the going tough. The commander of 'D' Company found himself pinned down with his company sergeant major and six other men in the shelter of a small stream outside the village of Cuitron when they came under fire from a nearby building. 'On either side we could still see a few unwounded men, the sole remnants of four Companies, carrying on with this unequal struggle against a dozen or so enemy machine guns …' Attempting to outflank the position, the group came under accurate sniper fire, forcing them to take cover in a ditch:

> I crouched in a small pool of water at the corner of the copse, not knowing where my enemies were. I lay 'doggo' in this two feet of water, surrounded by rank undergrowth and rushes, with the hot sun scorching the little of me which was above water. Any slight movement I made was immediately rewarded by a sharp crack from my attentive sniper and a neat little furrow curved along the rim of my shell hole refuge. They suddenly began to shell this corner of the copse. Heavies and gas shells followed each other in quick succession and I became covered with wet, muddy earth and almost choked on poison gas. This nightmare ceased after about twenty minutes.[18]

As the 5th Battalion came under intense and sustained fire, the two platoons on the right had been badly hit from the chateau grounds where Second-Lieutenant P. Moore, advancing with two platoons on a copse west of the village of Courmas, thought the woods were under the control of the 2/4th Y&L. Going forward to make contact, Moore's runner was killed. Gathering ten men, Moore attacked and soon five of his force had been killed and four wounded, as the Germans pulled back with a furious Moore in pursuit. Catching up, he killed the machine-gun crew and turned the weapon on the retreating Germans, firing until the weapon jammed. Collecting all the troops he could find, Moore next pushed on to reach the objective of Bouilly, but his group was too small to hold it and had to withdraw. Meanwhile, tasked with clearing the western edge of the Bois du Petit Champ, the rest of the battalion soon found itself stopped by machine gun and sniper fire. 'In all wood fighting', the 1915 training manual confidently asserted, 'the attackers should have an advantage over the defenders'. The logic was that, unable to observe what was happening on either side, the defenders would become demoralised and quickly surrender whilst the attackers would know that the attack was being pressed home all along the line. Thick woods, it said, would simply not be defended. Unfortunately, the Germans had not read the manual.

The men pushed forward in small groups and reached the Bois du Petit Champ, where one company quickly lost three officers killed and one wounded 'and very few of the company survived'.[19] Contact with the 8th West Yorkshires on their immediate left was soon lost in the thick woods, where, leading a platoon of the West Yorkshires, Lieutenant Burrows found that:

careful direction and keeping of formations soon became impossible. The thick undergrowth, some quite impassable, prevented any intelligent observation. Our own scouts sometimes carefully stalked each other. Then the Boches decided to join in at the game. A machine gun would spit out from some cunningly concealed position. At times an ingenious sniper would fire at us from his fortalice in some tree-top … Though it was quite light, the further we wormed our way into this tangle of wood the more 'nervy' we became … Once we had gone forward only to find a whole crowd of Boche behind us. We changed direction to avoid being cut off. This game of hide and seek continued for hours. The wood was certainly held in strength. The nervous excitement of scrambling through undergrowth, sometimes meeting a terrified Hun popping up from some hole, or sometimes finding oneself in the centre of an amazed group of attacking Germans, was rather wearing. Naturally enough the men were feeling exhausted. We had done our main task, for the edge of the wood had been cleared of enemy machine guns … However, we made another attempt, but only ran into many more Boches. Our next excitement was to run into some French, but fortunately no side suffered casualties. Then we tried a joint effort, but with no better success. The game was no nearer solution. We decided to hold on to the southern edge of the wood, for it was hopeless attempting too much.[20]

About ten minutes and 500 yards behind the 2/4th Y&L, the 2/4th KOYLI began its own advance with 'A' Company on the right, 'C' Company on the left and 'B' Company following behind. The German bombardment had fallen about 100 yards inside the wood where the battalion had been forming up, wounding Second Lieutenant McBeth and leaving Second Lieutenant Maylor in command of 'B' Company. In 'A' Company, Lieutenant Gilbert Hall's men doubled down the hill into the deserted village below 187th Brigade HQ (Hall's biography names this as Sermiers but the adjacent Chamery seems to be the more likely site):

The place was oddly quiet, the silence only broken by the crackle of burning timbers from one or two of the shelled houses and the muffled crunching of broken glass beneath the feet of the advancing infantry. As Gilbert picked his way through the rubble he was faced with an incongruous sight. Lying on the ground in front of him, glaringly conspicuous among the debris, was a magnificent silk Tricolor, bullion edged and bearing in gold embroidery the legend *Sapeurs Pompiers de Sermiers (Marne)*; it was the banner of the local fire brigade … Unthinkingly he reached down and scooped it up, and then, remembering with a sudden start, leaped sideways waiting for the inevitable explosion, convinced that his trophy must be wired to a booby trap. Against all the rules of probability, it was not, and Gilbert glanced sheepishly at his platoon, folded the flag carefully, pushed it into his valise and motioned them forward again.[21]

German POWs carry wounded British troops away from the fighting.

German trenches after the battle.

Pushing forward, 'A' Company soon reached the ridge outside Courmas with the chateau to their left when machine guns opened up on them, too. Caught in the open by enfilade fire was the worst possible situation for them to be in and within seconds around two-thirds of the company were dead or wounded. Recognising that the fire was being directed from a small spinney to the left, Gilbert directed the Lewis gun team onto the target, and a burst of fire silenced the hidden machine gun. A lone German stood, his arms raised in surrender. 'Gilbert looked back at the crumpled khaki figures laying behind him in the trampled grain; "I'm not looking," he said and another burst from the Lewis bowled over the German before he had finished speaking.' The survivors resumed their advance, still under heavy fire, and took cover in the sunken Courmas-Bouilly road. Late in the day, a French company joined them but Gilbert declined the suggestion that his few remaining men should take the chateau by bayonet charge. At the end of the day, the 2/4th's war diary noted that 'the majority of the survivors of "A", "B", "C" Companies were lined up along the Courmas-Bouilly road from Courmas to the cross roads at the N corner of the chateau wood facing the chateau. With them were details of the other two battalions.' That evening, orders were given to reorganise the remaining men ready for a further attack the next day. Gilbert's company had started the day with five officers and 120 men. As they dug in that evening, he had just thirty-nine men, himself included.[22]

Across the brigade front, the boys of the draft began to take stock. In all, eighty-nine men of the 5th Battalion died on the first day of the battle along with forty-nine of the 2/4th, and more succumbed to wounds over the next few days. By the time Arnold Ambler found his way to the main dressing station, his broken arms splinted with tree branches, one in ten of the men he had arrived in France with were dead. In the 5th Battalion, Harry Alderson, whose father was now a prisoner of war in Germany, lay dead somewhere among the corn, as did William Holmes, Charles Beckett, John Davis, George Depledge, George Fox, Arthur Goodings, John Henegan and Joseph Iredale. Of the 2/4th, John Meeking, whose brother Harry had served alongside Jimmy Wiseman and who himself had died with the Canadians, was gone; Clement Smith and Fred Sutcliffe, who had grown up together in Hebden Bridge, enlisted together and who had promised to contact each other's parents if need be, had now also died together. Victor Lister had gone. Arthur Field, whose brother had been missing on the Marne since May, was himself now missing in action, leaving a widowed mother who had now lost her last remaining family. No one had seen him fall and it would be many months before his body was found in the dense undergrowth, whilst his mother continued to search through the Red Cross for any information about him. Many more of the draft lay wounded, some seriously, and somewhere in the chaotic fighting, machine-gun bullets had hit John Carr 'a little above the ankles', leaving 'through and through' gunshot wounds and causing compound fractures that shattered both legs.[23] Perhaps it was some German phrase learned at his grandfather's knee that saved his life when two German soldiers found him. As his friends dug in a short distance away, Carr began the long journey to a German prison camp.

The brigade had reached its objective at Bouilly, but the western half of the Bois du Petit Champ was still in enemy hands and no progress could be made along the line between Marfaux and Cuitron until it was cleared. With no battalion in the brigade now fit to continue the attack, on 21 July the task fell to the divisional pioneers of the 9th Durham Light Infantry but they, too, charged into a 'perfect inferno of machine gun fire' and were halted. General Braithwaite ordered the DLI to be pulled out as soon as possible and for the rest of the 187th Brigade to consolidate their control of the ground they occupied as a new attack was launched by the 5th Duke of Wellington's Regiment of the 186th Brigade, but the initial progress they made was then lost to a counter-attack.

According to the divisional history, during 22 July the 187th Brigade 'spent a comparatively quiet day'. There is no real record of what actually happened as the 2/4th KOYLI held their positions that day, but at some point six men lost their lives, among them newcomers Harry Nutton and Arthur Tidswell, and it was perhaps one of these men that Harold Wiseman went to help. A short time later, Harold's parents received Army Form B104-82 with his name entered by hand and the words 'killed in action' rubber-stamped above a note explaining that details of the burial

Interrogation of a German POW.

would be supplied in due course. It was followed later by a pencilled note from his platoon officer:

> Your son was carrying a wounded chum to the rear of the line when a shell burst near him, killing him instantly. I have lost a good gunner and a noble soldier. He was a good lad, always jolly and never sad. He is missed by all his company and chums.[24]

The rapid turnover of officers and men sometimes meant such letters came from men who barely knew the man involved, but sometimes the sentiments were genuine. In every case, though, the story was the same. The man was hit in the heart or the head and died nobly, killed instantly and painlessly. No one wanted to tell grieving relatives the true version of often sordid deaths on the battlefield. Harold's body was placed in a shell hole and a rifle was stuck into the ground to mark his grave for the body recovery teams who would come along later.

The following day, Cuitron and the western edge of the Bois du Petit Champ finally fell. Divisional reserves were brought up to hold the line and the battered survivors of the KOYLI battalions began to regroup. As always, the end of the battle soon gave way to the 'pursuit of the loot':

> [I]t was those behind, such as the artillerymen and labour corps, who were the authentic human crows … [Passing corpses over a period of days] I got to know the dead … and I watched them daily grow more and more naked as successive waves of souvenir hunters went over them. There was a handsome German some six feet three, very well clothed, and the first time I saw him he was as he had fallen. Then his boots went – he had a good pair of boots. Then his tunic had been taken off. A few days later he was lying in his pants with many parts of the dead body exposed … I came home late one evening and fell in with [an artilleryman] … He was grubbily but methodically examining the corpses of the German machine-gunners and hoping to pick up a revolver. I watched him examine one without success and he gave the dead body a kick. 'The dirty barsted,' said he, as if he were accusing the corpse, 'somebody's bin 'ere before me.' The revolver or automatic pistol was the best prize of the souvenir-hunter. Money was sought, and watches and rings. There is something gruesome in the act of taking a marriage ring or even an ordinary ring from a dead man's hand and then wearing it or giving it to be worn in England. But very few German dead were left with rings, and the Roman Catholics were despoiled of their crosses. The legitimate tokens to take were the brightly coloured numerals from the shoulders of tunic or greatcoat, the officers' helmets (not the saucepans but the Alexander-the-Greats), field-glasses, pocket-books, etc. But the hope of each seeker was the pistol … I was wandering through a shattered and deserted military camp one morning and a questing Major burst upon me. I saluted, but he brushed formality aside.

'Hello, hello,' says he. 'Is it true that your regiment has a special privilege to look for automatic pistols?' ... I looked demure in the presence of such exalted rank and the Major regarded me searchingly ... 'I'm out to give fifty francs for every automatic pistol I can pick up,' said he. And that was a plain hint to me that if I could sell he would buy. He was Major in a regiment impolitely referred to by our haughty Spartans as a 'grabby mob'. There must have been many men who were not as lacking in imagination and impressionableness as the majority who ranged o'er the battlefield seeking for treasures. But I did not myself meet these. Even the best saw nothing in taking away any property which might remain with the dead. Such property was no good to corpses. It was curious what a great number of letters, both British and German, lay on the battlefield. These had been taken out of the pockets and pocket-books of the dead and since they were no use had been thrown to the winds – literally to the winds, for when the wind rose they blew about like dead leaves. There were photographs, too, prints of wife or sweetheart, of mother, or perchance of baby born whilst father was at the war – the priceless, worthless possessions of those whose bodies lay on the altar.[25]

Withdrawn to their start point at the Ferme d'Écueil, the exhausted men passed piles of packs left behind before the assault by friends who would now never reclaim

As the rest of the draft regrouped, Arnold Ambler was put aboard an ambulance train like this for the long journey home.

them. As the survivors of the draft sought news about their mates another, William Barr, a former shuttlemaker and Sunday school regular remembered for his 'quiet disposition', died in hospital of his wounds. After a brief rest, the men would be detailed to sort through the possessions of their dead friends and to salvage whatever they could find a use for.

Most men born in the late Victorian era, and especially those growing up in the crowded towns and cities, had known the death of family and neighbours and seen

Wounded troops await evacuation.

corpses laid out for burial. Grief and mourning had been open and acceptable at home but for soldiers in wartime, it became complicated. 'Men were touchy for a day or two afterwards when a mate was killed,' one man remembered:

> and it was nothing to see a man in a quiet part of the trench having a little weep. If a man did not cry, then often his voice broke down and he would not want to talk to anybody else, then he would perhaps take a quiet five minutes to pull himself together.[26]

After a few times, though, men learned to adapt to the loss:

> Men who you like and with whom you have been close suddenly get struck down. You feel sorry for them and for a fleeting instant you feel their poignant loss. But presently vain regrets are cast aside and one plunges back into the activities of the present; new people take their place and life goes on. It is no matter of callousness. The exigencies of war demand all one's energies.[27]

Within a short time, they were forced to 'become grossly selfish. We think only of … our own skins. It has to be that way. Our hearts would break if we shouldered

British POWs in a German camp. Conditions, especially towards the end of the war when Germany faced a famine, could be extremely harsh.

the burdens of others and let our minds dwell on their agonies and their deaths,'[28] The faith of the religious had been sorely tested and instead a protective shell of black humour formed. When rations were brought up, the first question was always, 'How many to a bun?' but after such heavy losses, there would be plenty of food for everyone that night. Those without appetites were advised to make the most of it – 'it might be your last' – and men teased each other about who would be next. For most, the overwhelming response was of simple resignation. Somewhere out there was the bullet or shell that would kill every single one of them sooner or later. A torpor set in that in the years since has come to be depicted as men going sheep-like to the slaughter. 'And I saw it then, as I see it now,' wrote the poet Siegfried Sassoon:

> a dreadful place, a place of horror and desolation which no imagination could have invented. Also it was a place where a man of strong spirit might know himself utterly powerless against death and destruction, and yet stand up and defy gross darkness and stupefying shell fire, discovering in himself the invincible resistance of an animal or an insect, and an endurance which he might, in after days, forget or disbelieve.[29]

There was, in any case, little time to reflect or to mourn. Platoons were reorganised and lance corporals suddenly found themselves promoted to sergeant and taking command of sections or even platoons because the battle was not over yet.

Progress along the Ardre was being held up by German defences on the high ground south of the river and a joint operation by the 51st and 62nd Divisions was ordered by the Corps Commander to clear the area on 26 July. Aware of how tired their men were, battalion commanders asked for, and were given, a twenty-four-hour postponement. The attack would start at 6 a.m. on the 27th. Unbeknown to the British, the Germans had begun to pull back the night before and so the attack met with less resistance than expected, and by 10 a.m. the 2/4th KOYLI had taken Espilly and Nappes; by 2 p.m. the 5th were in the village of Chaumuzy, where patrols found a single German soldier, left behind with a telephone to report on the British advance. Though regarded as light, the casualty list added two more members of the draft to the list of the dead: Ernest Carter, an only child from Keighley who had joined up with Harold Wiseman, was gone. So too was Ernest Wise from Bridlington. Originally destined for the East Yorkshires, Ernest had missed his draft and had been added to the KOYLI contingent as they prepared to leave back in May. Elsewhere, other elements of the division faced a few more days of fierce fighting on the high ground around the village of Bligny, but the 187th Brigade's part in the Second Battle of the Marne was over. The men could not know it, but the French counter-attack that began on 18 July was the turning point of the war. From now on, the Germans were never again able to mount an offensive as their casualty rates soared. But there was still a long way to go. On the last day of July, the remnants of the 62nd Division boarded trains for the long ride back to Couin.

'It would kill you, or just go …'

As the division returned to its billets to re-form and prepare for the next attack, two of the draft, both wounded on the same day, faced very different journeys. Helped by other 'walking wounded', Arnold Ambler had made his way back to the Regimental Aid Post (RAP) on the first stage of a long journey back to England. The RAP was established as close to the fighting as practical and run by the battalion medical officer with orderlies and stretcher bearers drawn from HQ Company to provide basic first aid to those men able to either make their own way or be carried by a friend to the RAP, where they would be patched up and either returned to the unit if the wound was minor or, if more serious, passed back to an Advanced Dressing Station (ADS). Those who were in need of further treatment were collected by Royal Army Medical Corps stretcher bearers sent out from the ADS and, in busy periods, Collecting Posts and Relay Posts were established to avoid congestion as teams of RAMC stretcher bearers strung out over miles of ground unpassable by motor or horsed transport, shuttled between the posts passing the wounded on to the next team. A 'carry' could be anything up to 4 miles back through the same woods that had caused so many problems such a short time before.

The ADS was run by the divisional Field Ambulance unit with the aim of collecting the sick or wounded from the RAPs and providing sufficient treatment so the men could be returned to their units in the line wherever possible. Although better equipped, they could still only provide limited medical treatment and if the casualty was not fit enough to be returned to his unit he was collected by horse or motor ambulance and taken to the Main Dressing Station (MDS). The MDS had a limited surgical capacity to enable emergency life-saving operations, but its main role was to hold stable casualties for up to a week if they could be returned to duty after that time. If not, they would be passed to a Casualty Clearing Station (CCS). With at least fifty beds and 150 stretchers, a CCS could handle 200 casualties at any one time and included specialist surgical teams, X-ray technicians, dentists, pathologists and nursing staff in large complexes about 20km behind the front. Patients would be sorted to be held for up to four weeks if they could be expected to be fit for duty in that time. If not, they would be sent back by Ambulance Trains or Inland Water Transport to a base hospital.

Base area hospitals were located on or near railway lines to facilitate movement of casualties from the Casualty Clearing Stations on to the Channel ports and were designed to hold up to 400 casualties. The holding capacity was such that a patient could remain there if it appeared he would recover to be returned to his unit or be sent aboard a hospital ship to the UK for either specialist treatment or discharged from the forces, and the evidence shows that in the British sector during a large offensive, the process was so well developed that a man wounded in the morning could be in a hospital in England by nightfall. Arnold's wounds were serious enough for him to be sent home, but the long journey would take a little longer, lasting a week in all before he found himself in the Brighton hospital where he would spend the rest of the war. Having lost two brothers, he was reluctant to have his mother visit but entertained himself by enjoying priority seats at local theatres and half-price treats from patriotic local shops and cafes.

The rest of the war for John Carr, though, was much less comfortable. Both legs broken, he was taken by his German captors and passed through their casualty system, receiving the basic care necessary before being moved to the rear and put on a train to Germany with other wounded prisoners. Fit men taken captive might be put to work close behind the lines, sometimes within artillery range of their own

Troops moving forward towards the Second Battle of Cambrai.

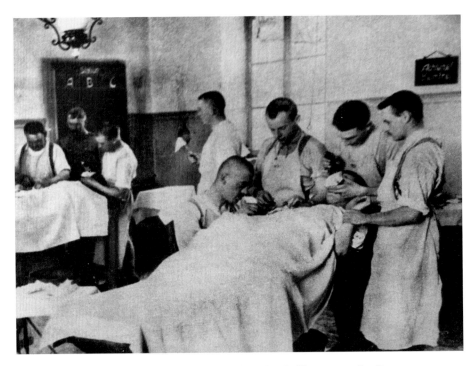

A German surgical team. John Carr was treated in such a facility en route for Germany.

guns in contravention of the Geneva Convention rules. Even this, though, came as a relief, because by 1918 the murder of prisoners by both sides was commonplace. In his memoir *Goodbye to All That*, Robert Graves described stories in which a game was played that involved placing a live hand grenade in the trousers of a prisoner and watching as he frantically tried to retrieve it in the seconds available to him. Stories of men gunning down groups of prisoners appear throughout many veteran accounts, but in general such actions seem to have been only against fit prisoners. Wounded men tended to be treated differently.

Like all prisoners, John Carr was quickly relieved of 'souvenirs', his army-issue clasp knife being among the first items to go. German accounts tend to downplay the extent to which Allied prisoners were relieved of their possessions, but complaints about having rings, watches, money and other personal valuables taken were commonplace. Sometimes they were taken by force, sometimes offered by prisoners hoping to buy their safety. The clasp knife, though, was the object of special attention. From the early days of the war rumours spread that the marlin spike on the knife (used – among other things – for prising stones from horses' hooves) was used by the British to gouge out the eyes of German wounded and the belief continued throughout the war, despite German knives having the same attachment. All the horror stories of German atrocities had been matched by similar claims about the

British and, as the trains carrying prisoners moved further and further from the front lines, anger and bitterness towards the prisoners grew. In the early days of the war, attacks on groups of prisoners by German civilians had been condoned and even encouraged by the authorities, but by 1918 these had become less common as people recognised that their treatment of Allied prisoners would influence how the Allies in turn dealt with captured Germans; ill treatment was nevertheless far from uncommon. Conditions aboard the trains taking prisoners back to Germany were harsh. The same 'forty and eights' were being used and, like those used by the Allies, were switched between different types of cargo. Wounded men sometimes lay among piles of horse manure for days with scarce food and water.

Carr found himself taken first to a *Lazarett* or military hospital for rudimentary treatment to stabilise his wounds and was lucky to avoid amputation – the most simple and common form of treatment provided – before being transferred to a *Mannschaftslager* (a camp for other ranks, as opposed to *Offizierlagers* for officers) outside the small West Prussian town of Czersk on the Danzig-Schneidemuhl railway. Initially built as a camp for Russian prisoners, it had been used to house British troops since 1916, and after four years of war conditions in the camps were becoming worse, especially after the stunning success of the March offensive. From the very

As the British push continued, German POWs began to flood in. These men are awaiting interrogation.

beginning of the war, the German authorities had found themselves confronted with an unexpected influx of prisoners. In September 1914 alone, 125,050 French soldiers and 94,000 Russians were held captive, crowded into forts, hangars, schools, tents and anywhere else they could be held securely. Special camps had been built, but were increasingly overcrowded as the prison population swelled to 1,625,000 in August 1916 and to 2,415,000 by October 1918.[1] Earlier in the war, Carr might have qualified for evacuation to neutral Switzerland or the Netherlands, but by now it was too late. To relieve the pressure on their prison camps, all sides had agreed in 1918 to repatriate older soldiers (over 45), those over 40 with at least three children and those who had been in captivity for at least eighteen months.[2] The rule did not apply to officers but over 200,000 men were eventually exchanged.[3]

According to the Second Hague Convention on the laws of war:

> The Government into whose hands prisoners of war have fallen is charged with their maintenance. In the absence of a special agreement between the belligerents, prisoners of war shall be treated as regards board, lodging, and clothing on the same footing as the troops of the Government who captured them.[4]

By 1918, the naval blockade of German ports was driving the country towards starvation and feeding 2.5 million prisoners proved an almost impossible task. Soup became the almost invariable meal of the day, served with 'KK bread' (from the German *Kleie und Kartoffeln* or bran and potatoes), and was barely enough to sustain the prisoners – but their guards did not fare much better, and the civilian population was itself nearing starvation. Most prisoners relied on food parcels supplied by the Central Prisoners of War Committee (CPWC), working for the Red Cross, or comforts sent from families or local relief committees back home. The CPWC laid down that every British prisoner held in Europe should receive three 10lb parcels dispatched from Britain and 13lb of bread from bakeries in Switzerland per fortnight.[5] Four variants of food parcels were sent containing tins of beef, salmon and herrings as well as bacon, sausage and vegetables, tea, milk, sugar and biscuits, and even cigarettes and soap. From December 1917, the CPWC also arranged delivery of a 'personal parcel' weighing between 3 and 11lb from a prisoner's family and containing a specified list of contents for personal care – boot and metal polish, bootlaces, medal ribbons, dominoes, brushes and razor blades. It is unlikely Carr ever received such a package because although he was released from captivity at the end of November, his name was still included in the December 1918 list of the missing published by the International Red Cross. In theory, every prisoner had the right to write four postcards and two letters (limited to six pages each for officers, and four pages for other ranks), on paper that he had to buy at the camp, but as the war progressed the mail system broke down. As a result, Carr's family would not have known where he was until shortly before he was able to begin the journey home.

The nature of the war had changed by late summer of 1918. Fighting now took place in open fields and built-up areas in fast-moving, open warfare.

An artist's impression of fighting along the Hindenburg Line.

As Ambler and Carr settled into their respective hospitals, Frederick Gaines was recovering from his own wounds. Not severe enough to get him home to England, they were enough to temporarily downgrade him and prevent his going back to the KOYLI. Instead, he was transferred to 48 Prisoner of War Company of the Labour Corps and would spend the remaining months of the war acting as guard and escort for the thousands of prisoners beginning to flood in as the British Army finally broke the trench stalemate and entered the final, bloody offensives of what historians would come to call 'the last 100 days'. Elsewhere, other members of the draft had varying luck in the lottery of treatment. Any wound requiring a man to be away from his unit overnight was enough to classify him as a casualty and, from 1916 on, to qualify for a special 'Wound Stripe'. This was to be worn on the lower left sleeve of the tunic and served both to recognise front-line service and to show new men that wounds were not always fatal, and would not automatically entitle them to go home. By now the draft had acquired a good many such stripes; Willie Landale, the neighbour of Charles Pickering from Tormorden, was wounded in the shoulder and ankle, and was taken back to a hospital in Sunderland for surgery. Charles Pickering himself had been hit in the neck on 26 July but returned to duty with the 2/4th. Harold Smith, known to his friends as Harry and frequently mixed up with the other Harry Smith in the draft, was hit by shell splinters in both legs, back and face, causing damage to his right lower jaw, and he was brought back to Southampton. On 1 August, his leg was amputated and more was taken on 3 November before he could be fitted with a 'Longmate's' artificial leg. By then, most of the draft carried at least one scar.

Earlier in the month of July, Australian troops had taken Hamel in a combined assault that had included tanks and air drops of supplies to keep the men on the ground moving forward. On 8 August Canadian, French and Australian troops had advanced a staggering 8 miles around Amiens, capturing around 27,000 men and 400 guns in what Luddendorf would later call 'the black day of the German Army in the war'. Sensing the Germans were near breaking point, Haig ordered General Byng's Third Army into the attack to maintain the momentum and on 19 August the 187th Brigade set out on a three-day journey to its starting point for an assault to relieve the 2nd Division. After a long trip by bus, they were in position and ready at 9 a.m. on 24 August, when, supported by the tanks of the 9th Battalion of the Tank Corps, the two KOYLI battalions advanced on the village of Mory. As the attack moved forward, German gas shells mixed with high explosives rained down, a lucky hit detonating shells in a British gas dump abandoned during the March retreat. Both sides had used gas widely over the past years as a cheap and effective way of incapacitating large numbers of troops (Captain W.H. Livens, inventor of the Livens Projector used by the British, had 'expressed the ambition of reducing the cost of killing Germans to a paltry sixteen shillings apiece'.[6] Four types of gas were used: lachrymators (tear gas), which caused intense eye irritation but were not lethal; sternutators (sneezing gas) that irritated the nose but were again non-lethal; suffocants such as phosgene and chlorine that affected the lungs and were extremely dangerous; and vesicants like mustard gas that blistered the skin and lungs. As the KOYLI pushed on in the August heat, they loosened their tunics and pushed back their sleeves. When the gas hit, men began to experience first and second-degree burns where mustard gas had landed on bare skin. Soon, large yellow liquid, filled 'blebs' or 'bullae' began to appear, the pus inside spreading contamination when the blisters burst. Respirators saved men from inhaling the gas – which would have led to their drowning in their own bodily fluids as the throat and lungs blistered – but the wounds to the skin forced them to seek medical attention and put them out of action for a few days.

The gas was soon dispersed by a strong breeze, but the main problem was the heavy high explosive shell fire. 'The Germans had been firing time-fused shells set to explode at just above head height, and many men, including two of the officers, were decapitated by these bursts. Percussion fused shells were also bursting on the hard ground and spraying splinters laterally, again causing many casualties.' At about 5 p.m., a German counter-attack began and Lieutenant Gilbert Hall led his men to meet it. After just a few paces:

> an air burst in front of him sent a shell splinter through his throat. He gulped and staggered, but did not fall, and fortunately the fragment had missed both spine and jugular vein. However, shock and loss of blood made him feel sick and dizzy and he was hard put to make it to the advanced dressing station ... From there he was speedily evacuated across the Channel and a few days later was lying in bed in a military hospital in Epsom.[7]

Hall's war was over.

On 27 August, the 62nd Division received orders for another attack, this time restricted to just two companies from each KOYLI battalion, on a sugar factory held by the Germans near Vraucourt. Almost immediately after they crossed the start line, the KOYLI came under heavy fire from machine guns from the appropriately named l'Homme Mort and found themselves pinned down for a time as the units on both flanks halted. Second Lieutenant Fisher managed to get the men moving again and led the assault into German lines, but they were again caught out in the open by machine guns. Company Sergeant John Byram, ignoring his own leg wound, rushed one gun and killed the crew, for which he would later be awarded the Distinguished Conduct Medal, but as a newspaper report at home explained, 'Of the 130 men who started out on the morning of the attack, only 24 returned'.[8] Among the dead was another draft member Joseph Vickers.

New drafts continued to arrive and it says much about the slick system now in place that after just four days the two battalions had been reinforced and were

'Mopping up' after capturing a trench. Bombers would usually deal with dugouts by throwing in grenades bayonet men would then deal with any survivors.

moving back up to the line. There is a tendency to assume that by this stage of the war the ranks were filled with war-weary volunteers and reluctant conscripts waiting only for the end of the war but, with no end in sight, the men arriving at the front could still show high levels of motivation. The newly promoted Lance Corporal Frank Earley, fresh from the KOYLI depot and his first action, wrote to his parents just after Vraucourt:

> It is a strange feeling to me, but a very real one, that every letter now that I write home to you or to the little sisters may be the last that I shall write and you shall read. I do not want you to think that I am depressed; indeed on the contrary, I am very cheerful. But out here, in odd moments, the realisation comes to me how very close death is to us ... Much as I hope to live thro' it all for your sakes and my little sisters, I am quite prepared to give my life, as so many have done before me. All I can do is put myself in God's hands for him to decide.[9]

On 2 September, the two battalions were sent forward to take a section of the infamous Hindenburg Line in a fight that at one stage hinged on Lance Sergeant Johnson holding back the Germans with his stock of bombs and, when they ran out, a supply of German stick bombs abandoned in a nearby trench as the enemy emerged from deep bunkers to attack the rear of the advancing troops. Nineteen-year-old Francis Turbutt Earley's letter had indeed been the last he would write and that his beloved little sisters would read from him. He died of wounds that day. Alongside him, another member of the draft, Huddersfield born John Beaumont was killed in action. Like Earley, Bradford-born Lewis gunner Edmund Walker was taken back to a Casualty Clearing Station where he died, aged 19, on the 5th.

A year after their first fight there, the KOYLI battalions found themselves back near Cambrai where, on 11 September, they joined the Second Battle of Havrincourt. 'The attack on Havrincourt unassisted by tanks and in face of strong opposition,' reported the brigade history, 'was undoubtedly a magnificent performance, carried out as it was by battalions under officered and with few NCOs who had borne the rank longer than 10 days.'[10] For three days, the 187th Brigade pushed forward, losing Cyril Scratcherd and William Fay on the 12th, Arthur Thorpe on the 13th, and on the 14th George Wheatley became the last of the June draft to die in action.

Since 20 July, the two battalions had been involved in four major battles and now needed time to regroup. The rest of September, and into October, would be spent in refitting and integrating the hundreds of reinforcements needed to bring them back up to strength. But in the supposed safety behind the lines, another danger

Victims of a gas attack await evacuation.

A Regimental Aid Post in action. These provided basic triage and first aid for the wounded before moving them back down the line for further treatment.

had emerged. In the spring of 1918, outbreaks of a disease that at first appeared to be nothing more dangerous than the common cold were reported across the world. On the Western Front, men began to complain of *la grippe* causing sore throats, headaches and a loss of appetite but although the illness was highly infectious, and the primitive, crowded conditions made rapid spread inevitable, recovery was swift and doctors at first called it 'three-day fever'. In May, the situation deteriorated rapidly as Glasgow began to report large numbers of influenza cases. This first wave caused illness, and death rates remained normal, but within weeks the illness had spread south, reaching London by June. Suddenly, in September, a second wave sent death rates soaring as the disease erupted all over the world. In the United States, army doctor Dr Roy Grist was working at Camp Devens near Boston:

> These men start with what appears to be an ordinary attack of la grippe or influenza, and when brought to the hospital they very rapidly develop the most vicious type of pneumonia that has ever been seen. Two hours after admission they have the mahogany spots over the cheekbones, and a few hours later you can begin to see cyanosis extending from their ears and spreading all over the face, until it is hard to distinguish the colored men from the white ... It is only a matter of a few hours then until death comes ... It is horrible. One can stand it to see one, two, or 20 men die, but to see these poor devils dropping like flies ... We have been

Back in the UK, rationing had become severe. These children have been sent to collect their coal ration, distributed by army lorries.

averaging 100 deaths per day ... It takes special trains to carry away the dead. For several days there were no coffins.[11]

Officially, it was referred to as Spanish Flu because of the media attention the outbreaks received in Spain, where neutrality had not led to press censorship, but Cyanosis, the blue colouring caused by lack of oxygen, soon gave the disease a new name – the Blue Death. It struck with such devastating speed that someone symptom-free at breakfast could be dead by evening, and over 200,000 people died in Britain alone. Unlike other strains, this flu appeared to strike healthy young people aged 20–30 more than the young or old and, it seemed, those who should have had the strongest immune systems were, unexpectedly, the most vulnerable. Across the battlefields of France, thousands were struck by it, among them Charles Edward Pickering.

In many cases, soldiers in the front line had no access to immediate medical care. One recalled that the men regarded being taken to hospital as a virtual death sentence:

It didn't last long – it would either kill you, or just go. The ones that went into hospital, we were hearing the day afterwards that they'd died. It would kill you in twenty-four hours – two days at most. That's when men started refusing to go into hospital. I know we lost more men from flu, day for day, than we did during the war.[12]

Food queues were commonplace and troops at the front suggested that their rations be cut in order to feed their families at home.

As field ambulances became swamped, units were left to look after their own. One veteran recalled how he became ill one day and the company officer was called: '[T]he major said ... "Fill him up with rum and let him take his chance. He's got Spanish flu".'[13] A strong dose of rum and leaving the man to either recover or die was the only option available in the front lines. When Pickering showed symptoms he was rushed into 29 Casualty Clearing Station, but about a fifth of those infected developed pneumonia or septicaemia which progressed to cyanosis. A letter from nursing staff to his grieving mother explained that Charles had died of pneumonia on 18 October.[14]

Two days after Pickering's death the battalions were practising assaults by two companies on a 1,200-yard frontage – unthinkable in 1914 and even now a measure of how deeply the manpower shortage was biting as the brigade tagged along in the wake of the Third Army. By now Harold Whitmam was the only one of the six boys still serving with the KOYLI when, on 3 November, they were warned to take part in a push to take the village of Orsinval. Just over a third of the 135 men had made it through the last five months. It was clear that the Germans were nearly beaten, but it seemed there was still a long way to go.

Again facing heavy machine-gun fire they waded through the river towards Orsinval, allowing the rear companies to build a makeshift bridge and to spread out for the attack. They had found that by now German infantry were often keen to surrender but machine-gun and artillery crews, working in teams, proved harder to dislodge. American research in the Second World War found evidence that riflemen might not use their weapons even when under attack themselves, so crew served weapons were more effective as gunners and loaders worked together and supported each other. Combat motivation and cohesion was one reason why the machine guns held out longest, but there was another factor. Stories were told of machine-gunners chained to their weapons to prevent them running away, but the simple fact was that infantrymen reserved special hatred for the men who scythed down their friends and few machine-gun crews stood much chance of being taken prisoner. They fought as if their lives depended on it for the simple reason that they probably did.

The battalions remained in action until the morning of 10 November. In its last week of the war, the 187th Brigade had advanced 20 miles in appalling weather conditions, opposed every step of the way. The next morning, 'At 08.30 hours,' the 2/4th War Diary recorded, 'a telephone message was received from Brigade to say that hostilities would cease at 1100 hours'. That day, three 5th Battalion men died of their wounds in hospital.

'What was one going to do next?'

And then it was over.

The decision to end the war at 11 a.m. on 11 November was an aesthetic one. The eleventh hour of the eleventh day of the eleventh month has a ring to it that the negotiators liked but, in fact, the ceasefire had been agreed hours earlier and could have been in place by dawn. At 9.30 a.m. on the eleventh day of the eleventh month of 1918, 40-year-old Private George Edwin Ellison of the 5th Royal Irish Lancers was on the outskirts of the Belgian town of Mons scouting forward to where German soldiers had been reported in a wood. A former coal miner from Leeds, Ellison had survived the trenches for the past four years and now was back at the town where his long war had begun. In five days' time, his only son, James, would be 5 years old and, almost unbelievably after all he had been through, Ellison knew he would soon be going home. Already word had spread that a ceasefire would come into effect at 11 a.m., just ninety minutes away. A single shot rang out and he was dead: the last British soldier to die in action during the Great War. At 10.45 a.m., another 40-year-old soldier, Frenchman Augustin Trébuchon, was taking a message to troops in a position on the River Meuse that soup would be served after the ceasefire. He too was killed by a sniper. At 10.58 a.m., 25-year-old Canadian Private George Lawrence Price had just entered a cottage as the Germans escaped through the back door. As he stepped back out into the street, he was shot and killed. To the south, an American private, Henry Gunther, was killed in the last sixty seconds of the war as he attacked a German position. The Germans were aware of the ceasefire but when the Americans launched one final, futile bayonet charge they had no choice but to open fire or be killed themselves. 'Soldiers may accept a need to be the first to die in a war,' wrote historian Max Hastings, 'but there is often an unseemly scramble to avoid becoming the last.' Inevitably, though, someone must be the last item on the butcher's bill. The attacks that had been launched that morning served no real purpose and as the last minutes approached, gunners along the front fired off their remaining rounds to avoid having to store and return the ammunition. Conscious now that the war was over, most fired blindly into open ground, making no real effort to kill the retreating enemy. At 11 a.m., whistles blew and, all across the Western Front, the firing stopped.

The first thing the men noticed was the sudden silence. After years of listening for the guns, men now listened to birdsong and the sound of the wind. An awed hush fell across no-man's-land. For the men who had yearned for this moment through long months of war, the first few minutes of peace brought an almost overwhelming sense of anti-climax. Some men wanted to keep going, to push the Germans back to Berlin. Some felt cheated of the chance to avenge friends and family. Few men who were in the front line as the news came through remember any wild celebrations, just the calm acceptance of another order to cease fire. There was another, widespread reaction to the end of the war – uncertainty. 'I was sitting at a table,' one young officer explained:

> with a major in the Scots Greys who had a large, old fashioned hunting watch which he put on the table and watched the minutes going round. When 11 o'clock came he shut his watch up and said, 'I wonder what we are all going to do next!' That was very much the feeling of everyone. What was one going to do next? To some of us it was the end of four years, to others three years, to some less. For many of us it was practically the only life we had known … Nearby there was a German machine-gun unit giving our troops a lot of trouble. They kept on firing until practically 11 o'clock. At precisely 11 o'clock an officer stepped out of their position, stood up, lifted his helmet and bowed to the British troops. He then fell in all his men in the front of the trench and marched them off.[1]

Captain L.W. Batten had served with the 1/5th KOYLI earlier in the war and on 11 November was attached to the Machine Gun Corps:

> … the armistice came and the whole show fell flat … and saw the demoralisation of an army without a job! Though the post Somme army was by no means that of June 1916 I am quite sure it would have pushed the Germans back to Berlin if invited to do so and would have voted for doing so had it been asked. It was not the 'men in the trenches' who made or were responsible for the armistice.[2]

The decision to stop was a largely political one. British resources were almost exhausted and fighting to the end would have been costly once the Germans began to defend their homeland, but Lloyd George's bitter dislike of Haig also played a part. Unwilling to allow Haig to be seen as the victor, the Cabinet held back the army to such a degree that even today the resounding success of the British Expeditionary Force in 1918 is barely acknowledged. Like Batten, many Germans believed that the war was stopped by politicians, but their belief turned to anger against the Jews and bankers they held responsible for Germany's surrender. It was a myth reinforced by the fact that no enemy troops marched through Berlin in 1918, only German soldiers with the oak leaf garlands of heroes wound around their helmets, a myth that would feed directly into the ideology that brought Great War veterans like Hitler, Goering and the rest of the Nazi hierarchy to power in the years to come.

As the firing ceased, thoughts inevitably turned to going home but there was still work to be done. This was not the end of the war, it was only an armistice to allow negotiators to work out the terms of the German surrender, and the risk of fighting breaking out again was still very real. The first task was to move into comfortable billets and to rest, but that in itself could be dangerous. Retreating Germans had left booby traps in dugouts and buildings. Gas cylinders had been left under floorboards to leak slowly, poisoning men before the levels of gas became noticeable; delayed action mines had been left under road slabs; trip wires had been placed inside doors where the sudden switch from daylight to gloomy interiors would make them hard to spot. The British fascination for souvenirs had not gone unnoticed. Wine bottles, helmets, pistols and other goodies were rigged to improvised explosive devices and took their toll as rear echelon troops came forward to see the battlefields for themselves and to plunder what they could. Alongside the traps, unexploded munitions had to be cleared to make the area safe and accidents handling supposedly dud shells claimed more lives.

Once the immediate battlefield threats had been dealt with, the next priority was to clear the dead who lay, often for years, where they had fallen. Even if not 'souvenired' of any personal items, flesh, uniforms and papers rotted, leaving little by which to identify the dead. Prior to the war, soldiers had been issued with a single aluminium identity disc bearing their name, rank, religion and regiment to be worn under the uniform on a 42in cord around the neck. The massive expansion of the army in 1914 meant that supplies of aluminium discs could not be maintained and instead a cheaper version made of red/brown vulcanised asbestos fibre was issued. Doubtful of the quality of these discs, many men bought their own identity discs or bracelets to ensure they could be identified if killed. The assumption was that bodies would be recovered and buried quickly enough for only one disc to be needed, but it soon became clear that the recovery of the dead would not be so simple. Following Army Order 287 of September 1916 the British Army followed the French model of now issuing two discs. 'Disc, identity, No 1' was also vulcanised asbestos fibre-coloured green and lozenge-shaped and attached on a cord around the neck and was to remain on a body after death for future identification. 'Disc, identity, No 2' was the original red/brown circular disc attached by a cord to the first disc. This would be removed from the body in order to account for losses on the battlefield. The system was logical, but it assumed that all men would wear the discs as directed. In the KOYLI and other regiments recruiting from mining districts where men were used to tally tags to identify themselves when working underground in case of accidents, it was common for men to attach their identity discs to their braces as they had done at work. Elsewhere, well-meaning burial parties had given the dead temporary graves but had mistakenly removed both tags and an order had to be issued in 1917 to remind them to take only one.

At the start of the war, responsibility for the marking, recording and registration of soldiers' graves rested with each man's own unit and soldiers took care to treat their dead comrades with respect, but as the war dragged on, hundreds of thousands of bodies were scattered across France either unburied or in makeshift graves and cemeteries that had been disturbed by later fighting. Men became accustomed to navigating the trenches by bodies in the walls and floors and, with death omnipresent, had learned to ignore the corpses. Now that the war was over, the time had come to retrieve them and give them a dignified resting place. In late 1914, a Mobile Ambulance Unit provided by the British Red Cross began to undertake the duties of identifying the battlefield dead on a voluntary basis alongside its other duties. As the army medical services expanded, the unit began to focus exclusively on this task. On 29 December 1915 the French Government granted plots of land in perpetuity to the

Crowds outside 10 Downing Street, 11 November 1918.

British Government to act as war cemeteries and a Director of Graves Registration and Enquires (DGR&E) was appointed to work with the French Government for the establishment of suitable sites. Located at Winchester House in London, the office oversaw the work of Deputy Assistant Directors (DADGR&E) assigned to each Field Army. Grave registration in the field fell squarely on the shoulders of the unit chaplains who were responsible for filling out the proper form (AF W3314) with information about each man killed and where his body lay, including map references using the 1/40000 or 1/20000 trench maps or detailed descriptions of localities on the back of the form. Where possible, a Graves Registration Unit would be formed to create cemeteries behind the lines, but these were usually simply a detail from any available unit and, in effect, grave registration fell to whoever happened to find the body.

With the fighting over, Burial Officers, frequently referred to as 'the cold meat specialists' or 'body snatchers', began a concerted effort to clear the battlefields and prepare permanent cemeteries. Men who had faced death many times found the work traumatic and, aware of the effect on the morale of men who may still yet be called upon to resume fighting, details were drawn from volunteers and from Labour Corps units. Attached to a clearing unit between August and November 1918 as he recovered from wounds, one man recalled that:

> [f]or the first week or two I could scarcely endure the experiences we met with, but I gradually became hardened … Often have I picked up the remains of a fine brave man on a shovel. Just a little heap of bones and maggots to be carried to the common burial place. Numerous bodies were found lying submerged in the water in shell holes and mine craters; bodies that seemed quite whole, but which became like huge masses of white, slimy chalk when we handled them. I shuddered as my hands, covered in soft flesh and slime, moved about in search of the disc, and I have had to pull bodies to pieces in order that they should not be buried unknown. It was very painful to have to bury the unknown.[3]

Elsewhere, another recalled that:

> The flesh had gone mainly from the face but the hair had still grown, the beard to some extent. They looked very ragged … and the rats were running out of their chests. The rats were getting out of the rain, of course, because the cloth over the rib cage made quite a nice nest and when you touched a body the rats just poured out of the front … to think that a human being provided a nest for a rat was a pretty dreadful feeling. And when the flesh goes from under a puttee, there is just the bone and if you stand on it, it just squashes.[4]

Given the horror of the task, it is surprising the extraordinary lengths many teams went to in order to try to find ways of identifying bodies. As they were found, remains were put onto cresol-soaked canvas for a careful search for identification. If any uniform remained, pockets were checked and badges and buttons identified. If a Scottish soldier was found, the tartan was recorded. Next they looked for identification discs and personal effects: watches, for example, sometimes had useful inscriptions or handkerchiefs might be initialled. Sometimes knives, forks and spoons that had been placed down the puttees carried the man's name, initials or number. Webbing was checked because that also often had soldiers' names and numbers stencilled on. The remains of officers could sometimes be recognised by their Bedford cord breeches and privately bought army boots and these too might yield some clues through maker's marks and labels. An intact skull or jawbone allowed a dental record of the teeth, fillings or dentures to be made in an effort to confirm the identification of the man. With the best will in the world, though, the task was overwhelming.

Harold Whitwam and the survivors of the draft were spared the nightmare job. Exactly one week after the Armistice, when the agreed pause to allow the Germans to evacuate France had elapsed, the two KOYLI battalions began their long march into Germany as the 62nd Division became the only Territorial division to form part of the Army of Occupation. In pouring rain on the morning of 17 December, the 5th KOYLI finally crossed the German frontier. As they moved east, a steady stream of released British, French and Belgian prisoners of war flowed in the opposite direction. In many German prison camps the guards had simply turned their charges loose and pointed them in the general direction of home. Exhausted, emaciated and ragged, the POWs brought tales of virtual famine among Germany's civilian population, who now watched in silence as British troops marched through their streets. Three days after crossing the border, the 5th KOYLI reached the barracks at Elsen while the 2/4th marched into Vlatten, where they would spend the next few months as part of the newly formed 1st Midland Brigade.

By the time the two battalions reached Germany, eighty-three of the 136 young men who had paraded at Étaples six months earlier were gone. More than one in four were dead; twenty-two were in hospital in England, and twenty-five had been wounded seriously enough that they had not been able to return to their battalions. After 149 days of service in France, only fifty-three had managed to escape serious injury, although many had suffered minor wounds. In December, the International Red Cross issued yet another list of those still missing. Eleven members of the draft remained unaccounted for, mostly from the 20 July attack. Arthur Field, like his brother Joseph, was missing, leaving their mother desperately searching for news. Clement Smith's parents had received the field postcard he had written as he waited to go forward on 19 July and told the local newspaper months later that they still 'cherish the hope' that he was being held prisoner. John Elsworth was making his way home from a prison camp and John Carr was still confined to bed in a German hospital. The rest were, eventually, assumed to be among the dead.

'The heart no greater sorrow knows'

As the new year dawned, men who had volunteered or had been conscripted for the 'Duration of War' reasoned that it was over and that they should be allowed to go home but, with over seven million men in uniform, it was clear that this was going to take time, not least because the war was not actually over. As late as May 1919, orders were issued to the two KOYLI battalions:

SECRET   COPY NO.14

5th BATTALION KING'S OWN YORKSHIRE LIGHT INFANTRY

OPERATION ORDER NO.1

May 30th 1919

Reference Map – Buskirchen

1. If the Peace Negotiations fail, notice of the termination of the Armistice in 72 hours will be given to the Germans. The day on which the Armistice ceases will be called 'J' Day.
2. In the event of this the 1st Midland Brigade will move to the Area East of DUREN with the object of guarding the communications by road and Railway along the DUREN-COLOGNE Line.[1]

Despite the continuing threat, by January 1919 men were being discharged at a rate of 10,000 per day, but this was not fast enough for many and soldier strikes became regular events at base camps in France. Some were spontaneous demonstrations, others part of a co-ordinated campaign by trade unions like the Calais Area

Soldiers' and Sailors' Association to organise protests about working conditions, poor food and slow demobilisation. At Folkestone, thousands of troops returning from leave refused to board ships for France whilst news reached Australia that:

[f]ive thousand members of the Army Service Corps broke camp at Brentford and commandeered four lorries. Part of 300 of them reached London and created a demonstration of a good natured character before the War Office. They protested against the delay at demobilisation. It is understood that the Government has decided that the army service corps shall be demobilised in concurrency with other units. Ten thousand soldiers were being demobilised daily during the past week. It is expected that the figure will soon become 20,000.[2]

Addressing complaints about demobilisation, Lord Milner explained:

Remember that, though the fighting may have ceased, all is not yet over. Impatience and overhaste might yet rob us of all that four long years of unexampled struggle and sacrifice have won. We have yet to make a just, strong and enduring peace. When the representatives of Great Britain go to the Council

British Army on the Rhine. A limited advance into Germany was made to provide a buffer zone in case the peace negotiations failed.

table to negotiate that peace, they must not have a disarmed and disunited nation behind them. If we are all at sixes and sevens at home, if what remains of our Army is not compact, disciplined, orderly, we shall never get the sort of peace, which we justly expect. The world, which is still in many parts seething with disorder, may not settle down for years, or let us get back to normal life and work in safety and tranquillity ... Our guiding principle was to demobilise in the way most likely to lead to the steady resumption of industry, and to minimise the danger of unemployment. Pivotal men first, basic industries like coal mining before those of less vital importance. In each industry those men first, who were assured of immediate employment. Subject to these ruling principles, we want to release the older men, and those of longest service, before the younger ones. That is the general idea. I don't say that it can ever be perfectly executed. Certainly the execution isn't perfect yet. When the huge engine began to move, some defects immediately appeared in the machinery. These are being remedied. Some officials may have been stupid or obstructive. I am afraid, where thousands of people have to co-operate, there will always be a good sprinkling of muddlers. But when all is said and done the big engine is moving. It is moving at a steadily increasing pace.[3]

Clearing the dead. Men of a Graves Registration Unit search a body for identification.

Men were allocated to demobilisation groups, each subdivided into discharge numbers. First to go would be civil servants who would then administer the system, followed by those who would create jobs for others. Next came 'slip men' with chits to prove they had work to go to, followed by those with good prospects of finding jobs. Many men who had chosen to leave work to volunteer in the heady days of 1914 were therefore among the last to be released, leading to even further discontent. For the older men, it would mean a return to the lives they had left behind, but many thousands were 19 years old and had come of age during the war. To them it was the beginning of their adult lives and they would have to start from scratch. For the survivors of the draft, like everyone else, it was a question of waiting.

It had taken several months to turn the boys of the draft into soldiers, but the process of turning them back into civilians was mainly a bureaucratic one. Before each soldier left his unit he was, once more, medically examined and given Army Form Z22, which allowed him to make a claim for any form of disability arising from his military service. At the same time he was given Army Form Z44 (Plain Clothes Form) and a Certificate of Employment showing what he had done in the army. A Dispersal Certificate recorded personal and military information and also the state of his equipment on discharge. If he lost any of it after this point, the value would be deducted from his outstanding pay. Any local currency had to be exchanged at an Army Post Office for a postal order in sterling.

Passing back through an Infantry Base Depot, he would be sent to a Dispersal Centre in England where he received more forms and a railway warrant or ticket to his home station. An Out-of-work Donation Policy was issued, which acted as an insurance against unemployment of up to twenty-six weeks in the year after he was discharged along with an advance of pay, a fortnight's ration book and also a voucher – Army Form Z50 – for the return of his greatcoat to a railway station during his leave. He could choose between being provided with a civilian suit on production of his Form Z44 or a clothing allowance of 52s 6d. In uniform and still holding his greatcoat and helmet, he then began his final leave. Still technically a soldier, he could now wear civilian clothes and could no longer legally wear his uniform twenty-eight days after leaving the Dispersal Centre. During the leave he had to go to a railway station to hand in his greatcoat and would be paid £1 for doing so as part of his war or service gratuity payment, with any other payments due to him sent in three instalments by money orders or postal drafts. As long as the Military Service Act was in force, all men liable for service who were not remaining with the colours in the regular army, had not been permanently discharged or who were not on a Special Reserve or Territorial Force Reserve engagement were discharged into Class Z of the Army Reserve and were liable to recall to a designated base in the event of a national emergency.

Released from hospital, Arnold Ambler celebrated the armistice in London, where he met a girl from Richmond. In January 1919, he was declared fit and discharged

Throughout the war, women volunteers had maintained cemeteries and cared for visiting relatives. These cemeteries began to expand as battlefield clearance operations began.

to the Class Z Reserve. To those awaiting their release, the discharge system seemed arbitrary and unfair. Arnold was one of six members of the draft discharged in January, followed by twelve in February and seven in March. In September:

> a new official order was published which seemed to cover my case, and it was reported … that all 'volunteers' would be demobbed before the end of the month. (Although I had finally entered the army as a conscript, by call up under the Military Service Act in 1917, I officially ranked as a volunteer for demob purposes by reason of my earlier rejections in 1914, 1915 and 1916).[4]

Although hopes were raised, only one member of the draft went home that month. Twenty-four men were released at the end of the year, including Harold Whitwam, who, still with the KOYLI, was finally discharged on 22 November 1919. Wilf Landale, former neighbour of Charles Pickering in Todmorden, waited until March 1920 for his discharge; Tom Hall, the 'immature' from Baildon waited until April. Last of all was Bradford-born Walter Robinson. Discharged in September 1920, Walter had by then served almost three years to Arnold's fifteen months. Not everyone, though, was keen to leave. Frederick Gaines found he enjoyed soldiering.

He took the opportunity to re-enlist and on 15 July 1919 became 88266 Private Gaines of the West Yorkshire Regiment. Several others stayed on, too, four draft veterans later serving in Iraq.

As Arnold Ambler began his discharge leave, a ship carrying wounded ex-prisoners docked at Leith. Taken by train from Czersk to the port of Danzig and then by ship via Denmark, John Carr was finally home. After a short stay at a military hospital in Edinburgh, he moved first to Bradford War Hospital where he was to remain until June, undergoing operations to drain and clean his wounds before being transferred to Royd Halls Hospital in Huddersfield for two months. In August he was moved again to Wharncliffe Hospital in Sheffield where he would remain for almost a year until on 22 July 1920, two years and two days after German bullets smashed his legs on a glorious summer's day, John Carr was discharged from the army, now 'permanently unfit'.

Isolated graves like this were spread across northern France. Many had fallen victim to later shelling and all evidence was lost.

At some point in 1919, like all the next of kin of British and Commonwealth war dead, a stiff cardboard envelope arrived for Ada Pickering. In it was a circular bronze plaque inscribed with her son's name and the words 'He died for freedom and honour' that soon became known as the 'dead man's penny'. A short time later came a cardboard tube containing a printed letter with a copy of the King's signature acknowledging Charles' service. Later still came a postal order for his outstanding wages. Ada had lost her first son aged 7 months in 1897 and her husband in 1901. In 1912 her 21-year-old daughter had died and now her last remaining child was also gone. Taking what comfort she could from the fact that Charles at least had a marked grave, she accepted the offer to add a personal inscription to his standard issue headstone, paying thrupence ha'penny per character to add:

The heart no greater sorrow knows
7, Brook St., Todmorden Yorks.[5]

Like Ada, James and Elizabeth Wiseman received their dead man's penny but could add no inscription. Harold had been killed, that was certain, but somehow his grave had been lost.

The Imperial War Graves Commission (IWGC) had been created on 21 May 1917 with three aims: to locate an estimated 160,000 isolated graves; to concentrate small, scattered cemeteries into larger ones; and to locate and identify the estimated half a million missing. On 18 November 1918 the Adjutant-General hosted a conference on the matter at GHQ and three days later exhumation work to gather in the dead began in the Fifth Army area and was extended to the Third and later First Army areas using volunteers given extra pay of 2s 6d per day. Although the British began to search the Aisne/Marne area for 1914 casualties, no search was completed for victims of the Second Battle of the Marne and responsibility for the whole area was later handed to the French. The sheer physical difficulties of the work were immense, starting with the need to build shelters to house the men and to find the transport and materials they would need to carry out their grim work. As the winter of 1918/19 set in, it typically needed five to six men each working day to exhume each body, transport it to the cemetery and re-inter it. When work resumed on 17 February 1919 after a harsh frost froze the ground, nine men were required per exhumation per day. By March 1919 it was estimated that 12,000 men, rising to 15,000 by May, would be needed but with demobilisation under way, the supply of volunteers began to dry up.[6]

At first, volunteers were men who had fought over these battlefields and who shared a common bond with the dead. The process was painstaking. Based on the records held by the DGR&E, 'body density' maps were created plotting the locations of known burials. A Survey Officer then marked out a 500-yard square to be searched, the body density map showing the Burial Officer the anticipated number of remains to be found. The accuracy of the maps varied. In one case eleven

Makeshift crosses were erected in the short term and, when they were replaced by headstones, the crosses were offered to the next of kin. Few accepted.

bodies were indicated but sixty-seven found. In another, 4 per cent of grave sites marked by crosses were empty. In the end, the IWGC acknowledged that experience was the only effective method of choosing where to dig based on indications on the battlefield:

i. Rifles or stakes protruding from the ground, bearing helmets or equipment;
ii. Partial remains or equipment on the surface or protruding from the ground;
iii. Rat holes – often small bones or pieces of equipment would be brought to the surface by the rats;
iv. Discolouration of grass, earth or water – grass was often a vivid bluish-green with broader blades where bodies were buried, while earth and water turned a greenish black or grey colour.[7]

The Wisemans couldn't afford to do it, but even before the fighting ended, more affluent British civilians had been in France searching for loved ones, sometimes for years. Women volunteers had been working with them to locate graves and arrange visits, but the end of the war had suddenly brought an influx of tourism into an area that had no infrastructure to accommodate them, adding a new dimension to the battlefield clearance work. On 17 April 1917, Australian Private W. Macbeath saw a grim reminder of what his work meant, recording in his diary, 'Working in cemetery. An English lady came over to see her son's grave, found him lying in a bag and fainted.'[8]

Among the troops awaiting discharge, discipline grew worse throughout the armies still in France and the Graves Registration Units were no exception. Often short of the materials and support they needed to do their job, the psychological stress took its toll and sickness rates rocketed. 'Souveniring' continued and the finders of officers' bodies sometimes came away with rewards of cash and valuables, which they saw as one of the few perks of the job. As time went on, men became less motivated to conduct their searches thoroughly, instead just trying to get the work finished as quickly as possible. As less and less care was taken with identification, the IWGC expressed concerns about the efficiency of the way the work was being carried out: 'Exhumation Companies,' it claimed, 'obsessed with the idea that their reputation depended on their concentrating the highest possible number of bodies in the shortest possible time have often paid little or no heed to the essential matter of identification.'[9] The revelation that serious identification errors had been made around Hooge led to an official inquiry at which Australian Major A. Allen accused some British units of 'chopping men in halves in order to double their body returns'.[10]

Finally, on 6 August 1921, the Colonel Commandant DGR&E certified that, with the exception of certain indicated areas, 'the whole of the battlefield areas of France and Belgium have been finally researched for isolated graves, both British and German. It cannot be guaranteed that no graves either with or without surface indication remained in the area ...'[11] By then over 200,000 remains had been concentrated and by the end of October, all the military search teams had returned to England. The 37th meeting of the IWGC on 18 October noted: 'if it was known to the public that bodies were being found at the rate of 200 a week at the time the search parties were disbanded, the public would want an explanation.'[12] Indeed, questions were being asked in parliament, prompting Sir L. Worthington-Evans, Secretary of State for War, to claim that '[s]ince the Armistice the whole battlefield area in France and Flanders has been systematically searched at least six times. Some areas in which the fighting had been particularly heavy, were searched as many as 20 times.'[13] With almost 300,000 men unaccounted for, the public remained sceptical.

Even had the will and the resources remained, the thick woods of the Bois du Petit Champ had regrown. Finding bodies in the tangled undergrowth would have been an almost impossible challenge. If the British Government no longer showed the same interest in identifying the dead, it comes as no surprise to learn that the clearance of the Marne battlefields by French teams had little emotional connection to begin with. The priority for the French was to reclaim the land and

The corpses of thousands of men lay where they had fallen, some for years before they were recovered.

to rebuild their farms. The 2-franc bounty offered for British remains hardly made up for the 7 or 8 francs lost by taking the time to trek to the nearest office to report the find; equally, however, the temptation to add a rusted British helmet to a pile of bones meant that even a man's nationality could be in question. Farmers ploughing up human remains might have been tempted to keep personal items that could have identified the body and simply collected the bones in a sack.

In their brief, ten-day stay on the Marne, between them the two **KOYLI** battalions had lost 203 men. Today, almost a century later, 108 remain unaccounted for, their names carved into the massive Soissons memorial to the missing: among them the two close friends Clement Smith and Fred Sutcliffe, Harold Wiseman and seven more of the young men of the draft.

'Known unto God'

'I'll tell you what will happen to you duration soldiers,' an old sweat explained. 'You'll have the time of your lives, you'll be hugged and kissed, treated and petted, they'll have banners strung out across the streets: "Welcome Home, Our Heroic Tommies." Then some morning they'll wake up and realise the war is over, and that's when you fellows will have to start using your own toilet paper. You'll get the cold shoulder, as they'll have no more use for a penniless, out-of-work fighting man who stinks of trench manners and speech.'[1]

He was soon proved right. In 1920 one journal reported that ex-officers:

are turning their hands to many things. Brigadier-Generals are acting as company cooks to the [Royal Irish Constabulary]. Colonels are hawking vegetables. Majors are travelling in proprietary goods. Captains are renovating derelict 'prams'. And subalterns are seeking anything which will keep them from having to fall back on charity or to beg in the streets.[2]

Men who had enlisted from lowly clerical jobs in 1914 and who had risen through the ranks to become highly decorated officers commanding companies and even battalions by 1918 now found their employers expected them to be grateful to be given their junior office posts back. For the 19-year-old conscripts of the draft, there had been no opportunity before call up to establish themselves in careers; now they found themselves rejected on the basis of having no experience – or rather, as more than one angry applicant explained, too much experience of the wrong kind.

Returning home to Halifax with his new girlfriend, Arnold Ambler moved back into the crowded terrace house and began looking for work. One mill offered him a job working alongside women and at the same substandard rate of pay, but it was not enough for him to save for his planned marriage. Through contacts at her church, his mother found work for him:

> I'm not a machinist, there's no kidding about it, I know I'm not a machinist. She gave me a job in an iron factory and, oh, for God's sakes, it was agony to me. The more I went in there the more madder I got. I said, 'I've got to get out of this somehow. How can I do it?'

Arnold's sister had emigrated to America before the war, but his knowledge of the country was confined to having read *Last of the Mohicans* at school. He decided to give it a try. In 1920 he married Emily Whiting on a Monday and set sail from Liverpool two days later. As his new wife lay suffering seasickness, Arnold sneaked upstairs from steerage class to read books in the second-class lounge until he was asked to leave, his service and his wounds counting for nothing. For the Ambler family, taking American citizenship was a big step and Arnold recalled that when his sister became a naturalised US citizen, 'my mother and father resented things like that, swearing against the flag, that's what it was. Swearing against your king and country.' In time, Arnold and Emily settled in Concord, Massachusetts and had a daughter, who died aged 18. There were no other children, but they remained in contact with nieces and nephews until Arnold died, the last survivor of the draft, in 1992.[3]

After his discharge, John Carr returned to Bradford and went back to work with his father as a printer. On 3 July 1926, he married Dora Graham and the couple settled down to a quiet life. There is no record of them having had children. John died in 1973, Dora in 1993.

Frederick Pease Gaines served his time in a regular battalion of the West Yorkshire Regiment before returning home to Leeds where, in 1923, he found work as a clerk, saving his wages to marry Nellie Devier in 1928. His name appears in local directories in the 1930s as manager of a local hotel but, again, the couple do not appear to have had children. Frederick died in 1953.

Harold Fewdale Whitwam returned home to Huddersfield after his discharge in November 1919 and married Margaret Priestley in 1925. There were no children. Harold died in 1981.

Stanley Wade, another member of the draft, returned to his Baildon home after recovering from his wounds and was discharged in March 1919. Finding work in the local mill, where hot, humid conditions mixed with a dust-laden atmosphere, Stanley became ill and died of tuberculosis at home, attended by his mother, on 1 September 1923. He was 23.[4]

John Edward Bowskill, a neighbour of John Carr in Bradford, was wounded on 20 July and was evacuated to hospital in Rouen, rejoining his unit on 24 August just in time for the September attack on Havrincourt. As he went forward in the attack, John was hit by a bullet in the right buttock, but it was not a simple flesh wound. The round had struck his hip, leaving a wound that kept him in a Sheffield hospital until March 1919. Transferred to the Army Service Corps, he trained as a driver and, after discharge, found work as a Bradford Corporation tram driver. In 1922 he married Blanche Smith and it seemed that he had coped better than most, although his wound still troubled him from time to time. In 1927, he began to suffer a fever, confusion and to hyperventilate. When a bullet is fired, it creates a shock wave in front of it that pulverises flesh before the bullet itself hits home. In its wake, comet-like, it trails the residue of the explosive charge used to fire it, along with any dust, gas or bacteria in the air, which is then sucked into the wound. That had happened to John. Even had antibiotics been available, they would not have been enough. He died, nursed to the last by Blanche, on 23 October 1927, his death certificate recording that he died of septicaemia and 'Gas Gangrene' directly resulting from a shot fired nine years before.[5]

On 26 July 1919, the British Government announced the award of the British War Medal to officers and men of the British and Imperial Forces who either entered a theatre of war or entered service overseas between 5 August 1914 and 11 November 1918 inclusive (later extended to service in Russia, Siberia and some other areas in 1919 and 1920). It was followed in September by the award of the Inter-Allied Victory Medal. Following a decision at the Inter-Allied Peace Conference at Versailles, Belgium, Brazil, Cuba, Czechoslovakia, France, Greece, Italy, Portugal, Romania, Siam, the Union of South Africa, the UK and the US all agreed to adopt a unified medal to commemorate war service, with slight variations for each country. Eligibility was also extended to government contractors and hospital staff as well as those involved in mine clearance operations after the war. Nicknamed 'Mutt and Jeff' after two cartoon characters, the medals did nothing to show what a man had done to earn them. A new recruit disembarking at Boulogne on 10 November 1918 would be entitled to the same medals as a man out since 1916. What really mattered, though, was the 1914 Star (often referred to as the Mons Star) issued in 1917 to all officers, warrant officers, non-commissioned officers and all men of the British and Indian Forces, including civilian medical and nursing staff as well as men of the Royal Navy, Royal Marines and the Naval Reserves who served with their unit in France and Belgium between 5 August 1914 and midnight of 22/23 November 1914. Those not qualifying for the 1914 Star were rewarded in 1918 by the issue of the very similar 1914–15 Star issued to officers and men of British and Imperial forces who served in any theatre of the war between 5 August 1914 and 31 December 1915 if they did not already have the 1914 Star.

The wearing of 'Pip, Squeal and Wilfred', as the War Medal, Victory Medal and either of the Stars were known (after a popular comic strip in the *Daily Mirror*), was an important status symbol. 'A few old soldiers,' notes Richard van Emden:

especially those who missed receiving the '14–15 Star by a matter of days, purchased and took to wearing the medal regardless, thus indicating two things to the casual observer: firstly, the man was a regular, territorial or a volunteer and not a conscript ... For 1914 Kitchener Volunteers, in particular, this was a very important distinction. They had enlisted at the beginning of the war and did not want people to think they had been coerced into serving their country. And secondly, the 1914–15 Star carried the clear implication that the wearer might have served abroad for some considerable time, and had probably seen front line action.[6]

Equally, of course, a man could qualify for the '14–15 Star by working as a clerk at HQ or as a Canary at Étaples whilst those arriving after the qualifying date might well be conscripts but had faced the Somme, Passchendaele, the Spring Offensive and the last hundred days.

The perception of those enlisting after 1916 as 'shirkers' had by now firmly taken root. As memoirs and histories appeared on the bookshelves, the experiences of the Kitchener volunteers were described in detail but the men who followed later remained quiet, to the degree that historian Ian Beckett notes 'it is not without significance that the voluminous canon of published Great War memoir contains but a handful of accounts by conscripts'.[7] So ingrained is the view that the Great War was a war fought primarily by Kitchener volunteers that even the Official History of the war admits 'it would seem that events in the earlier part of the war made greater impression than did later adventures'.[8] In the only study of the conscript experience to date, Ilana Bet-El describes how, when producers of the BBC's seminal documentary series *The Great War* began work in 1963, they sought contributions only from 'those who served on any front up to the end of 1915', reinforcing this later with a prominent advert in the *Radio Times* announcing, 'The BBC invites anyone who served on any front during the First World War, UP TO THE END OF 1915 [original emphasis] to write briefly ...'[9]

On 7 November 1920, four ambulances, each carrying an officer and two men, arrived at cemeteries in the four main battle areas of the British front – the Aisne, the Somme, Arras and Ypres – to each exhume one unidentified body. From those four, one would be selected to be interred at Westminster Abbey as a focus for national mourning and a symbol of all those men still missing in France, and to represent all who had been killed in the service of the British Empire, be they British, Indian or 'dominion'. Privately, though, instructions had been given to ensure that the body was not only British, but from the early part of the war. After exhuming the body, the teams were to search for any identification (itself an indication of the doubts expressed by the IWGC about earlier searches) and, if any were found, to re-inter the body and choose another. By examining the equipment found, such as the presence of a soft cap rather than a helmet or by the type of respirator with the body, it was possible to identify early war casualties and four were taken to GHQ at Saint-Pol-sur-Ternoise. The next day, after a brief service, one body, chosen at random by Brigadier Wyatt, was placed in an ambulance and began its journey to London, the

British streets thronged by people hoping to catch a glimpse of what may be their son, their husband, their father. It was suggested that the need to choose an early war body was to avoid polluting the atmosphere of the Abbey during the planned ceremony, but after two years even the corpses of 1918 were in an advanced state of decay. The decision, whether by accident or design, to find an early war soldier meant that whatever else he may be, the Unknown Soldier would not be a conscript …

On a warm summer's day, the village of Courmas is quiet and still. A slight breeze ripples across the ripening corn and swallows swoop low across the fields. It is, as the men of the 187th Brigade noted almost a century ago, nearly impossible to imagine war in such a tranquil spot. Stepping off the track into the woods, though, the broken ground soon shows the scars of foxholes and shell craters. The field boundaries and woods remain almost identical to my 1920s map taken from the regimental history and, looking at it, I began to trace where the men had been and to walk within a few yards of where the boys of the draft had walked. In this field, men whom I probably passed in the street as a child without a second glance had bled and watched friends die. Men from houses I now pass daily on my way to work but whose occupiers have no knowledge of how their tiny terraces are forever linked to this sunny French field. In the middle of a field of ripening corn stands a small Commonwealth War Graves cemetery. From here, it is only a couple of hundred metres to where Harold Wiseman was killed and it is tempting to think that perhaps one of the graves marked 'An Unknown soldier of the King's Own Yorkshire Light Infantry' is his. Growing up, I'd heard about Harold from his younger sister, my grandmother, Annie. Aged 14 when he died, Annie never forgot her big brother but, as with all the draft, time went on and pictures, medals and letters fell victim to house clearances as their closest relatives grew old and followed after their long lost loved ones. All traces of Harold had gone by the time I had developed an interest in military history and the photos I remember from childhood are gone. Somewhere, perhaps, his dead man's penny sits in a collection. Alfred Smith, killed on 20 July, earned one for his family. It sold at auction in 2009 for £185. The buyer cares, I hope, that the 18-year-old former Boy Scout worked at Joseph Marton's Brickyard in Halifax before he joined up in November 1917; that he was remembered by his friends at All Saints' church and by a mother who had lost her husband and her only child. Alfred was never found. His medal roll simply states that he was 'presumed dead' on that terrible day. Even if she could have afforded the trip, there was nowhere for Agnes Smith to go to mourn her son.

In researching this story, I have contacted many people whose online family trees include the boys of the draft, but the story has almost always been the same. He was an uncle or distant relative and there are no photos or memories kept alive within the family. None of the draft wrote about their experiences. Only Arnold Ambler, it seems, was ever asked about them. The Great War was not fought and won by great heroes whose deeds will echo down the centuries, but by millions of unknown soldiers doing what was asked of them and enduring because they thought it was the right thing to do. To say, as so many do, that they were led to the slaughter by incompetents is to belittle them, 'for to believe', wrote H.E.L. Mellersh:

> that one has been badly led but at the same time to acknowledge that one obediently followed is to write oneself down as a fool … we did not believe, I am sure, that our top generals, and in particular our C-in-C, Sir Douglas Haig, were criminally inefficient and bloody minded nincompoops. We did not have much strategical or historical knowledge. But as fighting men we did know one thing, that war is a difficult game played mostly in the dark, and that it is much too easy for the critic to be wise after the event.[10]

The years following the Great War were marked by political turmoil. It suited trades unions and others to create the image of lions led by donkeys and for later writers of the 1950s and '60s to follow their lead in the anti-nuclear age. In the complex political and social atmosphere of the 1920s and '30s, a clear agenda arose of a war fought by willing but naive patriots putting their trust in their leaders only for it to be betrayed. The disillusionment felt by those who had answered the call was no doubt genuine as the economy crashed, but the popularity of magazines like *Twenty Years After* and *I Was There* in the late 1930s shows that a sizeable number, perhaps the majority, of veterans saw their war as worth fighting and their part in it as something to be proud of.

Remembered – if at all – as shirkers who had to be forced to serve their country, conscripts were championed by no one and today their role remains the least studied of all those who served in the First World War. More attention has been paid to pets in the trenches than to half the men who served there. Yet the war-winning army of 1918 was largely made up of teenage conscripts who formed the largest force Britain has ever put into the field and, at that time, the most professional and capable army it had ever known. Despite devastating losses, battalions of soldiers who in 1917 would have been regarded as too young to serve formed and re-formed to keep pressing home the attack and never lost cohesion, never followed the examples of the French, Russian and German armies by mutinying, and never lost their motivation to fight.

Too young to be able to maintain the pretence long enough to serve as Kitchener volunteers, but willing enough to serve their country when their time came; condemned as shirkers solely by accident of age and so forgotten by the country they served, the tale of Arnold Ambler, John Carr, Fredrick Gaines, Charles Pickering, Harold Whitwam and Harold Wiseman doesn't amount to much.

But I can tell you of many a thousand such.

Appendix

5th Battalion

62479   Private Alfred Aspinall
Born 25 Sep 1899, died 1970. Discharged to Z Reserve 17/10/19. Second son of William and Eliza of Armley Mill Yard, Leeds.

62480   Private Frank Ayrton formerly 5/93785 8th Training Reserve Battalion.
Birth registered Oct–Dec 1899, died of wounds 12/8/18. Buried St Germain-au-Mont-D'or. Youngest of three sons of John and Annie of Gargrave.

62481   Private John Acroyd
Born 27 Sep 1899, died 1969. Discharged to Z Reserve 24/1/19. Second son of William and Minnie of Sowerby Bridge.

62482   Private Arnold Ambler
Born 28 Sep 1899, died 1992 in USA. Discharged to Z Reserve 24/1/19.

62483   Private Harry Alderson formerly 96216 7th Training Reserve Battalion.
Birth registered Oct–Dec 1899, Killed in action 20/7/18. Buried Jonchery-sur-Vesle. Son of Tom and Mary Ellen of Birstall, Leeds. Tom was missing in action when Harry was killed but later found to be a prisoner of war.

62484   Private William Barr
Born Sep 1899, died of wounds 24/7/18. Buried Marfaux Cemetery. Son of Matthew and Mary of Todmorden. William's 25-year-old brother, Fulton, was killed near Arras in 1917.

62485   Private Harold Buckley
Born November 1899, died 1959. Discharged to Z Reserve 15/12/19. Son of Walter and Emily of Sowerby Bridge, Harold enlisted in the Army Service Corps in 1915 and was discharged aged 16 years and 2 months in February 1916.

62486   Private Frank Leslie Baxter
Born 20 Sep 1899, died 1987. Discharged to Z Reserve 28/1/20. Second son of John and
Edith of Linthwaite, Huddersfield.

62487   Private Charles Beckett
Birth registered Oct–Dec 1899, killed in action 20/7/18. Buried Courmas Cemetery. Son of
Charles and Charlotte of Spennymoor, Middlesbrough.

62488   Private Wilfred Berry
Birth registered Oct–Dec 1899, died 1951. Discharged to Z Reserve 24/1/19. Son of Joseph
and Elizabeth of Fell Lane, Keighley.

62489   Private Frank Bates later served as 615925 Pte Bates of the Labour Corps. To
date it has not been possible to positively identify this man.

62490   Private John Henry Beaumont later 629402 Labour Corps.
Born 11 Oct 1899, died 1974. Only son of widowed insurance agent Fred of Lidget Lepton,
Huddersfield.

62491   Private George Henry Ernest Bishop
Birth registered Apr–Jun 1899, died 1964. Discharged to Z Reserve 9/12/19. Son of William
and Florence of Leicester.

62492   Private Norman Alfred Bundy
Born 23 Mar 1899, died 1972. Discharged to Z Reserve 17/10/19. Son of Norman and
Harriet of Headingley, Leeds.

62493   Private John Willie Brown wounded in action August. Later 4682223 KOYLI.
Born 15 Sep 1899, died 1987. John re-enlisted into the regular army and later served in Iraq.

62494   Private Lionel Blenkinsop
Birth registered Jun 1899, died 1978. Enlisted underage on 13/2/17 and was discharged
23/4/19. Son of William and Rebecca of Hartlepool.

62495   Private John Edward Bowskill (or Bouskill) 5/93741 8th TRB, later M/412377
Army Service Corps. Born 3 Oct 1899, died 1927. Son of John Bowskill of Globe Fold,
Bradford.

62496   Private John Victor Beaumont
Born 14 Oct 1899, killed in action 2/9/18. Buried Vaulx Hill Cemetery. Still listed as missing
Dec 1918. Son of Wilson and Hannah of Meltham, Huddersfield.

62497   Private Ernest Cressy formerly 5/93687 8th Training Reserve Battalion later
M/411818 Army Service Corps.
Born 29 Sep 1899, died 1955. Son of William and Elizabeth, Pudsey.

62498   Private Kenneth Ely Crosland formerly 5/93636 8th Training Reserve Battalion.
Birth registered Oct–Dec 1899, killed in action 20/6/18. Buried Bienvillers Cemetery. Son of
Amy of New Hey Road Huddersfield.

62499   Private Edward Chilton
Birth registered Oct–Dec 1899, died ? Canada. Discharged to Z Reserve 9/3/19. Son of Edward and Fanny of Primrose Hill, Bingley.

62500   Private Benjamin Crawshaw
Born 26 Oct 1899, died 1950. Discharged to Z Reserve 11/10/19. Son of Thomas and Clara, West Lane Keighley. Ben enlisted in the Notts & Derby Regiment for one month in May 1916. His older brother Clayton served alongside the brothers of Meeking and Wiseman.

62501   Private John Cameron
Born 27 Sep 1899, died 1965. Discharged 27/3/19. Son of John and Ada of New Wortley, Leeds. Enlisted as part of the extension of the Derby Scheme on 1/9/16. Right arm amputated after being wounded during the Marne battle.

62502   Private Ernest Carter 'C' Company. Formerly 5/93632 8th Training Reserve. Born 28 Sep 1899, killed in action 27/7/18. No known grave, commemorated on Soissons Memorial. Only son of John and Lavinia of Keighley.

62503   Private Richard Crabtree
Born 30 Sep 1899, died 1979. Discharged to Z Reserve 21/2/19. Son of Bernard and Isabella of Todmorden.

62504   Private Percival Snowden Child
Born 8 Oct 1899, died 1964. Discharged to Z Reserve 17/7/19. Son of Arthur and Jane of Claverley, Huddersfield.

62505   Private John William Crowther I Platoon, 'A' Company. Formerly 5/93707 8th Training Reserve Battalion.
Born 17 Oct 1899, killed in action 2/9/18. Listed as wounded and missing December 1918. Buried Vaulx Hill Cemetery. Son of William and Hannah of Pepper Hill, Cleckheaton.

62506   Private John Crossley
Believed to have been born 17 Sep 1899. Discharged 14/6/19. Son of George and Annie of Bradford.

 62507   Private Harry Cunnington formerly 5/93637 8th Training Reserve Battalion.
Birth registered Oct–Dec 1899, killed in action 27/7/18. Buried Marfaux Cemetery. Son of William and Fanny, Exeter St, Salterhebble, Halifax.

62508   Private John George Cox
Born 28 Sep 1899, died 1936. Discharged to Z Reserve 22/11/19 Son of Richard and Elizabeth, Paddock, Huddersfield.

62509   Private Rowland Clifford later 619877 Labour Corps.
Born 18 Oct 1899, died 1981. Son of Anthony and Alice, Cowcliffe, Huddersfield.

62510   Private John Carr IV Platoon, 'A' Company. Formerly 5/93631 8th Training Reserve Battalion.
Born 28 Sep 1899, died 1973. Listed as missing December 1918. Discharged 22/7/20. Son of John and Robina, Bradford.

62511   Private Harold Calvert formerly 5/92658 8th Training Reserve Battalion. Later 44316 Leicestershire Regiment.
Born 2 Sep 1899, died 1948 (?). Son of Alfred and Minnie, Leeds.

62512   Private Harry Oldfield Cherry later 222236 and 1415398.
Born Sep 1899, died 1960. Served in Iraq with 5th Medium Battery Royal Garrison Artillery.

62513   Private Irvin Darlington
Born 8 Oct 1899, died 1973. Discharged Z Reserve 6/3/19. Son of George and Mary Ann of 635 New Hey Road, Huddersfield.

62514   Private George Depledge formerly 5/93688 8th Training Reserve Battalion.
Born 2 Sep 1899, killed in action 20/7/18. Buried Courmas Cemetery. Son of George and Mary, Elland, Halifax.

62515   Private Harry Verity Dennison formerly 5/93638 8th Training Reserve Battalion.
Birth registered Oct–Dec 1899, died of wounds 4/7/18. Buried St Sever Extension, Rouen. Son of Louisa of Bramley, Leeds.

62516   Private Hubert (possibly Herbert) **Denison**
Born 28 Sep 1899, died 1975. Son of Fred and Maria, High Street Yeadon. Previously enlisted 1915 into Duke of Wellington's Regiment. Discharged to Z Reserve 15/6/19.

62517   Private John Davis
Believed born Sheffield 10 Sep 1899. Killed in action 20/7/18. No known grave.

62518   Private George William Evans
Born 29 Sep 1899, died 1989. Discharged (wounds) 20/11/18.

62519   Private John W Elsworth 'A' Company. Later 050411 Army Ordnance Corps.
Born 1 Oct 1899, died 1964. Listed as wounded and missing December 1918 believed taken prisoner 20/7/18.

62520   Private William Emmott
Born 2 Oct 1899, died 1980. Discharged to Z Reserve 21/2/19. Son of Frederick and Lucy, The Gardens, Cliffe Castle Keighley.

62521   Private Ernest Frankland
Born 25 Sep 1899, died 1980. Discharged 19/9/19. Son of Louis and Eliza, Great Horton, Bradford.

62522   Private Samuel Walter Ellison
Birth registered Oct–Dec 1899, died 1967. Discharged to Z Reserve 28/1/19 son of John and Margaret, Consett, Co. Durham.

62523   Private Alfred Flack
Born 3 Oct 1899, died 1975. Discharged (wounds) 8/1/19. Son of Catherine, Salt Lake, Ingleton.

62524   Private Harry Firth
Discharged (wounds) 4/2/19. No other details.

62525   Private George Fox formerly 5/82819 8th Training Reserve Battalion.
Born 1899, killed in action 20/7/18. Buried Jonchery-sur-Vesle. Son of James and Lily, Arnold, Notts.

62526   Private Arthur Goodings formerly 5/93750 8th Training Reserve Battalion.
Birth registered Oct–Dec 1899, presumed killed in action 20/7/18. Buried Bouilly Crossroads. Son of George and Georgine, Bingley.

62527   Private Francis Leo Grogan
Born 2 Oct 1899, died 1973. Discharged to Z Reserve 15/12/19. Son of Francis and Mary, Jonas Gate Bradford.

62528   Private Frederick Pease Gaines later 48 POW Company Labour Corps.
Born 28 Sep 1899, died 1953. Re-enlisted in West Yorkshire Regiment 15/7/19. Son of Brother James was killed aged 17 in 1915.

62529   Private Albert Edward Gillman
Birth registered Apr–Jun 1899 in Essex. Died 1964. Enlisted 13/9/16, discharged 6/6/19. Son of William, Grimsby.

62530   Lance Corporal William Fay
Birth registered Oct–Dec 1899. Listed missing Dec 1918. Killed in action 12/9/18. Buried Vis-en-Artois Cemetery. Headstone reads, 'His memory is cherished with pride'. Son of Emma, Ancoats, Manchester.

62531   Private Frederick H Fox later S/3325 and 7577862 Army Ordnance Corps.
Birth registered 1899. Died 1951. Enlisted 6/12/15, discharged 13/9/19. Son of Frederick and Mary, Brightside, Sheffield.

62532   Private Robert Farrand
Born 21 Aug 1899. Died 1960. Enlisted May–Aug 1915 in Royal Field Artillery. Re-enlisted 24/9/16 and discharged 3/4/19. Son of Albert and Ellen, Todmorden.

62533   Private John Thomas Horne
Born 30 Sep 1899, died 1987. Discharged 22/11/19. Son of Herbert and Emma, Birdsedge, near Wakefield.

62534   Private Joseph Hainsworth
Born 1 Oct 1899, died 1972. Enlisted 3/9/17, discharged 9/4/19. Son of Arthur and Mary, Greetland, near Halifax.

62535   Private Albert Harrison formerly 5/93698 8th Training Reserve Battalion.
Born 29 Sep 1899. Killed in action 2/9/18. No known grave. Commemorated on Vis-en-Artois Memorial. Son of widowed Thomas, Kirkstall, Leeds.

62536   Private Albert Hirst
Birth registered Oct–Dec 1899, died 1967. Discharged 24/1/19. Son of George and Harriet, Longwood, Huddersfield.

62537   Private Tom Ellis Hall later GS/107948 10th Battalion Royal Fusiliers.
Born 14 Oct 1899, died 1980. Transferred to No. 5 Convalescent Camp as 'immature' 9/6/18. Discharged 10/4/20. Son of Fred and Lucy, Baildon.

62538   Private James Willie Hewitt
Birth registered Oct–Dec 1899 Barnsley. Discharged 21/2/19. No other details.

62539   Private Edwin Hepworth
Born 30 Sep 1899, died 1981. Discharged 6/3/19. Son of Walker and Ada, Siddal, Halifax.

62540   Private William Holmes formerly 5/93758.
Birth registered Oct–Dec 1899. Killed in action 20/7/18. No known grave and commemorated on Soisssons Memorial. Son of Wainman and Ann, Burley-in-Wharfedale.

62541   Private William Edward Howard
Birth registered Oct–Dec 1899, died 1966. Discharged 26/11/19. Son of Edward and Harriet, West Bowling, Bradford.

62542   Private Ernest Alfred Haw
Born 21 Feb 1899, died 1971. Discharged 28/11/19. Son of John and Mary Ann, Craghead, Durham.

62543   Private John W Holt later GS/83982 Royal Fusiliers.
Born 13 Sep 1899, died 1976. Son of Michael and Eliza, Bradford.

62544   Private John Henegan formerly 5/93757 8th Training Reserve Battalion.
Birth registered Oct–Dec 1899, killed in action 20/7/18. No known grave. Commemorated on Soissons Memorial. Son of William and Bridget, Bradford.

62545   Private Joseph Iredale formerly 5/93807 8th Training Reserve Battalion.
Birth registered Oct–Dec 1899, killed in action 20/7/18. No known grave. Commemorated on Soissons Memorial. Son of Herbert and Bertha, Kings Cross, Halifax.

62546   Private Gilbert Henthorn
Birth registered Oct–Dec 1899, died 1951. Discharged 11/02/19. Son of Thomas and Hannah, Oldham.

62547   Private Lewis Hamer later 60186 West Riding Regiment.
Born 13 Aug 1899, died 1969. Son of John and Emma, Halifax Brother Jack killed in action 21/3/18.

62548   Private John Kane
Birth registered Apr–Jun 1899. Discharged 17/4/19. Son of James and Mary, Middlesbrough.

2/4th Battalion

62549 Private John Lightowler
Born 16 Sep 1899, died 1922. Discharged 11/10/19. Son of James and Florence, North Brierley, Bradford.

62550 Private Wilfred Landale Later 53422 Lincolnshire Regiment.
Born 27 Sep 1899, died 1974. Son of Thomas and Sarah, Todmorden.

62551 Private Charley Lumb
Born 30 Sep 1899, died 1984. Discharged 16/10/19. Son of David and Ellen, Sowerby Bridge.

62552 Private George Latimer
Birth registered Apr–Jun 1899, died 1958. Discharged 20/2/19. Son of John and Jane, Newcastle.

62553 Private Victor Albert Lister formerly 5/93636 8th Training Reserve Battalion.
Birth registered Oct–Dec 1899. Listed as missing Dec 1918. Killed in action 20/7/18. No known grave, commemorated on Soissons Memorial. Son of Harry and Harriet, Clayton Heights, Bradford.

62554 Private Arthur Field formerly 5/93748 8th Training Reserve Battalion.
Born 3 Oct 1899. Listed as missing Dec 1918. Killed in action 20/7/18. No known grave, commemorated on Soissons Memorial. Son of Clifton and Annie, Skelmanthorpe, Huddersfield. Brother Joseph killed 27/5/18 also listed on Soissons Memorial.

62555 Private James Morley later 276637 Royal Field Artillery.
Born 1 Nov 1899, died 1989. Son of Robert and Dulcibella, West Hill Park, Halifax.

62556 This number does not appear to have been allocated.

62557 Private Alexander McDonald formerly 98520 Training Reserve.
Birth registered Oct–Dec 1899. Discharged 24/1/19. Son of Peter and Hannah Middleton, Co Durham.

62558 Private John Meeking formerly 5/93707 8th Training Reserve Battalion.
Birth registered Oct–Dec 1899. Listed as missing Dec 1918. Killed in action 20/7/18. No known grave. Commemorated on Soissons Memorial. Son of Tom and Mary, West Lane Keighley. Brother Harry was killed serving with the Canadian army 1915.

62559 Private George Edward McGrann formerly 5/93812 8th Training Reserve Battalion.
Birth registered Oct–Dec 1899, died 1948. Discharged 27/2/19. Son of Patrick and Alicia, Skipton.

62560 Private William Middlemass
Born 22 Oct 1899, died 1971. Discharged 7/10/19. Nephew of James and Alice, South Moor, Middlesbrough.

62561 Private Joseph McNulty later GS/107947 10th Royal Fusiliers.
Born 15 Oct 1899, died 1962. Son of John and Elizabeth, Skipton. Transferred with Tom Hall to No. 5 Convalescent Camp 9/6/18.

62562   Private Alfred Miller
Born 3 Oct 1899, died 1979. Discharged 10/12/19. Son of Samuel and Elizabeth, Leeds.

62563   Private George William Moyns later 80230 KOYLI served in India 1920.
Birth registered Oct–Dec 1899, died 1967. Son of George and Florence, Bradford.

62564   Private Edward Nowland
Born 26 Mar 1899, died 1976. Discharged 14/12/18 due to wounds Son of Charles and Sarah, Holbeck, Leeds.

62565   Private Harry Nutton formerly 5/93816 8th Training Reserve Battalion. Born 12 Oct 1899. Killed in action 22/7/18 No known grave, commemorated on Soissons Memorial. Only son of Whitely and Ada, Greetland, Halifax.

62566   Private Charles Nicholl
Born 29 Sep 1899, died 1957, Discharged 2/1/19 (wounds). Son of James and Rosie, Sowerby Bridge.

62567   Private Thomas W Nutt
Birth registered Jul–Sep 1899 Fleckney, Leicester. No other details.

62568   Private Fred Pearson
No details.

62569   Private Frank Edward Poucher
Born 18 Sep 1899, died 1959. Discharged 1/9/19. Son of Edward and Ann, Marsden, Huddersfield. Brother Joseph killed 1917.

62570   Private Charles Edward Pickering formerly 5/93706 8th Training Reserve Battalion.
Born 28 Sep 1899, died of pneumonia 18/10/18. Buried Delsaux Farm Cemetery. Son of Ada, Todmorden.

62571   Private Arthur Pedder
Birth registered Oct–Dec 1899, died 1957. Discharged 17/10/19. Son of James and May, Bradford. Brother Herbert killed 1915.

62572   Private Harry Pearson
Believed born 17 Oct 1899, died 1973. Discharged 21/12/19. Son of Joe and Edith, Golcar, Huddersfield.

62573   Private Willie Rollinson later 79773 Royal Northumberland Fusiliers.
Birth registered Oct–Dec 1899, died 1946. Went on to serve in Iraq, 1920.

62574   Private Walter Robinson
Birth registered Oct–Dec 1899. Discharged 14/8/20. No other details.

62575   Private John Rose later 619467 Labour Corps.
No details.

62576   Private Harry Robinson formerly 5/93644 8th Training Reserve Battalion.
Born 29 Sep 1899, died 1970. Discharged 12/9/19 (sickness). Son of William Robinson, Huddersfield.

62577   Private Albert E Rawnsley
Birth registered Oct–Dec 1899, died 1967. Discharged 21/2/19. Son of Evelyn, Baildon.

62578   Private Fred Sutcliffe formerly 5/93712 8th Training Reserve Battalion.
Born 22 Sep 1899, killed in action 20/7/18. No known grave, commemorated on Soissons Memorial. Son of Henry and Mary Alice, Hebden Bridge.

62579   Private Clement Smith formerly 5/93714 8th Training Reserve Battalion.
Born 20 Sep 1899, listed as missing Dec 1918, killed in action 20/7/18. No known grave. Commemorated on Soissons Memorial. Son of Edwin and Fanny, Hebden Bridge.

62580   Private Norman Storey
Birth registered Oct–Dec 1899, died 1954. Discharged 23/4/19 (wounds). Son of Frank and Amy, Bradford.

62581   Private Alfred Smith formerly 5/93824 8th Training Reserve Battalion.
Birth registered Oct–Dec 1899, listed as missing, later killed in action 20/7/18. No known grave. Commemorated on Soissons Memorial. Son of Agnes, Halifax.

62582   Private Cyril Scratcherd formerly 5/93822 8th Training Reserve Battalion.
Birth registered Oct–Dec 1899, listed as missing Dec 1918. Presumed killed in action 12/9/18. No known grave. Commemorated on Vis-en-Artois Memorial. Son of Fred and Lucy, Halifax.

62583   Acting Corporal Harry Smith formerly 5/93715 8th Training Reserve Battalion.
Birth registered Oct–Dec 1899. Discharged 13/12/19. No further details but known to be discharged to Bradford.

62584   Private Harold Smith formerly 5/93791 8th Training Reserve Battalion.
Born 3 Oct 1899, discharged 27/5/19 after amputation of arm. Son of Henry and Ada, Slaithwaite, Huddersfield.

62585   Private Edgar Telford Stainton
Birth registered Oct–Dec 1899, died 1923. Discharged 7/1/19. Son of Tom and Hannah, Sedburgh.

62586   Private Frank Strong
Born 27 Sep 1899, died 1988. Discharged (wounds) 27/2/19. Son of William and Annie, Moldgreen, Huddersfield.

62587   Private Samuel Maurice Sanderson
Born 1 Oct 1899, died 1974. Discharged 7/2/19. Son of Fred and Ann Mary, Saddleworth.

62588   Private Norman Smith
Born 3 Oct 1899, died 1979. Discharged 4/2/19. No other details.

62589   Lance Corporal George Henry Spencer
Born 2 Oct 1899, died 1978. Discharged 22/12/19. Son of John and Beatrice, 635 New Hey Road, Huddersfield (62513 Pte Darlington lived at No. 629).

62590   Private Harry Stevens
Discharged 13/2/19. No positive identification. Probably son of Albert and Mary Ann, Menston.

62591   Private James Scott
Discharged 17/10/19. Probably born 7 Oct 1899. Son of James Robert and Sarah Ann, Dewsbury.

62592   Private Stanley Rowley
Born 27 Sep 1899, died 1970. Discharged 16/10/19. Son of William, Leeds.

62593   Private Gilbert Townend
Born 8 Oct 1899, died 1971. Discharged 22/12/19. Son of Joe William, Towngate, Huddersfield.

62594   Private Arthur Tidswell formerly 5/93828 8th Training Reserve Battalion.
Birth registered Oct–Dec 1899, listed as missing Dec 1918, presumed killed in action 22/7/18. Buried St Imoges Churchyard. Son of William and Margaret, Denholme. Also listed as 'Tidsdale'.

62595   Private Arthur Thorpe formerly 5/93827 8th Training Reserve Battalion.
Birth registered Oct–Dec 1899, listed as missing Dec 1918, presumed killed in action 13/9/18. Buried Ruyalcourt Military Cemetery. Son of Albert and Hannah, Manningham, Bradford.

62596   Private Joseph Turley formerly 5/31141.
Birth registered Jan–Mar 1899. Killed in action 4/11/18. Buried Ruesnes Communal Cemetery. Son of Edwin and Edith, Wolverhampton.

62597   Private Joseph Vickers formerly 5/93668 8th Training Reserve Battalion.
Birth registered Oct–Dec 1899. Died of wounds in UK hospital 28/8/18. Buried Bradford (Bowling) Cemetery. Son of Fenton and Elizabeth, Bradford.

62598   Private George Walter Wheatley formerly 5/93722 8th Training Reserve Battalion.
Born 24 Sep 1899, killed in action 14/9/18. No known grave. Commemorated on Vis-en-Artois Memorial. Son of George and Sarah Anne, Bradford.

62599   Private Harry Tunnicliffe Waite later 618778 Labour Corps.
Born 26 Sep 1899, died 1973. Son of Alfred and Ada, Potter Newton, Leeds.

62600   Private Harold Wiseman formerly 5/93672 8th Training Reserve Battalion.
Born 28 Sep 1899. Killed in action 22/7/18. No known grave. Commemorated on Soissons Memorial. Son of James and Elizabeth, Keighley.

62601   Private George Arnold Webster
Born 18 Oct 1899, died 1969. Discharged 28/5/19. Son of Ernest and Mary, King Cross, Halifax.

62602   Private Stanley Wade
Born 25 Sep 1899, died 1923. Discharged 9/3/19. Son of Herbert and Isabell, Manningham, Bradford.

62603   Private Samuel Sydney Wells
Birth registered Oct–Dec 1899, died 1980. Discharged 29/12/19. Son of Samuel and Alice, East Ham.

62604   Private Richard Wilson later 050465 Army Ordnance Corps.
Believed born 18 Oct 1899, died 1981. Discharged 8/1/20.

62605   Private Harold Fewdale Whitwam
Born 28 Sep 1899, died 1981. Discharged 22/11/19. Son of Benjamin and Mary Jane, Moldgreen, Huddersfield.

62606   Private James Woodrow later 631920 Labour Corps.
Born 11 Oct 1899, died 1982. Son of Albert and Clara, Bowling, Bradford.

62607   Private Edmund Walker formerly 5/93833 8th Training Reserve Battalion.
Birth registered Oct–Dec 1899. Died of wounds 5/9/18 buried Bac-Du-Sud British Cemetery, Bailleulval. Son of Frederick and Elizabeth, Saltaire.

62608   Acting Corporal Horace Wakelin
Birth registered Apr–Jun 1899, died 1928. Discharged 18/2/19. From Tamworth area.

62609   Private Jack Wood formerly 5/93724 8th Training Reserve Battalion.
Discharged 7/3/19 to Bradford area. No other details.

62610   Private Ernest Martin Wise formerly 5/90493.
Birth registered Apr–Jun 1899. Killed in action 27/7/18. Buried Marfaux Cemetery. Son of Headley and Jane Elizabeth, Bridlington.

62611   Private James Woodyet
Born 28 Mar 1899, died 1985. Discharged 18/2/19. Son of Richard and Jane, Dewsbury.

62612   Private Tom B Watson later 3300559 Highland Light Infantry.
Birth registered Oct–Dec 1899, died 1931. Son of James and Elizabeth, Bramley, Leeds.

62613   Private Lawrence Wright later GS/107752 Royal Fusiliers.
Probably birth registered Oct–Dec 1899. Son of William and Emily, Bramley, Leeds.

62614   Private Henry Wheelwright
Born 25 Sep 1899, died 1977. Discharged 16/10/19. Son of Harry and Sarah, Leeds.

62615   Private John Warwick
Born 17 Sep 1899, died 1954. Enlisted Oct 1915 and again Jan–Apr 1916 discharged due to age. Discharged 27/2/19. Son of George, Hunslet, Leeds.

Notes

Introduction

1. Hamilton, J.A., *The Siege of Mafeking* (London: Methuen & Co., 1900), pp.43–4.
2. Ibid., p.43.
3. Ibid.

Chapter 1

1. Corrigan, Gordon, *Mud, Blood and Poppycock: Britain and the First World War* (London: Cassell Military Paperbacks, 2004), p.354.
2. Newman, Sir George, *Infant Mortality: A Social Problem* (New York: E.P. Button and Company, 1907), Appendix IX.
3. Morris, Joseph E., *The West Riding of Yorkshire* (London: Methuen & Co., 1911), p.6.
4. Ibid., p.10.
5. Ibid., p.8.
6. Ibid., p.9.
7. Dewhirst, I., *A History of Keighley* (Stroud: Tempus, 2006), p.57.
8. Ibid.
9. Mr Garlick's Statement in Ranger, W., *Report to the General Board of Health, on a Preliminary Inquiry as to the Sewage, Drainage and Supply of Water, and the Sanitary Conditions of the Inhabitants of the Town of Halifax in the County of York*
10. Ibid., p.35.
11. Ibid., Appendix C, pp.115–20.
12. Ibid., p.18.

13. *Consultative Committee Report Upon the School Attendance of Children Below the Age of Five (The Acland Report)* (London: HM Stationery Office, 1908), p.18.
14. Ibid., p.19.
15. Hansard, 13 March 1912, 35 H.C. Deb., col. 111.
16. Rowntree, B.S., *Poverty: A Study of Town Life* (London: Macmillan, 1901), pp.86–7.
17. Ibid., pp.133–4.
18. Hammal, R., 'How Long Before the Sunset? British Attitudes to War, 1871–1914', *History Review* (2010). Available at http://www.historytoday.com/rowena-hammal/how-long-sunset-british-attitudes-war-1871-1914.

Chapter 2

1. Fichte, J., *Addresses to the German Nation (1807), Second Address: 'The General Nature of the New Education'* (Chicago and London: The Open Court Publishing Company, 1922), p.21.
2. Marriott, J.A.R. and Grant Robinson, C., *The Remaking of Prussia: The Making of an Empire* (Oxford: Clarendon Press, 1917), p.237–8.
3. Penn, A., *Targeting Schools: Drill, Militarism and Imperialism* (London: Woburn Education Series, 1999), p.11.
4. Blyth, W.A.L., *English Primary Education: A Sociological Description Vol. II: Background*

(London: Routledge and Kegan Paul, 1965), p.21.

5. Board of Education, *General Reports of HM Inspectors on Elementary Schools and Training Colleges for the Year 1902* (London: HMSO, 1903), p.91.
6. Penn, op. cit., p.125.
7. Ibid., p.21.
8. Ibid., p.82.
9. Bloomfield, A., 'Muscular Christian or Mystic? Charles Kingsley Reappraised', *The International Journal of the History of Sport*, vol. 11, no. 2 (1994), p.174.
10. Chisholm, H. (ed.), 'Boys' Brigade', *Encyclopædia Britannica*, 11th ed. (Cambridge: Cambridge University Press, 1911).
11. Springhall, J., *Youth, Empire and Society: British Youth Movements, 1883–1940* (London, 1977), p.57.
12. Freeman, M., 'Muscular Quakerism? The Society of Friends and youth movements in Britain, *c*.1900–1950', *English Historical Review*, vol. 125, no. 514 (2010), pp.642–69.
13. Wilkinson, P., 'English Youth Movements, 1908–30', *Journal of Contemporary History*, vol. 4, no. 2 (April 1969), pp.3–23.
14. Cotton Minchin, J.G., *Our Public Schools: Their Influence on English History; Charter House, Eton, Harrow, Merchant Taylors', Rugby, St. Paul's Westminster, Winchester* (London: Swan Sonnenschein & Co., 1901), p.113.
15. Code of Regulations for Day Schools, Education Department (London: HMSO, 1900), p.4.
16. Withers, H.L., 'Memorandum on the Teaching of History in the Schools of the London School Board', reproduced in Withers, H.L., *The Teaching of History and Other Papers* (Manchester: Sherrat and Hughes, 1904).
17. Welton, J., *Principles and Methods of Teaching* (London: University Tutorial Press, 1906), p.136.
18. Garlick, A.H., *A New Manual of Method*, 6th ed. (London and New York: Longmans, Green and Co., 1904), p.259.

19. Welton, J., *Principles and Methods of Teaching* (London: University Tutorial Press, 1906), p.267.
20. Fletcher, C.R.L. and Kipling, R., *A School History of England* (Oxford: Clarendon Press, 1911), p.247.
21. Ibid., p.21.
22. Ibid., p.220.
23. Ibid., p.245.
24. Anon., *Britannia History Readers* (London: Arnold's School Series, *c*.1902), pp.9–10.
25. Warner, G.T., *A Brief Survey of British History* (London: Blackie and Son, 1899), pp.248–9.
26. Board of Education, *General Reports of HM Inspectors on Elementary Schools and Training Colleges for the Year 1902* (London: HMSO, 1903), p.20.
27. Yeandle, P., 'Empire, Englishness and Elementary School History Education, *c*.1880–1914', *International Journal of Historical Learning, Teaching and Research*, vol. 3 (2003).
28. See Cipolla, C.M., *Literacy and Development in the West* (London: Penguin, 1967).
29. Gardiner, A.G., *Prophets, Priests, and Kings* (London: Alston Rivers Ltd, 1908), pp.269–70.
30. Boyle, A., *The Riddle of Erskine Childers* (London: Hutchinson, 1977), p.111.
31. Le Queux, W., *The Invasion of 1910* (1906)
32. Ibid., pp.167–8.
33. Porter, B., *The Origins of the Vigilant State* (Woodbridge: Boydell & Brewer, 1991), p.172.
34. Ramsden, J., *Don't Mention the War: The British and the Germans since 1890 – The British and Modern Germany* (London: Abacus 2007), p.73.
35. Ibid., pp.73–4.
36. Johnson, M., *Saturday Soldiers: The Territorial Battalions of the KOYLI 1908–1919* (Doncaster: Doncaster Museum Services, 2004), p.7.
37. Howard, M., 'Empire Race and War', *History Today*, vol. 31, no. 12 (1981), pp.4–11.

Chapter 3

1. Pearce, C., *Comrades in Conscience: The Story of an English Community's Opposition to the Great War* (London: Francis Boutle, 2001), p.57.
2. Scott, W.H., *Leeds in the Great War: A Book of Remembrance* (Leeds: The Libraries & Arts Committee of the Leeds Corporation, 1923), p.4.
3. Hansard, 25 March 1914, 60 H.C. Deb., cols. 392–458.
4. Hansard, 28 April 1914, 61 H.C. Deb., cols. 1529–38.
5. www.curragh.info/articles/mutiny. htm. See also Ian D. Colvin's *Carson the Statesman* (Kila, MT: Kessinger Publishing Co., 2005).
6. www.curragh.info/articles/mutiny.htm.
7. *Belfast Evening Telegraph*, 25 April 1914.
8. Stewart, A.T.Q., *The Ulster Crisis: Resistance to Home Rule 1912–14* (London: Faber & Faber, 1967; reprinted 1969); see appendix for numbers and sources.
9. James, D., *Class and Politics in a Northern Industrial Town: Keighley 1880–1914* (Keele: Keele University Press, 1995), p.69.
10. Ibid.
11. See Engels, F., 'The War Office and the Volunteers', *The Volunteer Journal for Lancashire and Cheshire*, vol. II, no. 40 (8 June 1861), p.125; Chaloner, W.H. and Henderson, W.O., *Engels as Military Critic* (Manchester: Manchester University Press, 1959), pp.37–8.
12. See Dalton, R.D., *Labour and the Municipality: Labour Politics in Leeds 1900 -1914* (PhD thesis, University of Huddersfield, October 2000).
13. Morris, P.M., *Leeds and the Amateur Military Tradition: The Leeds Rifles and their Antecedents, c. 1859–1918* (PhD thesis, University of Leeds, 1983), pp.132–3.
14. Dewhirst, I., *A History of Keighley* (Stroud: Tempus, 2006), p.112.
15. Marwick, A., *The Deluge: British Society and the First World War* (1973), p.29.
16. *Huddersfield Daily Examiner*, 31 July 1914.
17. *The Worker*, 8 August 1914.
18. Lee, J.A., *Todmorden and the Great War* (Todmorden: Warrington & Sons 1922), p.2.
19. Ibid., p.3.
20. *Huddersfield Daily Examiner*, 6 August 1914.
21. Macdonagh, M., *I was There*, vol. 1, p.17.
22. Gregory, A., *The Last Great War: British Society and the First World War* (Cambridge: Cambridge University Press, 2008), p.11.

Chapter 4

1. Lee, J.A., *Todmorden and the Great War* (Todmorden: Warrington & Sons, 1922), p.3.
2. Taylor, A.J.P., *A Personal History* (New York: Atheneum, 1983), p.27, cited in Gregory, op. cit., p.298.
3. Scott, W.H., *Leeds in the Great War: A Book of Remembrance* (Leeds: The Libraries & Arts Committee of the Leeds Corporation, 1923), p.10.
4. Hammerton, Sir J. (ed.), *A Popular History of the Great War Vol I: The First Phase 1914* (London: Amalgamated Press, 1933), p.69.
5. Ibid., p.71.
6. McDonald, L., *1914: Days of Hope* (London: Penguin, 1987), pp.213–14.
7. Hammerton, op cit., p.73.
8. Hayward, J., *Myths and Legends of the First World War* (Stroud: Sutton Publishing, 2002), p.24.
9. Ibid., see pp.31–45.
10. Humphries, S. and van Emden, R., *All Quiet on the Home Front: Life in Britain during the First World War* (London: Headline Publishing, 2003), pp.68–9.
11. Graves, Robert, *Goodbye to All That* quoted in Ramsden, J., *Don't Mention the War* (London: Abacus, 2006), p.114.
12. Lynch, T., *Dunkirk 1940 'Whereabouts Unknown': How Untrained Troops of the Labour Divisions were Sacrificed to Save an Army* (Stroud: The History Press, 2010), p.135.
13. Macdonald, L., *1914*, p.209.
14. Haste, C., *Keep the Home Fires Burning: Propaganda in the First Word War* (London: Allen Lane, 1977), p.87.
15. Read, J.M., *Atrocity Propaganda 1914–1919* (New Haven, CT: Yale University Press, 1941), p.30.

16. See Read, *Atrocity Propaganda*, pp.37–8; Haste, *Keep the Home Fires Burning*, p.84.
17. Ramsden, op. cit., p.126.
18. Turner, E.S., *Dear Old Blighty* (London: Michael Joseph Ltd, 1980), pp.81–3.
19. MacDonald, op. cit., p.214.
20. *Yorkshire Post*, 1 September 1914.
21. MacDonald, op. cit., p.215.
22. Ramsden, op. cit., pp.93–4.

Chapter 5

1. Holmes, R., *Tommy: The British Soldier on the Western Front* (London: HarperCollins, 2004), p.135.
2. Sheffield, G., *Officer-Man Relations, Morale and Discipline in the British Army, 1902–22* (PhD thesis, King's College, London, 1994), p.5.
3. Caddick-Adams, P., *Monty and Rommel: Parallel Lives* (London: Arrow Books, 2012), p.91.
4. Dunn, Captain J.C., *The War the Infantry Knew* (London: Abacus Books, 2003), pp.429–30.
5. See French, D., *Military Identities: The Regimental System, the British Army, and the British People c. 1870–2000* (Oxford: OUP, 2008).
6. Holmes, op. cit., p.121.
7. 8 May 1912, RMC Register of Letters File index 1910–12, 4843, RNASA, quoted in Sheffield, op. cit., p.5.
8. Scott, *Leeds in the Great War*, p.10.
9. www.ludditclink.org.uk.
10. Gregory, op. cit., p.78.
11. Morris, P., *Leeds and the Amateur Military Tradition: The Leeds Rifles and their Antecedents, c. 1859–1918 Vol. 1* (PhD thesis, University of Leeds, 1983), p.397.
12. Cunningham, H., *The Volunteer Force: A Social and Political History 1859–1908* (London: Croom Helm, 1975), chap. 1, passim.
13. Watson, Major F.L., *A Territorial in the Salient* (London: J.M. Dent & Sons Ltd, 1930), republished as *True World War I Stories* (London: Constable & Robinson, 2009), p.33.
14. Beckett, I.F. and Simpson, K.A. (eds), *Nation in Arms: A Social Study of the British Army in the First World War* (Manchester: Manchester University Press, 1985), p.132.
15. Nicholson, Col W.N., *Behind the Lines* (London, 1939), pp.15, 19–20.
16. Beaumont, S.G., *The Reminiscences of S.G. Beaumont* (Private publication, n.d.), p.18, quoted in Johnson, M., op. cit., p.65.
17. Beckett, op cit., p.135.
18. Hankey, D., *A Student in Arms* (London: Melrose, 1916), p.19.
19. Gregory, op. cit., p.74.
20. Hughes, C., 'The New Armies' in Beckett, Ian and Simpson, Keith (eds), *A Nation in Arms* (Barnsley: Pen & Sword Books, 2004), p.102.
21. *Yorkshire Observer*, 7 September 1914.
22. Scott, *Leeds in the Great War*, p.177.
23. Powell, M., *Below Stairs* (London: P. Davies, 1968), p.24.
24. National Archives, CAB24 GT406.
25. Scott, *Leeds in the Great War*, pp.12–14.
26. Service record of 2242 Frederick John Adams of Docks Bn, Liverpool Regiment, available at www.ancestry.co.uk.
27. War Office, *Statistics of the Military Effort of the British Empire during the Great War, 1914–1920* (London: HMSO 1922), p.364.
28. Cartmell, H., *For Remembrance* (Preston: Toulmin & Sons Ltd, 1919), p.40.
29. Gregory, op. cit., p.90.
30. Ibid., p.88.
31. Adams, R.J.Q. and Poirier, Philip P., *The Conscription Controversy in Great Britain, 1900–18* (Columbus, OH: Ohio State University Press 1987), pp.90–91.
32. Harrison, B., *Bill's Book* (Beverley: Hutton Press, 1990), p.41.
33. Wolfe, H., *Labour Supply and Regulation* (Oxford: Clarendon, 1923), p.15.
34. National Archives, MUN 5/199/1700/4.
35. Adams, R.J.Q., *Arms and the Wizard: Lloyd George and the Ministry of Munitions. 1915–1916* (London: Cassell, 1978), pp.101–2; Jordan, Gerald H.S., *The Politics of Conscription in Britain, 1905–1916* (unpublished PhD thesis, University of California, Irvine, 1974), pp.127–9.

36. See Adams, R.J.Q. and Poirier, Philip P., *The Conscription Controversy*.

37. Memo to the Cabinet 21 March 1916, in Lloyd George, D., *War Memoirs Vol 1* (London: Oldhams Press, 1938), p.438.

38. Bet-El, I., *Conscripts* (Stroud: The History Press, 2009), p.9.

39. Dewhirst, I., *The Story of a Nobody: A Working Class Life, 1880–1939* (Mills & Boon, 1980), p.63.

40. Wilson, W., *The Myriad Faces of War: Britain and the Great War 1914–1918* (Cambridge: Polity Press, 1986), p.400.

41. Dewhirst, I., *A History of Keighley* (Stroud: Tempus, 2004), p.114.

42. Gregory, op. cit., p.101.

43. Ibid., p.105.

44. Empey, A.G., *From the Fire Step: The Experiences of an American Soldier in the British Army. Together with Tommy's Dictionary of the Trenches* (London: G.P. Putnam's Sons, 1917), p.235.

45. Dyer, G., *The Missing of the Somme* (London: Hamish Hamilton, 1994), p.3.

46. In 1982, the British Army lost a number of 17-year-olds in the Falklands and others were sent to serve in the Gulf War, Iraq and Afghanistan. Despite the popular image of boy soldiers in the First World War, their presence was not officially condoned and it was not until the end of the twentieth century that Britain knowingly deployed child soldiers.

47. Service record John Warwick letter dated 6 August 1917.

48. Banning, Lt Col S.T., *Military Law Made Easy*, 11th ed. (London: Gale & Polden Ltd, 1917), p.298.

49. Ellis Island Oral History Project, series KECK, no. 044: Interview of Arnold Ambler (Alexandria, VA: Alexander Street Press, 2003).

50. Van Emden, R., *Britain's Last Tommies* (London: Abacus, 2006), p.280.

51. Gregory, op. cit., p.102.

Chapter 6

1. Military Service Act 1916 No. 2, June 1916.

2. Hodges, F., *Men of 18 in 1918* (Ilfracombe: Arthur H. Stockwell Ltd, 1988), p.22.

3. Harrison, B., *Bill's Book*, p.41.

4. Messenger, C., *Call to Arms: The British Army 1914–18* (London: Weidenfeld & Nicolson, 2005), p.107.

5. Winter, J.M., *The Great War and the British People* (London: Macmillan, 1986), p.52.

6. Dunn, Capt J.C., *The War the Infantry Knew, 1914–1919: A Chronicle of Service in France and Belgium* (London: Abacus, 1988), p.245.

7. MacPhail, Sir A., *Official History of the Canadian Forces in the Great War 1914–19: The Medical Services. Minister of National Defence, Under Direction of the General Staff* (n.d., pre-1923) pp.211–12.

8. Hodges, op. cit.

9. WO 95/5460.

10. Dunn, op. cit., pp.245–6.

11. Mellersh, H.E.L., *Schoolboy into War* (London: HarperCollins, 1978), p.125.

12. Messenger, op. cit., p.157.

13. Charles Carrington quoted in Arthur, M., *Forgotten Voices of the Great War* (London: Ebury Press, 2003), p.135.

Chapter 7

1. Cole, H., *The Story of Catterick Camp 1915–72* (Catterick: Catterick Garrison HQ, 1972), p.15.

2. Mellersh, p.125.

3. Whitehouse, C.J. and G.P., *Great War Camps on Cannock Chase – A Town for Four Winters* (self-published, 1983), p.7.

4. Bet-El, *Conscripts*, pp.45–6.

5. Haking, Brigadier R.C.B., *Company Training* (London: Hugh Rees, 1915), pp.11–12.

6. Noakes, F.E., *The Distant Drum: A Memoir of a Guardsman in the Great War* (London: Frontline Books, 2010), p.4.

7. Haking, p.11.

8. Kiernan, R.H., *Little Brother Goes Soldiering* (London: Constable & Co., 1930), pp.22–3.

9. Hodges, p.26.

10. Quoted in Bet-El, pp.42–3.

11. Taylor, F.A.J., *The Bottom of the Barrel* (Bath: Chivers Press, 1986), pp.48–9.
12. Hodges, pp.27–8.
13. See Kiernan, pp.29–32.
14. Voight, F.A., *Combed Out* (London: The Swarthmore Press, 1920), pp.11–12.
15. Vickers, L., *Training for the Trenches* (London: George H. Doran Co., 1917).
16. Kiernan, p.24.
17. National Archives, MAF 60/243.
18. Dewhirst, *History of Keighley*, p.118.
19. Taylor, p.43.
20. Cole, p.22.
21. Bet-El, p.54.
22. Cole, p.22.
23. Baxby, D., 'The End of Smallpox', *History Today*, vol. 49, no. 3 (1999).
24. Vickers, p.84.
25. Taylor, pp.23–4.
26. Napoleon Bonaparte, *Maxims of War*, 5th ed. (Paris, 1874).
27. Ministry of Defence, *Army Doctrine Publications: Operations 2010*, www.mod.uk/dcdc.
28. Haking, p.1.
29. Hockey, J., *Squaddies: Portrait of a Subculture* (Exeter: University of Exeter, 1986), p.23.
30. *Reminiscences of S.G. Beaumont* quoted in Johnson, p.64.
31. Vickers, p.18.
32. Noakes, p.21.
33. Vickers, pp.60–1.
34. Kiernan, p.32.
35. Hockey, p.22.
36. Taylor, *The Bottom of the Barrel*, pp.63–4.
37. Haking, p.13.
38. General Sir Edward Bruce Hamley, quoted in *Blackwood's Magazine* (London, between 1851 and 1863).
39. Carrington, C., *Soldier from the Wars Returning* (Barnsley: Pen & Sword, 2006), p.225.
40. Turner, P.W. and Haigh, R.H., *Not for Glory* (London: Robert Maxwell, 1969), p.81.
41. General Staff, *Bayonet Training* (London: HMSO, 1918), pp.1–2.
42. Vickers, p.69.
43. Vickers, pp.118–19.
44. *Bayonet Training*, p.9.
45. Graves, Robert, *Goodbye to All That: An Autobiography* (London: Penguin, 1969), p.195.
46. Blacker, C.P., *Have you Forgotten Yet? The First World War Memoirs of C.P. Blacker, M.C., G.M., M.A., M.D., F.R.C.P, M.R.C.S.* (London: Leo Cooper, 2000), p.157.
47. Kiernan, p.31.
48. Harrison, *Bill's Book*, p.46.
49. Carrington, p.230.

Chapter 8

1. Terrraine, J., *To Win a War: 1918, the Year of Victory* (London: Phoenix, 2000), p.48.
2. National Archives, NATS 1/912.
3. See Cahill, L., *Forgotten Revolution: Limerick Soviet, 1919. A Threat to British Power in Ireland* (Dublin: O'Brien Press, 1990).
4. Terraine, p.50.
5. Hansard, 20 June 1918, 107 H.C. Deb., cols. 522–3W.
6. Hodges, pp.39–40.
7. Carrington, p.231.
8. Bet-El, p.37.
9. Ibid., p.66.
10. Hodges, p.37.
11. Abraham, Alfred J., IWM, Document no. 546, p.9.
12. Noakes, p.37.
13. Kiernan, p.46.
14. Bet-El, p.68.
15. National Archives, Service Record of 62537 Tom Ellis Hall.
16. Gill, D., and Dallas, G., 'Mutiny at Etaples Base in 1917', *Past & Present*, vol. 69 (1975), pp.88–112.
17. Bet-El, p.71.
18. Ibid., pp.74–5.
19. Harris, R. and Paxman, J., *A Higher Form of Killing: The Secret Story of Gas and Germ Warfare* (London: Chatto & Windus, 1982), p.16.
20. Van Emden, *Britain's Last Tommies*, p.261.
21. Haigh, R., *Life in A Tank* (Boston and New York: Houghton Mifflin Company, 1918), p.18.

Chapter 9

1. Bond, R.C., *History of the King's Own Yorkshire Light Infantry*, vol. II (London: Lund Humphries, 1929), p.776.

2.   Beaumont in Johnson, op. cit., p.71.
3.   Johnson, p.82.
4.   Skirrow, F., *Massacre on the Marne* (Barnsley: Pen & Sword, 2007), p.106.
5.   NA WO185/54 Third Army GS 56/244 of 18/12/17.
6.   Johnson, p.135.
7.   Turner and Haigh, p.87.
8.   Van Emden, *Britain's Last Tommies*, p.240.
9.   Campbell, P.J., *Ebb and Flow of Battle* (Oxford: OUP, 1979), p.135.
10. Holmes, R., *Firing Line* (London: Jonathan Cape, 1985), p.331.
11. Hadden, quoted in Daddis, G.A., 'Beyond the Brotherhood: Reassessing US Army Combat Relationships in the Second World War', *War & Society*, vol. 29, no. 2 (2010), pp.97–117.
12. Borthwick, A., *Sans Peur: The History of the 5th (Caithness and Sunderland) Battalion, the Seaforth Highlanders, 1942–1945* (Stirling: Eneas Mackay, 1946), p.380.
13. Babcock, J.B., *Taught to Kill* (Washington, DC: Potomac Books, 2005), p.128.
14. Hodges, *Men of 18 in 1918*, p.48.
15. General Staff, Instructions for the Training of Platoons, 1917.
16. Taylor, pp.72–3. The term 'Coot' was also used and adopted by American troops, hence 'cooties' is still used to describe infestations of lice and nits in the US.
17. Graham, J.H.P., 'A Note on a Relapsing Febrile Illness of Unknown Origin', *The Lancet*, vol. 186, no. 4804 (1915), pp.703–4.
18. Sundell, C.E. and Nankivell, A.T., 'Trench Fever', *The Lancet*, vol. 191, no. 4933 (1918), pp.399–402.
19. MacPherson, W.G., 'Prevention of Infestation by Lice', in MacPherson, *Official History of the War – Medical Services – Hygiene of the War*, vol. 2 (London: HMSO, 1921–23), pp.327–88.
20. Hodges, p.57.
21. Trench fever has not gone away; in the last twenty years it has re-emerged as 'urban trench fever' in populations of the homeless and alcoholics, the causative organism now renamed Bartonella quintana. See Atenstaedt, R.L., 'Trench Fever: The British Medical response in the Great War', *Journal of the Royal Society of Medicine*, vol. 99, no. 11 (2006), pp.564–8.
22. Hodges, p.44.
23. Ibid., p.64.
24. Pte Vero Garratt, RAMC in van Emden, *The Soldier's War: The Great War through Veterans' Eyes* (London: Bloomsbury, 2008), p.93.
25. Eric Hiscock, quoted in Holmes, R., *Tommy*, p.286.
26. Noakes, p.51.
27. Simpson, A., *Hot Blood and Cold Steel: Life and Death in the Trenches of the First World War* (London: Tom Donovan Publishing Ltd, 1993), pp.33–4.
28. Lt Bernard Pitt, Border Regiment, quoted in Simpson, *Hot Blood and Cold Steel*, p.36.
29. Ibid.
30. Morris, *Leeds Rifles*, vol. 2, p.703.
31. Arthur, M., *Forgotten Voices of the Great War* (London: Ebury Press, 2003), pp.175–6.
32. Graves, R., *Goodbye to All That* (London: Penguin, 1960), p.112.
33. 'A Halifax Territorial', *Yorkshire Post*, 21 May 1915.
34. Morris, *Leeds Rifles*, p.690.
35. Burnett, J., *Plenty and Want: A social history of diet in England from 1815 to the present day* (London and Edinburgh: Penguin, 1966), p. 214.
36. Roosevelt, Lt Col T., *Average Americans* (New York and London: G.P. Putnam's Sons, 1919), pp.117–18.
37. Graham, S., *A Private in the Guards* (London: MacMillan, 1919), p.219.
38. Wyrall, E., *History of 62nd (West Riding) Division 1914–1919*, vol. 1 (London: The Bodley Head Ltd, 1930), p.159.
39. See King, Anthony, *The Combat Soldier: Infantry Tactics and Cohesion in the Twentieth and Twenty-First Centuries* (Oxford: OUP, 2013).

Chapter 10

1.   Corrigan, *Mud, Blood and Poppycock*, p.194; see also Davies, F. and Maddocks, G.,

Bloody Red Tabs: General Officer Casualties of the Great War 1914–1918 (London: Leo Cooper, 1995).

2. Skirrow, F., *Massacre on the Marne* (Barnsley: Pen & Sword, 2007), p.188.
3. *Barnsley Chronicle*, 10 August 1918.
4. Ambler Oral History transcript.
5. *Barnsley Chronicle*, 10 August 1918.
6. Wyrall, p.173.
7. *Yorkshire Observer*, 9 August 1918.
8. Wyrall, p.178.

Chapter 11

1. Wyrall, p.181.
2. Campbell, P.J., *In the Cannon's Mouth* (London: Hamish Hamilton, 1977), p.80.
3. Tobin in Stephenson, M., *The Last Full Measure* (New York: Crown Publishers, 2012), p.235.
4. Wyrall, p.181.
5. Haking, *Company Training*, p.112.
6. General Staff, *Infantry Training* (London: HMSO, 1914), chapter X, para. 121.
7. Cru, J.N., *War Books: A Study in Historical Criticism*, originally published as *Du témoignage*, translated by Cru, edited and annotated by Ernest Marchand and Stanley J. Pincetl, Jr (San Diego: San Diego University Press, 1976), p.84.
8. General Staff, *Instructions for the Training of Platoons* (London: HMSO, 1917).
9. Haking, *Company Training*, p.116.
10. See MacCurdy, J.T., *The Structure of Morale*, quoted in Holmes, R., *Acts of War* (London: Jonathan Cape, 1985), p.170. As Holmes points out, on 1 July 1916, the British fired some 224,221 artillery rounds, while the Germans suffered under 6,000 casualties – around thirty-seven shells for every casualty.
11. Haking, *Company Training*, p.127.
12. Ibid., p.131.
13. Laffin, J., *Combat Surgeons* (London: J.M. Dent, 1970), p.152.
14. Barbusse, H., *Under Fire* (originally published as *Le Feu*, Paris: Flammarion, 1916) (London: Penguin 2003), p.226.
15. Wyrall, p.184.
16. Ambler Oral History transcript.
17. Wyrall, p.187.

18. Wyrall, pp.187–8.
19. War Diary 5th Bn.
20. Morris, *Leeds Rifles* vol. 2, p.639.
21. Turner and Haigh, *Not for Glory*, pp.89–90.
22. Ibid., p.90.
23. Service Record, 62510 John Carr.
24. *Keighley News*, 17 August 1918.
25. Graham, S., *A Private in the Guards*, pp.244–6.
26. W. Green quoted in van Emden and Humphries, S., *Veterans: The Last Survivors of the Great War* (Barnsley: Leo Cooper, 1998), p.128.
27. Anon. quoted in Winter, D., *Death's Men: Soldiers of the Great War* (London: Penguin, 1979), p.208.
28. Burrage, A.M., *War is War*, available at http://www.firstworldwar.com/diaries/burrage_intro.htm (accessed 26 July 2011).
29. Sassoon, S., *Memoirs of an Infantry Officer* (London: Faber, 1944), p.153.

Chapter 12

1. Hinz, U., *Gefangen im Großen Krieg. Kriegsgefangenschaft in Deutschland 1914–1921* (Essen: Klartext Verlag, 2006), pp.98, 128, 320.
2. Yarnall, J., *Barbed Wire Disease: British & German Prisoners of War, 1914–19* (Stroud: Spellmount, 2006), pp.164–6.
3. Auriol, J.-C., *Les barbelés des bannis: La tragédie des prisonniers de guerre français en Allemagne pendant la Grande Guerre* (Paris: Tirésias, 2003), p.16.
4. Article 7 of the Convention (IV) respecting the Laws and Customs of War on Land and its annex: Regulations concerning the Laws and Customs of War on Land, The Hague, 18 October 1907.
5. *The British Prisoner of War*, vol. 1, no. 1 (January 1918), p.1, and no. 8 (Aug 1918), p.94.
6. Griffith, P., *Battle Tactics of the Western Front: The British Army's Art of Attack* (New Haven, CT: Yale University Press, 1994), p.118.
7. Turner and Haigh, p.94.
8. *Ossett Observer*, 28 December 1918.
9. Johnson, p.164.

10. WO95/3089 187th Infantry Brigade Narrative of Operations September 12th to 15th 1918.
11. Stephenson Carter, L., 'Cold Comfort', *Dartmouth Medicine*, available online at http://dartmed.dartmouth.edu Winter 2006.
12. Arthur, M., *Last Post: The Final Word from Our First World War Soldiers* (London: Weidenfeld & Nicholson, 2005), p.84.
13. Ibid., p.82.
14. *Todmorden Advertiser*, 1 November 1918.

Chapter 13

1. Arthur, *Forgotten Voices*, pp.310–11.
2. Batten, Capt LW GS0101, Liddle Collection.
3. Pte J. McCauley, IWM DOCS 97/10/1.
4. Collins, W.N., quoted in van Emden & Humphries, *Veterans*, pp.130–1.

Chapter 14

1. 5th Bn War Diary.
2. *Northern Territory Times and Gazette*, Saturday 11 January 1919.
3. National Archives, 30/30/8.
4. Noakes, p.237.
5. Gough, P., 'Loci Memoriae' (The Architecture Centre, Bristol and the Centre for Contextual, Public and Commemorative Art at UWE, Bristol, 2001), p.8.
6. For details of the body clearance work, see Hodgkinson, P., 'Clearing the Dead', *Journal of the Centre for World War I Studies*, vol. 3, no. 1 (Sept. 2007).
7. Christie, N., *The Canadians on the Somme* (Ottawa: CEF Books, 1999), p.59.
8. Macbeath, W.F., Diaries, AWM PR00675.
9. Revised Instructions – Records Branch (Undated, *c.* 1922), CWGC WG 1294/3 Pt. 1 Cat. No. 268 Box 1082.
10. Allen, Major A., Evidence given to Inquiry 30/3/1920. NAA: MP367/1,

AA446/10/1840, quoted in Zino, B., *A Distant Grief: Australians, War Graves and the Great War* (PhD thesis, University of Melbourne, 2003).
11. Commonwealth War Graves Commission 1294/3/3 Cat. No. 270 Box 1083.
12. Hodgkinson.
13. *The Times*, 10 November 1921.

Chapter 15

1. In van Emden, R., *Boy Soldiers of the Great War: Their Own Stories for the First Time* (London: Headline Books, 2005), quoted in Anderson, J., *World War I Witness Accounts* (Leicester: Abbeydale Press, 2009), p.149.
2. Petter, M., '"Temporary Gentlemen" in the Aftermath of the Great War: Rank, Status and the Ex-Officer Problem', *Historical Journal*, vol. 37, no. 1 (1994), p.130.
3. Ambler, Oral History transcript.
4. Death Certificate, Stanley Wade.
5. Death Certificate, John Edward Bowskill.
6. Van Emden, R., *The Soldier's War* (Bloomsbury, 2008), p.311.
7. Beckett, I., 'The Real Unknown Army: British Conscripts, 1916–1919', in Becker, J.J. and Audoin-Rouzeau, S., *Les sociétés européennes pendant la guerre de 1914–1918, Actes du colloque du Centre d'histoire de la France contemporaine de l'Université de Paris X-Nanterre de décembre 1988* (Nanterre: Publications de l'Université de Nanterre, 1990).
8. Edmonds, J.E. and Maxwell-Hyslop, R., *History of the Great War: Military Operations France and Belgium 1918 Volume V: 26th September–11th November: The Advance to Victory* (London: MacMillan, 1947), viii.
9. *Radio Times*, 4 July 1963, quoted in Bet-El, I., *Conscripts: Forgotten Men of the Great War* (Stroud: Sutton, 2003), p.203.
10. Mellersh, H.E.L., *Schoolboy into War* (London: Wm Kimber, 1978), p.191.

Selected Bibliography

Unit Histories

Bond, R.C., *History of the King's Own Yorkshire Light Infantry*, Vol. II (London: Percy Lund, 1929)

Johnson, M., *Saturday Soldiers: The Territorial Battalions of the KOYLI 1908–1919* (Doncaster: Doncaster Museum Services, 2004)

Magnus, L., *The West Riding Territorials in the Great War* (London: Kegan, 1920)

Morris, P.M., *Leeds and the Amateur Military Tradition: The Leeds Rifles and their antecedents 1859–1918* (PhD thesis, University of Leeds, 1983)

Wyrall, E., *History of 62nd (West Riding) Division 1914–1919*, Vol. I (London: The Bodley Head Ltd, n.d.)

Local Histories

Cole, H., *The Story of Catterick Camp 1915–72* (HQ Catterick Forces Press, 1972)

Dalton, R.D., *Labour and the Municipality: Labour politics in Leeds 1900–1914* (PhD thesis, University of Huddersfield, 2000)

Dewhirst, I., *A History of Keighley* (Stroud: Tempus, 2006)

James, D., *Class and Politics in a Northern Industrial Town: Keighley 1880–1914* (Keele: Keele University Press, 1995)

Lee, J.A., *Todmorden and the Great War* (Todmorden: Warrington & Sons, 1922)

Morris, J.E., *The West Riding of Yorkshire* (London: Methuen & Co., 1911)

Pearce, C., *Comrades in Conscience: the story of an English community's opposition to the Great War* (London: Francis Boutle, 2001)

Scott, W.H., *Leeds in the Great War: A book of remembrance* (Leeds: The Libraries & Arts Committee of the Leeds Corporation, 1923)

Whitehouse, C.J. & G.P., *Great War Camps on Cannock Chase: a town for four winters* (self-published: Whitehouse, 1996)

British Army 1914–18

Arthur, M., *Last Post: the final word from our First World War soldiers* (London: Weidenfeld & Nicholson, 2005)

Corrigan, G., *Mud, Blood and Poppycock: Britain and the First World War* (London: Cassell Military Paperbacks, 2004)

Empey, A.G., *From the Fire Step: the experiences of an American soldier in the British army. Together with Tommy's dictionary of the trenches* (London: G.P. Putnam, 1917)
French, D., *Military Identities: the regimental system, the British Army, and the British people c. 1870–2000.* (Oxford: OUP, 2008)
Holmes, R., *Tommy: the British soldier on the Western Front* (London: HarperCollins, 2004)
Messenger, C., *Call to Arms: the British Army 1914–18* (London: Weidenfeld & Nicolson, 2005)
Sheffield, G., *Officer-Man Relations, Morale and Discipline in the British Army, 1902–22* (PhD thesis, King's College, London, 1994)
Vickers, L., *Training for the Trenches: a practical handbook based upon personal experience during the first two years of the war in France* (London: George H. Doran Co., 1917)

Conscription
Adams, R.J.Q. & Poirier, P., *The Conscription Controversy in Great Britain, 1900–18* (Ohio: Ohio State University Press, 1987)
Beckett, I., 'The Real Unknown Army: British conscripts, 1916–1919' in Becker, J.J. & Audoin-Rouzeau, S., *Les sociétés européennes pendant la guerre de 1914–1918* (Nanterre: Actes du colloque du Centre d'histoire de la France contemporaine, 1988)
Beckett, I.F. & Simpson, K., *A Nation In Arms* (Barnsley: Pen & Sword, 1985)
Bet-El, I., *Conscripts* (Stroud: The History Press, 2009)
Jordan, Gerald H.S., *The Politics of Conscription in Britain, 1905–1916* (PhD thesis, University of California, Irvine, 1974)

Memoirs & Biographies
Blacker, C.P., *Have You Forgotten Yet?* (Barnsley: Pen & Sword, 2000)
Campbell, P.J., *In the Cannon's Mouth* (London: Hamish Hamilton, 1977)
———, *Ebb and Flow of Battle* (Oxford: OUP, 1979)
Carrington, C., *Soldier from the Wars Returning* (Barnsley: Pen & Sword, 2006)
Dunn, Capt J.C., *The War the Infantry Knew: 1914–1919: A Chronicle of Service in France and Belgium* (London: Abacus, 1988)
Graham, S., *A Private in the Guards* (London: MacMillan, 1919)
Halken, P. & Harrison, B., *Bill's Book* (Beverley: Hutton Press, 1990)
Hodges, F., *Men of 18 in 1918* (Ilfracombe: Arthur H. Stockwell Ltd, 1988)
Kiernan, R.H., *Little Brother Goes Soldiering* (London: Constable, 1930)
Mellersh, H.E.L., *Schoolboy into War* (London: HarperCollins, 1978)
Nicholson, Col W.N., *Behind the Lines* (London: Cape, 1939)
Noakes, F.E., *The Distant Drum: a memoir of a guardsman in the Great War* (London: Frontline Books, 2010)
Taylor, F.A.J., *The Bottom of the Barrel* (London: Chivers Press, 1986)
Turner, P.W. & Haigh, R.H., *Not For Glory* (London: Robert Maxwell, 1969)
Voight, F.A., *Combed Out* (London: The Swarthmore Press, 1920)

National Archives
Home Office Files
HO 45/10944/257142	Anti-German Disturbances
HO 45/10801/307402	No Conscription Fellowship

War Office Files
WO 95/3068	62nd Division War Diary
WO 95/3088	187th Brigade War Diary

WO 95/3089   187th Brigade War Diary
WO 95/3091/1   2/4th Bn KOYLI War Diary
WO 95/3091/2   5th Bn KOYLI War Diary
WO 95/3091/3   2/5th Bn KOYLI War Diary
WO 95/1626/3   1st Midland Brigade War Diary

Ministry of Food and Board of Trade Food Departments
MAF 60/243   Rationing. Food Queues: notes and memoranda on their prevention.

Ministry of National Service
NATS 1/912   Recruitment Costs
NATS 1/964   Recruiting Exemptions. 'Comb Out' of hunting and racing establishments
                     of persons evading military service

Newspapers
Armley and Wortley News
Barnsley Chronicle
Batley News
Cleckheaton Advertiser
Colne Valley Guardian
Halifax Evening Courier
Halifax Guardian
Halifax Weekly Courier
Huddersfield Daily Examiner
Huddersfield Weekly Examiner
Keighley News
Ossett Observer
Telegraph and Argus (Bradford)
Todmorden Advertiser
Wharfedale and Airedale Advertiser
Yorkshire Observer
Yorkshire Evening Post (Leeds)
Yorkshire Post

Acknowledgements

In trying to go beyond the stereotypes and find out who my great uncle, Harold Wiseman, and his friends were and why they fought I have had the help and support of too many people to list in full but special thanks need to go to Alison Hine of the Guild of Battlefield Guides and the University of Birmingham's First World War Studies programme, who was extremely generous in her support and encouragement. Thanks, too, to Dr John Bourne and Professor Peter Simkins of the Birmingham course for reading some of my material and providing a much-needed boost to morale with their kind comments. From the Western Front Association, Malcolm Johnson allowed me to steal freely from his work 'Saturday Soldiers' and David Tattersfield's enthusiastic interest in the Marne along with his position as Development Trustee provided invaluable assistance in tracking down some vital information. Steve Rogers of the War Graves Photographic Project (www.twgpp. org) found photographs and details of the graves of the draft from his extensive archive.

My mother, Violet, was Harold Wiseman's niece and provided her recollections of how his death affected her mother and the rest of the family. Unfortunately she died just before publication of the book. She and my father, Albert, are among the last of their generation born into a country still mourning its dead when another war came. A family holiday to Belgium in 1970 sparked an interest in the First World War and military history that has grown steadily ever since.

As ever, my greatest thanks go to my wife, Jacqueline and my kids, Bethany and Josh (yes OK Josh, and Monty the dog). Writing a book is hard work and they have always been patient when I've drifted off into my own little world, writing the next chapter in my head or sitting in the car as I tramped across a muddy field in northern France instead of standing in a line at Euro-Disney which was what I was supposed to be doing at the time. Thanks guys.

Tim Lynch
2013

Index